From the Cape to Cairo

by

Ewart S. Grogan and Arthur H. Sharp

The Echo Library 2014

Published by

The Echo Library

Echo Library
Unit 22
Horcott Industrial Estate
Horcott Road
Fairford
Glos. GL7 4BX

www.echo-library.com

Please report serious faults in the text to complaints@echo-library.com

ISBN 978-1-40684-949-3

From the Cape to Cairo

The First Traverse of Africa from South to North

BY

EWART S. GROGAN

AND

ARTHUR H. SHARP

T. Nelson & Sons, Ltd.

4

TO

THE MEMORY OF

THE GREATEST AND MOST FAR-SEEING

OF

BRITISH IMPERIAL STATESMEN,

THE RT. HON. CECIL JOHN RHODES,

THIS VOLUME

IS RESPECTFULLY DEDICATED

BY

EWART SCOTT GROGAN

AND

ARTHUR HENRY SHARP.

Government House,
Buluwayo,
7th Sept., 1900.

My Dear Grogan,

You ask me to write you a short introduction for your book, but I am sorry to say that literary composition is not one of my gifts, my correspondence and replies being conducted by telegrams.

I must say I envy you, for you have done that which has been for centuries the ambition of every explorer, namely, to walk through Africa from South to North. The amusement of the whole thing is that a youth from Cambridge during his vacation should have succeeded in doing that which the ponderous explorers of the world have failed to accomplish. There is a distinct humour in the whole thing. It makes me the more certain that we shall complete the telegraph and railway, for surely I am not going to be beaten by the legs of a Cambridge undergraduate.

Your success the more confirms one's belief. The schemes described by Sir William Harcourt as "wild cat" you have proved are capable of being completed, even in that excellent gentleman's lifetime.

As to the commercial aspect, every one supposes that the railway is being built with the only object that a human being may be able to get in at Cairo and get out at Cape Town.

This is, of course, ridiculous. The object is to cut Africa through the centre, and the railway will pick up trade all along the route. The junctions to the East and West coasts, which will occur in the future, will be outlets for the traffic obtained along the route of the line as it passes through the centre of Africa. At any rate, up to Buluwayo, where I am now, it has been a payable undertaking, and I still think it will continue to be so as we advance into the far interior. We propose now to go on and cross the Zambesi just below the Victoria Falls. I should like to have the spray of the water over the carriages.

I can but finish by again congratulating you, and by saying that your success has given me great encouragement in the work that I have still to accomplish.

Yours,

C. J. RHODES.

PREFACE TO NEW EDITION.

Since bringing out the first edition of this book, I have revisited the United States, Australasia, and Argentina in order that I might again compare the difficulties before us in Africa with the difficulties which these new countries have already overcome. I am now more than ever satisfied that its possibilities are infinitely great. Of the fertility and natural resources of the country I had no doubt. But two great stumbling-blocks loomed ahead: they were the prevalence of malaria and the difficulty of initial development owing to the dearth of navigable waterways. The epoch-making studies by Major Ross and other scientists of the influence of the mosquito on the distribution of malaria have shewn that we are within measurable distance of largely minimising its ravages, if not of completely removing it from the necessary risks of African life. A comparison of the death-rates in Calcutta, Hong-Kong, and other malarious regions with the present rates has also proved how immense is the influence of settlement on climate. As to the other obstacle, the question of access, I was amazed to find that in the United States the railways practically have absorbed all the carrying trade of the magnificent waterways, which intersect the whole country east of the Rockies. Naturally, these waterways were of immense assistance in the original opening up of the country, but now that the railways are constructed, they are of little importance.

I would also point out to those who still profess mistrust of the practical objects of railway construction in Africa, the object-lesson which the trans-American lines afford. They were pushed ahead of all settlement into the great unknown exactly as the Cape to Cairo line is being pushed ahead to-day. But there is this difference: in America they penetrated silent wastes tenanted by naught else than the irreconcilable Redskin, the prairie marmot, and the bison; while in Africa they pass through lands rich in Nature's products and teeming with peoples who do not recede before the white man's march.

Another point: when the main railway system of Africa, as sketched out by Mr. Rhodes, is complete, there will be no single point as remote from a port as are some of the districts in America which are to-day pouring out their food-stuffs along hundreds of miles of rail.

In the words of the old Greek, "History is Philosophy teaching by examples." The world writhes with the quickening life of change. The tide of our supreme ascendancy is on the ebb. Nations, like men, are subject to disease. Let us beware of fatty degeneration of the heart. Luxury is sweeping away the influences which formed our character. It is as though our climate has been changed from the bleak northern winds to the tropic's indolent ease. Yet we have still a chance. While we sleep, broad tracks have been cut for us by those whom we revile. Far and wide our outposts are awake, beckoning to the great army to sweep along the tracks. Let each man with means and muscles for the fray go forth at least to see what empire is. Clive, Hastings, Rhodes, a thousand lesser men whose tombs are known only to the forest breeze, have left us legacies of which we barely dream. Millions of miles of timber, metals, coal, lie waiting for the breath of life, "pegged out" for Britain's sons. In these our destiny lies. We live but once: let us be able, when the last summons comes, to say with the greatest of us all, "Tread me down. Pass on. I have done my work."

CONTENTS.

FROM THE CAPE TO CAIRO.

CHAPTER I.

THE CAPE TO BEIRA AND THE SABI.

To describe the first stage of the route from the Cape to Cairo, that is to say, as far as the Zambesi, which I accomplished four years ago, would, if time be counted by progress, be reverting to the Middle Ages. The journey to Buluwayo, which meant four dismal days and three yet more dismal nights, in a most dismal train, whose engine occasionally went off on its own account to get a drink, and nine awful days and nine reckless nights in a Gladstone bag on wheels, labelled coach, can now be accomplished in, I believe, two and a half days in trains that rival in comfort the best efforts of our American cousins. When I think of those awful hundreds of miles through dreary wastes of sand and putrefying carcases, the seemingly impossible country that the Buluwayo road passed through, the water-courses, the hills, the waterless stages, and the final oasis, where one could buy a bottle of beer for 10s. 6d., and a cauliflower for 36s., and that now men sit down to their fresh fish or pheasant for breakfast, where the old scramble daily took place for a portion of bully beef and rice; and when I think that the fish and pheasant epoch is already old history, then I know that the hand of a mighty wizard is on the country, and that yet one more name will go down to the coming ages which will loom big midst the giants that have built up an Empire such as the world has never seen. When I think, too, of my numerous friends in the country who have given their heave, some a great heave, some a little heave, yet a heave all together, and who toil on unaware of their own heroism, turning aside as a jest the vituperation of their countrymen; and when I think how I have seen the old Viking blood, long time frozen in Piccadilly and the clubs, burst forth in the old irresistible stream, then I know that it is good to be an Englishman, and a great pity fills me for those whose lives are cast in narrow ways, and who never realise the true significance of *Civis Britannicus sum*.

My first experience of Africa was gained in the second Matabele war, when Rhodesia was yet young. The railway had only reached Mafeking, and my experiences were not such as to make me desire a second visit. But the spirit of the veldt was upon me, and in comfortable England these trials sank into the misty oblivion of the past, and a short twelve months after I again started for those inhospitable shores.

However, I will not weary the reader with what he has had dinned into his ears for the last four years, by describing Rhodesia; nor will I dilate on how, at Lisbon, through a Bucellas-induced haze, I noticed that all the men had a patch in their trousers, all the women were ugly, all the food was dirty, and all the friendly-disposed were thieves, nor will I hurt the feelings of the Deutsch Ost Afrika Cie. by telling how badly managed their boats are; how they are perambulating beershops, disguised as liners; how conducive to sleep is a ten-strong brass band at five yards, seized with religious enthusiasm at 7 a.m. on Sunday morning—all these I will pass over, knowing that a *Cicero redivivus* alone could do justice to the theme.

Beyond this, suffice it to say, that on February 28th of the year of our Lord 1898, Arthur Henry Sharp and Ewart Scott Grogan, in company of sundry German officers and beer enthusiasts, took part in the usual D.O.A.'s Liner manoeuvre of violently charging a sandbank in the bay of Beira on a flood-tide, to the ear-smashing accompaniment of the German National Anthem. In the intervals of waiting to be floated, and finding out how many of our loads had been lost, we amused ourselves by catching sharks, which swarmed round the stern of the vessel. Beira, as every one knows, is mainly composed of galvanized iron, sun-baked sand, drinks, and Portuguese ruffians, and is inhabited by a mixed society of railway employés, excellent fellows, Ohio wags, and German Jews. The Government consists of a triumvirate composed of a "king," who also at odd times imports railways, the British Consul, and the *Beira Post*, and sundry minor Portuguese officials, who provide entertainment for the town, such as volley-firing down the main streets, dredging operations in the lagoon at the back of the town, bugle-blowing, etc., etc. The dredging operations and the subsequent depositing of the mud on the highways were undertaken, I believe, in a friendly spirit of rivalry as to the death-rate with Fontesvilla (a salubrious riverside resort about thirty miles inland); a consequent rise to thirty in one day established a record that, I believe, is still unbeaten. There was a Portuguese corvette in the bay, and I had the pleasure of dining on board; the doctor, a most charming specimen of the Portuguese gentleman (and a Portuguese gentleman is a gentleman), helped me to pass my things through the Custom House, and those who know Beira will understand what that means. At Beira I met many old friends, amongst them the ever-green Mr. Lawley, indefatigable as of yore, and was surprised to see the immense strides that the town had made in fourteen months. If it is not washed away some day, it should become second only in importance to Delagoa Bay. Before starting north, we determined to have a few months' shooting, and with this end in view took train to Umtali with the necessary kit. The new site of Umtali township is a more commanding position than the old one, and already a large number of fine buildings had been put up, but now that the temporary activity consequent on its being the railway terminus has passed away, I cannot foresee much future for the place, as the pick of the mines appear to be over the new Anglo-Portuguese boundary, and will be worked from Macequece.

We decided to try the Sabi, a river running parallel to, and south of, the Pungwe, having heard great accounts of the lions in that part; and with this end in view, hired a wagon, which after many days landed us and ours at Mtambara's Kraal on the Umvumvumvu, a nice stream running into the Udzi, which is a tributary of the Sabi. Mtambara was formerly a chief of considerable importance, but the advent of the white man has reduced him to the position of a mere figurehead; he is a phthisical old gentleman of no physique, decked out in a dirty patch of cloth and a bandolier of leather and white beads; he squats and takes snuff, takes snuff and squats, and had not yet joined the Blue Ribbon Army. There being no road to the Udzi, we had to send the wagon back and collect carriers for our loads. Two days' hard walking brought us to the edge of the high veldt, whence the path dived down the most fantastic limestone valley, between high cliffs thickly clothed with foliage, and topped by rows of square rock pillars, splashed with the warm tints of the moss and lichens that festooned their sides. At our feet lay the bush-clad plain of the Udzi, a carpet of green picked out with the occasional silver of the river itself, and in the hazy distance stretched an unbroken range of purple hills, backed by the silvery green and dull smoke-red of sunset. On the third day we camped on the Udzi, about six miles above its junction with the Sabi. The whole country is covered with low black scrub, and though there are many impala[1] and small buck, there are very few large antelopes, so after a few days' inspection we came to the conclusion that it was not good enough, and decided to return to Umtali and risk the climate of my old shooting grounds on the Pungwe.

Sharp went back by the road to pick up the loads and sick men at Mtambara's, while I followed up the Udzi for about twenty miles, and then struck across country to reach Umtali quickly in order to send out a wagon. After leaving the river-basin, I camped on a kopje about 1,000 ft. high, where I had one of the finest views it has ever been my fortune to see.

Beyond the valley lay range upon range of hills, stretching far as the eye could reach; fleecy clouds covered the sun, bursting with every conceivable shade, from delicate rose to deepest purple, backed by that wondrous green (or is it blue?) that so often in the tropics accompanies Phoebus to his rest; rarely one may see it at home in summer-time, as intangible as it is delicate, and, permeating the whole landscape, a sinuous mesh of molten red, a ghostly sea from which the peaks reared their purple silhouettes, until they faded into the uncertainty of lilac mists, like some billowy sea nestling to the bosom of the storm-cloud. From here I walked to Umtali, a distance of sixty miles, in nineteen hours, as I was anxious about the sick men at Mtambara's, and long will the ripple of the ensuing brandy-and-soda linger in my memory. After securing the services of a wagon, I had to lay up for a couple of days with fever and a bad foot, but turned out for a concert given as a house-warming by the latest hotel. It was a typical South African orgie, in a long, low, wooden room, plainly furnished with deal tables, packed to overflowing with the most cosmopolitan crowd imaginable, well-bred 'Varsity men rubbing shoulders with animal-faced Boers, leavened with Jews, parasites, bummers, nondescripts, and every type of civilized savage. Faces yellow with fever, faces coppered by the sun, faces roseate with drink, and faces scarred, keen, money-lustful, and stamped with every vice and some of the virtues; a substratum of bluff, business advertisement, pat-on-the-back-kick-you-when-you're-not-looking air permeated everything, and keen appreciation of both musical garbage and real talent.

Starting for Salisbury, where I wanted to look up some old friends, I was made the victim of one of those subtle little jests so much appreciated by many of the petty

---

[1] A small antelope (*Æpyceros melampus*).

officials in South Africa, who are for ever reminding one of their importance. I turned up at three, the advertised time for the coach's departure, and, finding no mules or signs of activity, learned that (being an official case) three meant three Cape time, or four Umtali time. So I went back to my hotel, and again turning up at ten to four, found that the coach had left at a quarter to four without blowing the bugle, and knowing that there was one passenger short; this necessitated a nine-mile walk to old Umtali in the rain, which, after three days' fever, was very enjoyable. The company, a pleasant one, was somewhat marred by the presence of a fat Jew of the most revolting type; unkempt curly black hair, lobster-like, bloodshot eyes with the glazed expression peculiar to tipplers and stale fish, a vast nose pronouncedly Bacchanalian, the hues of which varied from yellow through green to livid purple, and lips that would shame any negro, purple as the extremity of the nose, a small, straggling moustache and a runaway chin, the whole plentifully smeared with an unpleasant exudation, kept perpetually simmering by his anxiety lest some one should steal a march on him, made a loathsome *tout ensemble* that is by no means rare in South Africa. The way that creature fought for food! Well! I have seen hyænas and negroes fighting for food, but never such hopelessly abandoned coarseness as he displayed at every meal on the road, and for no apparent reason, as there was plenty for all, and by general consent he had the monopoly of any dish that he touched.

Salisbury, which is quite the aristocratic resort of Rhodesia, had made very little progress during my eighteen months' absence, though there had been some activity in the mining districts. The business of ferreting out the murderers in the late rebellion was still proceeding, and I saw about thirty condemned negroes in the gaol, and more were daily added. I went to one of the sittings and saw so many gruesome relics, burnt pipes, charred bones, skulls, etc., that I did not repeat my visit. I was forcibly struck by the absolute justice meted out: the merest technicality of law or the faintest shade of doubt sufficing for acquittal. Many of the natives in custody thus escaped, although their guilt was certain and well known. My return journey to Umtali was enlivened by the company of one of the civic dignitaries of Salisbury, who was going to "give it hot to Rhodes," shake him up a bit, and generally put things straight. In one day I had the whole future policy of Rhodesia and all outstanding difficulties like labour, etc., disposed of as though they were the merest bagatelles. So struck was I with the masterly grasp of gigantic questions that I fell into a profound slumber, whereupon, realizing that after all I was but an ordinary mortal, and consequently possessed of but ordinary intelligence, he roused me, and in five minutes sketched out a plan that would make my intended trip north a certain success; this, with more personal advice on a score of points, lasted till Umtali, where we found so-called celebrations in full swing. These celebrations (or barmen's benefits, as they should more appropriately be called) are of common occurrence, and are invariably got up on any sort of excuse; they take the outward form of a few pieces of bunting, and result in every one but the licensed few finding themselves next morning considerably poorer, and in an abnormal demand for Seidlitz powders. Society at Umtali groups itself into two classes, those who have liquor and those who have not, and each class into three divisions:

first, a small number who have killed lions and say very little about it; secondly, a large number of persons who have not killed lions, but tell you they have, and say much about it; and thirdly, a very large number who have not killed lions, but think it necessary to apologize for the fact by telling you that they have not lost any.

CHAPTER II.

THE PUNGWE AND GORONGOZA'S PLAIN.

"The bulky, good-natured lion, whose only means of defence are the natural ones of tooth and claw, has no chance against the jumping little rascal, who pops behind a bush and pokes a gun straight at the bigger brute's heart."—MARIE CORELLI.

Instead of following the Urema as on a previous trip, we marched up the Pungwe almost as far as Sarmento, an old Portuguese settlement, and then struck off north to a long lagoon that lies on the western extremity of Gorongoza's plain. Here we found enormous quantities of game, thousands of wildebeeste and zebra, and many impala, waterbuck, and hartebeeste. At night a hyæna came and woke us up by drinking the soapy water in our indiarubber bath, which was lying just outside our tent. We turned out and drove him away, but had no sooner climbed into our beds again than he returned and bolted with the bath, and, before we could make him drop it, had mauled it to such an extent that it was of no further use.

As after the first night we heard no lions, we decided to move across to the Urema. On the way we sighted three eland, but though Sharp and I chased them for about eight miles we were unsuccessful.

Towards the Urema the plain opens out to a great width and becomes very swampy, and as the water had just subsided, it was covered with short sweet grass. Here we saw between 40,000 and 50,000 head of game, mostly wildebeeste, which opened out to let us pass and then closed in again behind. It was a wonderful sight; vast moving masses of life, as far as the eye could reach. A fortnight later they had eaten up the grass, and most of them were scattered about the surrounding country. Some of the swamps were very bad, and we were finally compelled to camp in the middle far from any wood.

The next day we struck camp and marched up the Urema to a belt of trees which we could see in the distance. Several good streams, the most important being the Umkulumadzi, flow down from the mountains, and meandering across the plain, empty themselves into the Urema. Sharp and I went on ahead of our caravan, and keeping well to the south-west to avoid swamps, came on a nice herd of buffalo which we stalked. At our shots a few turned off into some long tufts of grass, while the main body went straight away. One, evidently sick, came edging towards us, and I gave him two barrels, Sharp doing likewise; I then gave him two more and dropped him. I kept my eye on where he lay as we advanced to get a shot at the others, who had again stood about 100 yards farther on, and he suddenly rose at thirty yards and charged hard, nose in air, foaming with blood, and looking very nasty. I put both barrels in his chest without the slightest effect, and then started for the river, doing level time and shouting to Sharp to do likewise; all the crocodiles in the universe seemed preferable to that incarnation of hell. But Sharp had not yet learnt his buffalo, and waited for him. I heard a shot, and stopped in time to see the beast stagger for a second with a broken jaw, then come on in irresistible frenzy; but still Sharp stood as though to receive a cavalry charge, crack rang out the rifle, and the great brute came pitching forward on to its nose, and rolled within three yards of Sharp's feet with a broken fetlock. It was a magnificent sight, and the odd chance in a hundred turned up. Now Sharp knows his buffalo, and is prepared to back himself, when one turns nasty, to do his hundred in 9-4/5 seconds.

Except an elephant, there is nothing harder to stop than a charging buffalo, as, when once he has made up his mind, he means business; there is no turning him, and if he misses he will round and come again and hunt a man down like a dog. Holding his head in the air as he does in practice, and not low down as in the picture-books, he gives no mark except the chest, which is rarely a dropping shot. Having hacked off his head (the buffalo's), we went in pursuit of our caravan, and found that Mahony had pitched camp in the most perfect spot imaginable. A strip of open park-like bush ran down from the mountains, cutting the vast Gorongoza plain into two portions, and abutting on the river, where it had spread into a small lagoon with banks 20 ft. high. Beyond lay another plain stretching away to the bush that lies at the foot of the ridge which runs north and south, and is the watershed of the Urema and the coast. In all directions from our camp we could see herds of game grazing. Flocks of fowl flighted up and down the watercourse, huge crocodiles leered evilly at us as they floated like logs on the oily water, broken only by the plomp-plomp of the numerous fish, and now and then the head of a mud-turtle rose like a ghost from below, without even a ripple, drew a long hissing breath, and as silently vanished. As there was lions' spoor by the water, we strolled out after tea and dropped a brace of zebra by the edge of the bush. After an eventful night, during which leopards coughed, lions roared, hyænas dashed into camp and bolted with my best waterbuck head, we all turned out early. Sharp went down the river, while Mahony and I went to our baits. The first had completely vanished, and the second had been dragged some three hundred yards under the shade of a palm-tree. Here we picked up the spoor of a big lion, who had evidently got our wind as we left camp. We followed for about a mile along the bush, when Mahony saw him watching us round the corner of an ant-hill. The lion, seeing that he was observed, doubled like a flash, and before Mahony could fire, had dashed into a small patch of thick jungle. We lost no time in following, and were carefully picking our way through the undergrowth, when I heard a deep grunt about twenty yards to my right, and saw him, tail straight in the air, vanishing through the bush. Mahony rushed along the jungle; while I made a desperate burst through the thorn into the open. I just caught a glimpse of the lion going through the scattered palms towards the open plain. When I reached the end of the palms, he was going hard about two hundred yards away. Using the double .500 magnum, I removed his tooth with the first barrel, and with the second pulled him up short with a shot in the hind leg. Mahony then arrived on the scene and gave him a .500, while I finished him off with two shots from the .303. He was a very old lion with his teeth much broken, but had a good mane, and measured as he lay from tip to tip 9 ft. 10-½ in.

As the moon was now full, I determined to sit up, and having killed a zebra close to two small palms, I built a screen of palm-leaves and awaited events. The first two nights nothing came but mosquitoes, and the third night two hunting dogs turned up, but I didn't fire for fear of disturbing some lions which I could hear in the distance. These dogs are very beautiful animals with long bushy tails. They hunt in large packs, and must destroy an immense quantity of game. Shortly after the dogs had vanished a lion came to the jungle which was about four hundred yards away, and apparently detecting my scent, in spite of the competition of the zebra, which was three days old, vented his disapproval in three stupendous roars. This is one of the few occasions on which I heard a lion really roar, though every night for months I have heard packs of them in all directions. The usual cry is a sort of vast sigh taken up by the chorus with a deep sob, sob, sob, or a curious rumbling noise. The true roar is indescribable. It is so deceptive as to distance, and seems to permeate the whole universe, thundering, rumbling, majestic. There is no music in the world so sweet. Let me recommend it to the Wagner school! Thousands of German devotees, backed by thousands of beers, could never approach the soul-stirring glory of one *Felis leo* at home. I then heard him going away to the north, rumbling to himself at intervals, and at 5 a.m. left my scherm [2] and started in pursuit, hoping to come up with him at daybreak in the plain. I could still hear his occasional rumblings, and, taking a line by the moon, made terrific pace. After leaving the ridge, I plunged into a dense bank of fog that lay on the plain, but still managed to keep my line, as the moon showed a lurid red and remained visible till sunrise. The lion had stopped his meditations for some time, and imperceptibly the light of day had eaten into the fog, when suddenly my gun-boy "Rhoda" gripped me by the arm, his teeth chattering like castanets, and said that he saw the lion in front. At the same instant I thought that I saw a body moving in the mist about seventy yards away, now looking like an elephant, now like a jackal. Then the mist swirled round, wrapping it in obscurity once more. I followed carefully, when suddenly an eddy in the fog disclosed a male lion thirty yards away, wandering along as if the whole world belonged to him. He rolled his head from side to side, swished his tail, poked his nose into every bunch of grass, then stopped and stood broadside on. I raised the .500, but found that I had forgotten to remove the bunch of cloth which served for a night sight, and, before this was remedied, the chance was gone. Again I followed and again he turned, when I dropped him with a high shoulder shot. As the grass was only 3 in. high and the lion not more than thirty yards distant, we lay flat and awaited the turn of events. He lashed out, tearing up the ground with his paws, then stood up and looked like going away. I fired again. This gave him my whereabouts. He swung round and began stalking towards me to investigate matters, so I snatched my .500 and knocked him over with one in the chest. We then retired to

---

[2] Fence or screen.

a more respectful distance. But he rose again, and once more I fired. Still he fought on, rolling about, rumbling, groaning, and making frantic efforts to rise, till I crept up close and administered a .303 forward shot in the stomach, which settled him. He died reluctantly even then. It is astonishing how difficult lions are to kill, if the first shot is not very well placed. I attribute it to the fact that after the first shot there is practically no subsequent shock to the system. This is especially remarkable in the larger brutes, such as the elephant, rhino, or buffalo. If the first shot is misplaced, one can fire shot after shot, even through the heart, without immediate effect. He was a good lion, in the prime of life, with mane, teeth, and claws perfect.

Sharp meanwhile had been making his first acquaintance with that ingenious device of the devil's, the jigger,[3] which confined him to the camp for a week with a very ugly foot.

Mahony, who had gone down-river, saw a male lion, but failed to stop him with a long shot, but the next day in the same place came unexpectedly on two lionesses, both of which he wounded. As they took refuge in the grass, which was very extensive and thick, and he saw a cub, he sent into camp for another gun. Sharp turned out in spite of his foot, and I followed immediately when I returned to camp and found the note. After a hard spurt of six miles, I met them coming back in triumph with the pelt of one lioness and five small rolls of fur and ferocity slung on poles. The cubs had been captured with difficulty. One only succumbed after being bowled over with a sun helmet. They were great fun in camp, and throve amazingly on cooked liver, of which they devoured enormous quantities. Two of them were males, and three of them (one male and two females[4]) are now disporting themselves in the Society's Gardens in Regent's Park.

Hoping to see something of the other lioness or the lion I returned to the same place next day, and after examining the neighbourhood of the grass, pushed on still farther to the centre of the swamp. In this swamp the river spreads out into a vast network of channels, with a small central lagoon. Owing to the dryness of the season, it was possible to cross most of the channels, which were then merely mud-troughs, and to reach the lagoon, which was about four hundred yards wide. Here I witnessed a most extraordinary sight. About fifty hippo were lying about in the water, and on the banks. As the water was not in most parts deep enough to cover them, they presented the appearance of so many huge seals basking in the sun. They climbed in and out, strolled about, rolled in, splashing, shouting, blowing, and entirely ignoring my presence. After watching them for some time, I sent my boys to the far end to drive them past. The boys yelled and threw stones at them. Suddenly the hippo took alarm and rushed *en masse* for the narrow channel of the waterway. Down this they swarmed, kicking the water 30 ft. in the air, throwing their heads back, roaring,

---

[3] *The jigger*, the "pulex penetrans."

[4] One female has since died.

thundering, and crashing along, while I stood on the bank at twenty yards and took photographs, all of which unfortunately failed.

The banks of every channel and mud-hole were lined with huge yellow masses of crocodiles; thousands and thousands of wildfowl (mainly Egyptian and spur-wing geese), which were nesting in the hippo holes, kept up a ceaseless din; herds and herds of game appeared as though dancing in the mirage, and the whole scene was one to delight the heart of a lover of nature. There indeed one felt one was far from the madding crowd.

During the night we were awakened by the most terrific yells, and found that some crocodiles had gone into the boys' quarters. Fortunately they contented themselves with removing about two hundredweight of meat.

As the lions appeared to have left the country, we moved up the river to our original camp for a week to give the plain a rest, and bagged an eland. Sharp secured a good lioness in the lion donga.

On our return I shot a zebra for bait in the strip of bush. Turning out somewhat reluctantly at 5.30 a.m. with no hopes of success, as the lions had been very quiet all night, I was cutting the wind rather fine when I saw a number of birds sitting at a respectful distance from the carcase. Approaching cautiously, I saw some brute apparently pulling at something, but could not see clearly what it was, as it was still more or less dark. I knew it must be a lion from its bulk, yet dared not think so. I retraced my steps for the wind and crept up to within sixty yards under cover of a stunted palm. Peering cautiously round, I saw, in the middle of a circle of some two hundred vultures, a grand old lion, leisurely gnawing the ribs. Behind him were four little jackals sitting in a row. It would be difficult to imagine a more perfect picture. In the background stretched the limitless plain, streaked with mists shimmering in the growing light of the rising sun. Clumps of graceful palms fenced in a sandy arena where the zebra had fallen. Round its attenuated remains, just out of reach of the swish of the monarch's tail, was a solid circle of waiting vultures, craning their bald necks, chattering and hustling one another. The more daring quartette sat within the magic circle like four little images of patience, while the lion in all his might and matchless grandeur of form, leisurely chewed and scrunched the tit-bits, magnificently regardless of the watchful eyes of the encircling *canaille*. Loath to break the spell, I watched the scene for fully ten minutes, then, as he showed signs of moving, I took the chance afforded of a broadside shot and bowled him over with the .500 magnum. I tried to reload but the gun jammed. The lion rose, and after looking round for the cause of the interruption, without success, started off at a gallop. With a desperate effort I closed the gun and knocked him over again. He was a fine black-maned lion, and measured as he lay in a straight line from tip to tip 10 ft. 4 in.—a very unusual length.

Another morning, taking an early stroll, I met an old cow hippo and a calf, wandering about far from the river. I accompanied them for some time watching them, but when I caught the youngster by the tail the old lady turned round in answer to its squeals, and opening her mouth to its fullest extent, some 6 ft., gave vent to a terrific roar, which reminded me that it was breakfast-time. On another occasion presumably the same pair strolled past within one hundred yards of our breakfast-table, but they out-distanced the boys who went in pursuit, and plunged into the river, easy winners.

As Sharp had shot a brace of hippo in our pool, we had them dragged out on to the sandbank opposite, and built a grass screen at the lower end of the hippo tunnel which led down through the bush from the high ground above the river. Fortunately, as it afterwards transpired, we took the precaution to block up the top entrance with stones. Here Sharp and I posted ourselves for the night in hopes of lions. When all was quiet, scores of vast crocodiles came out of the pool, and so successfully did they rend and tear the huge carcases that in the morning nothing remained but a few bones. It was a gruesome sight, the great loathsome reptiles tearing vast blocks of hide like brown paper, then crawling away to digest their morsel, then again advancing to the attack, while a row of hyænas sat silhouetted against the sky on the high bank opposite, or trotted uneasily to and fro, moaning and howling unceasingly, yet fearing to approach the evil mass of reptiles. Crowds of mosquitoes and sandflies added their plaintive song. Suddenly with a mighty rush five hippo dashed down the bank, then, recovering from their alarm, strolled quietly by at five yards, the moonlight gleaming white on their wet backs.

Having heard some lions at sunrise to the east I started in pursuit, and, following along an extensive dry donga that cut through the plain, found some fresh spoor which I lost in the endless sea of dry long grass that covered the greater part of the plain. This I fired, and then came round by the river, hoping to see some of them if they were driven from their cover. When nearly home I saw a lion stand up in the low scrub about a thousand yards away. He had our wind, and started across the bare plain at a gallop, making for the long grass. I set off in hot pursuit with my gun-boy. When the lion stopped to look I stopped, hoping that he would think I was not following him. Whereupon my boy, who would never learn the trick, sailed gracefully over my shoulder. The lion, apparently taking us for some harmless mountebanks, slackened his pace, and only reached the grass about five hundred yards ahead of me. Rushing in on his tracks, I was fortunate enough to catch a glimpse of his mane above the grass, as he crossed a place where the grass was rather shorter than elsewhere. He had turned at right angles from his course, and had ceased to worry himself about me. Following hard, I got a chance at sixty yards, and knocked him over with a shot from the .500 magnum high on the shoulder. Owing to the smoke, the lack of landmarks, and the height of the grass (about 4 ft. 6 in.), I lost his exact whereabouts, and after slipping in another cartridge, walked past him. He suddenly rose at twenty-five yards and charged straight. The incredible rapidity of his onslaught and the cover afforded by the grass rendered aiming impossible. I merely swung the gun on him and dropped him at four yards with a shot in the neck, then hastily retired. After waiting for some time and hearing no sound, I again advanced, this time with the greatest caution. I could soon distinguish his shoulder at ten yards between the grass. Not wishing to damage his skin unnecessarily, I took my small rifle and fired at his shoulder. The shot had hardly struck when he again rose and charged like lightning. Another lucky shot from the second barrel, which entered the old wound, laid him out. His head was within three yards of my feet. Even then he would not die, although unable to rise, and it needed three more shots to finish him. This was the first time I had been charged by a lion, and I was amazed at the incredible rapidity of their movements. My respect for friend lion increased a thousandfold.

The following day was evidently a lion's holiday, for Mahony and I, following the river to where I had dropped a zebra, put up two lionesses out of some scrub. I hit them both with a right and left. Mahony also hit one, which we secured. But the other one crossed the river, making a clean jump of 34 ft., and reached a large patch of long grass where we lost her. The wind dropped, and consequently the grass would not burn. Nor could we follow her spoor. Sharp, crossing the plain to the Umkulumadzi, met a lion and a lioness, and killed the lion with a shot in the neck. On his way home he met another lion, and with a shot at ten yards from the 10-bore removed a bunch of the mane. The lion jumped into a small patch of impassable reed from which he could not be induced to move, so was wisely allowed to stay, as handling a gun inside would have been impossible. This was our grand finale at lion camp, and we again moved to our old spot by the water-hole in the jungle, but without success.

The variation in the Lichtenstein hartebeeste was very remarkable, the type in this jungle being a heavy beast without face markings, the frontal bone very prominent and the white rump indistinct, while near Gorongoza's hills they were smaller, had a white blaze on the forehead, and were without the peculiar frontal prominence, the rump, too, being very white. The nocturnal attentions of the hyænas were most annoying, diabolical peals of laughter in rapid succession making sleep almost impossible. Failing to find buffalo, we again marched up the Pungwe, and to the lagoon where we had started proceedings.

The first morning after losing a splendid eland, in company with Mahony, I met a fretful porcupine taking his morning constitutional. We waited till he walked within five yards and then gave chase. For a time the pace was hot, till I headed him off, and grabbed him, by the long hair on his neck, which promptly gave way (I mean the hair). I was again closing on him, when he suddenly backed, driving one quill through my boot, 1-½ in. through my little toe, and a dozen others into my leg, one through the tendon. One of my boys was badly mangled in a similar manner, and it was only after giving the fretful one a playful tap on the skull that we made him fast. I regret to say that two days afterwards he died.

As the officials of a so-called Gorongoza Development Co., with its headquarters on the Dingi-Dingi, had seized our boys on their way to Fontesvilla with trophies, and ill-used them, we marched to the Pungwe, where I branched off to arrange matters, the others following the river towards Sarmento. I found seven or eight yellow-visaged creatures, a Portuguese-French mixture, who in three years had disposed of a capital of, I believe, some hundreds of thousands of francs, with the stupendous result of an asset comprising about fifty acres of castor oil (one of the most ineradicable weeds of the country). The Governor, who was very polite, told me that he was entitled to levy shooting licences, and after some talk we closed the matter with a payment of £10, which I should advise the shareholders of the Gorongoza Development Co. to keep an eye on, as it is the only return they are ever likely to see. He also told me that he should like a lion hunt, and had even sat up by his fowl-house for that purpose. Not long after we met him, vinously inclined, in Beira—the cheque had been cashed. On the Pungwe we watched some native blacksmiths at work. Several of their tools were very ingenious.

Again we marched north, and striking the Pungwe by Tiga's Kraal, crossed the island and the Dingi-Dingi, and eventually camped at the junction of a broad sandy river with the Urema. Sharp bagged a good buffalo with a 42-inch head the first night; and the following morning we found that a male lion had visited the carcase, but retired before our arrival. We tossed up as to who should sit up that night, and I was unlucky enough to win; unlucky, in that I spent one of the most awful nights it has ever been my lot to endure. Having built a small platform, 6 ft. from the ground, I repaired thither with a thick blanket at sunset. Soon about thirty hyænas appeared, and continued fighting, snarling, and uttering diabolical yells all night; while battalions of mosquitoes refreshed themselves at my expense, biting my knees, even through a camel's-hair blanket and flannel trousers.

At last, about an hour before dawn, I fell asleep, and was awakened at sunrise by a scuffling noise behind me. I turned round, on murder intent, expecting to find a belated hyæna, and beheld, ten yards away, a grand old lion slowly dragging the carcase under the shade of a tree. Still half asleep, I reached for the 10-bore, and killed him with a shot high on the shoulder, and went back to breakfast, feeling thoroughly ashamed of myself. I consider sitting up over a bait an unpardonable form of murder, if there is the remotest possibility of shooting a beast in fair hunt.

A few days later, when on the way to our camp in the jungle, I overshot the track in some long grass, and spent a terrible day in consequence. I could not be certain that I had crossed it, or if I had crossed, of not doing so again if I returned. The only safe course was to follow some definite direction. I judged the whereabouts of the junction of the Gorongoza plain and the Urema, and went straight ahead through thick and thin. Some of the bush was terrible, and the only way to pass was by climbing along the boughs of the trees above. The experience gave me a clear idea of how people lose themselves irretrievably, as I found it needed a tremendous effort of will to compel myself to go on and on. The temptation to try another direction is almost invincible, and nothing is easier than to lose one's nerves on these occasions. However, I at length emerged, torn and bleeding from head to foot, and throwing myself into the river, regardless of crocodiles, lay there, drinking in the water through every pore. Much refreshed, but with the unpleasant prospect of spending the night there, I climbed up on to the path that runs along the river-bank, and saw to my amazement the spoor of two horses; this I followed up; and half an hour later, as it was getting too dark to see, I caught the glimmer of a fire in the distance. Here I found Mr. H. S. H.

Cavendish of Lake Rudolph fame, and Mr. Dodson of the British Museum, who had just arrived on a shooting trip.

After an uncomfortable night in a horse's nose-bag and a cloud of mosquitoes, I hurried to my camp to relieve Sharp's anxiety, meeting a search-party of natives on the road. Next day I returned to Cavendish, to see how the fever from which he was suffering had progressed. During lunch a native rushed in, saying that he had been bitten by a night-adder (one of the most deadly snakes in Africa). I promptly collared him by the arm, stopped the circulation with some string, slit his finger crosswise with my pocket-knife, exploded some gunpowder in the cut, while Dodson administered repeated subcutaneous injections of permanganate of potash. Meanwhile the arm, chest, and left side swelled to the most appalling proportions. Cavendish then appeared on the scene with a bottle of whisky, three parts of which we poured down his throat. Then we told off three strong men to run the patient round the camp till he subsided like a log into a drunken stupor. The following morning he was still alive, but the swelling was enormous, and the colour of his nails indicated incipient gangrene. Not knowing what else to do, we put a pot on the fire, and made a very strong solution of the permanganate which we kept gently simmering, while six stalwart natives forced the unfortunate's hand in and out. His yells were fearful, but the cure was complete. The swelling rapidly subsided, the nails resumed their normal colour, and the following morning, with the exception of the loss of the skin of his hand, he was comparatively well.

A note from Sharp informed me that the Portuguese ruffians of the Gorongoza Development Co. had again raided our camp when he was out shooting, had removed the whole concern, beaten, threatened to shoot, and eventually made prisoners of all our boys.

This considerate proceeding they repeated with Mr. Illingworth's party. Needless to remark, our protests were received by the British Consul with the diplomatic interest due to the subject, a request to formulate them on paper, and an intimation that our trouble would be superfluous, as nothing could be done.

Having heard that another Portuguese official, who was reported to be looking for me, was in the vicinity, I asked him to come to dinner. Whereupon he refrained from arresting me, and asked me to stay with him instead; accordingly I returned with him to his station, and the following morning marched into Fontesvilla and caught the train to Beira, where I found Sharp busy packing and sending off the trophies.

CHAPTER III.

THE ZAMBESI AND SHIRÉ RIVERS.

Though very loath to leave our happy hunting-grounds, we had to tear ourselves away and make preparations for the long march north, so went down to Durban to lay in a few necessaries, an extra .303 in case of accidents, and to obtain the time and rate of our chronometer from the observatory.

On our return to Beira we embarked on the *Peters* for Chinde, finding as fellow-passengers the Congo Telegraph Expedition under Mr. Mohun—six white men, one hundred Zanzibaris, thirty donkeys, and a few cows, etc.

To our horror, on disembarking the next day, we found that all our heavy luggage, tents, etc., had been put on the wrong boat at Beira, and were on their way to Delagoa Bay. As the telegraph line is generally in a state of collapse, owing to the white ants eating the posts, and to vagaries on the part of the Portuguese or natives, it took some days to inform the agent.

Chinde offers no attractions except to those who are waiting for a home-going boat, so we made up our minds to go on to Chiromo, and have a little shooting till our things turned up, and we could proceed on our journey.

The African Lakes Corporation, to whom we had consigned a splendid full-plate camera, denied any knowledge of it. We afterwards found that it had passed through their hands, and had been stowed on a sunny and rain-swept verandah for three months, with a result that may be imagined. They had also inadvertently overlooked thirty of our cases of provisions, which we found at the last moment in their store.

Having borrowed a tent from Mr. Mohun, and being tired of sardines as a staple article of diet, we made a start up-river, only to find ourselves worse off afloat than we had been ashore, the Company we had the misfortune to travel by having apparently realized how to provide the minimum of comfort with the maximum of charge.

On each side of the steamer a barge was made fast, so progress was not rapid. It was the dry season. The river was very low, and intervals of rest on sandbanks were of frequent occurrence. The banks being very high, one very rarely saw the neighbouring country. No game was ever to be seen, while on the broad river only an occasional native canoe or a gunboat, bustling down-stream, broke the monotony.

Every night the boat tied up to lay in a supply of wood, sometimes near a native village, and occasionally near a sugar plantation; at the latter we were generally given some green vegetables, which were a great boon.

The water is pumped up from the river and distributed by channels over the cane-swamps, and in the time to come, as more of the river-banks are taken up by these Sugar Concessions, this drain on the water will make a considerable difference to navigation in the dry season.

Amongst the legitimate productions of the cane, they here manufacture Scotch whisky, the labels and bottles being imported from the home markets in large quantities. The most important estate is managed by a French company, superintended by ten Europeans (mainly French). The system of irrigation is very complete, and the work of cleaning is done by steam-ploughs, managed, of course, by Scotchmen. Mills are in course of erection, and the bottles, thistle and all complete, will soon be in requisition. Three hundred hectares are already planted, and the Company intend immediately planting five hundred more.

There is another important Sugar Company, owned by the Portuguese and managed by a Scotchman. The output from its extensive plantations during the season, which lasts three months, amounts to one hundred and twenty tons a week.

It is a dreary, hot, monotonous journey.

The river is most uninteresting, of great breadth, with low grass-covered banks and destitute of trees, except near the delta, where there are some thriving cocoanut plantations. The stream is cut up by numerous islands and sandbanks, haunted by vast flocks of geese, pelicans, and flamingoes.

At Senna there are a few miserable huts, and a few yet more miserable Portuguese, and at Songwe there is an Indian settlement, where there is some trade from the interior.

On reaching the Shiré we were transferred to an animated tea-tray, by courtesy called a steamer, which carried us to Chiromo. The food for five Europeans for two and a half days consisted of one ancient duck, three skinny fowls, and a few tins of sardines. There was no bread, butter, milk, or Worcester sauce, without which life, or rather native cookery, is intolerable. Luckily, at the villages on the way we were able to buy fowls, eggs, and tomatoes.

Before reaching Chiromo we put in at the first B.C.A. post, Port Herald, where dusky Napoleons ponder over wild orgies of the past. A broad road planted with shade trees leads up to the collector's house, and cross-roads, similarly planted, give quite a pleasant appearance to the place, backed in the distance by a high mountain.

Chiromo is laid out at the junction of the Ruo and Shiré rivers, while on the north-west side the station is hemmed in by the vast Elephant Marsh, now a closed game preserve, owing to the inconsiderate slaughter in time past. Lions can be heard almost every night, and the day previous to our arrival a lion appeared in the town in broad daylight, and carried off a native. Though the available population turned out to slay, he escaped untouched. Many shots were fired at him from many varieties of guns, and the range varied from five to five hundred yards. But still he wandered round, the least excited individual in the place. Eventually the Nimrod of Chiromo, who arrived late, hurt his feelings by tumbling off a tree on to his back. This was too much, and he majestically stalked off into the Marsh, wondering at the inscrutable ways of men.

Leopard spoor was also a common sight in the street in the morning, while in the Ruo the crocodiles lived an easy life, with unlimited black meat at their command near the bathing-places.

From its position, the town is the inland port of British Central Africa, and with the fast-growing coffee industry will become a place of considerable importance. Already the building plots command a high price, and stands are being eagerly bought up by the African Flotilla Company and Sharrers' Transport Company, who are rapidly ousting the African Lakes Corporation from their position of hitherto unquestioned monopolists. There are also several German traders who display considerable activity, apparently with satisfactory results, and there are rumours of a coffee combination, financed by a prominent German East Coast firm, making their headquarters here.

A large estate on the right bank of the Shiré, called Rosebery Park, is owned by the African Flotilla Company, which makes excellent bricks, and opposite the town a fibre-extracting company has started work. The company has obtained Foulke's patent fibre-cleaning machine, and a concession of the fibre-gathering rights over all Crown lands, and another similar concession in the Portuguese territory.

The plant employed is Sanseveira, of which there are about twenty varieties, the most common in the neighbourhood being *S. cylindrica* and *S. guiniensis*; the former, owing to the greater ease with which it can be worked, being the most valuable. The length of leaf is 3 to 6 ft., and the diameter about ¾ in. I found it growing in immense quantities on the plains round Chiperoni.

The treatment is very simple. The green stuff is put over rollers, which take it past a rapidly revolving brush under a strong jet of water. The resulting fibre is then dried in the shade, tied into bundles, and is ready bleached for the market. Consequently the cost of production is very low. The fibre is fine, strong, and clean, and the waste is very small, the proportion of fibre to reed being 4 per cent. The strength is estimated at two and a half times that of the best manilla.

The cost of fuel (wood) to run one engine for a day is only four shillings, and as the fibre needs no cleaning, only one process is necessary.

Mr. H. MacDonald, the Collector and Vice-Consul, royally entertained us at his house, the only cool spot in Chiromo. His method of providing fish for dinner was to fire a round from his .303 into the edge of the river, when one or two fish would rise stunned to the surface.

The climate of the vicinity is very trying to Europeans; the heat is intense, and, being a moist heat, is at times insufferable. We repeatedly registered 115° and 120° in the shade, and owing to the amount of vapour held suspended in the air, there was very little diminution of temperature at night.

Periodical waves of fever prostrate the population when the wind blows from the Elephant Marsh, and the death-rate assumes alarming proportions. A form of Beri-Beri is also prevalent.

Large numbers of natives frequently apply for permission to come over from the Portuguese country and settle in British territory, and the population is thus becoming very dense, and food is easily obtainable in large quantities.

CHAPTER IV.

CHIPERONI.

The Ruo, the main tributary of the Shiré river, which two rivers at their angle of confluence enclose Chiromo (native word, "the joining of the streams"), rises in the Mlanje Hills, whence it flows in two main streams which join about twenty-five miles north of its junction with the Shiré. Ten miles south of this are the beautiful Zoa Falls.

As there was every prospect of having to wait some weeks for the errant loads, we made arrangements for some shooting, having heard great tales of the rhinoceros on Mount Chiperoni, which lies about forty miles east of the Ruo in Portuguese territory. Having been provided with porters by Mr. MacDonald, and obtained a permit from the Portuguese, which entitled us to carry a gun and shoot meat for the pot, we crossed the river and marched up towards Zoa.

The country was exceedingly dry and burnt up: consequently the little game that remained in the vicinity was concentrated near the water. After some hard days' work under an impossible sun, I shot a klipspringer, which, curiously enough, was down in the flat country, and fully twenty miles from the nearest hills. The bristly hairs reminded me of a hedgehog, and came out in great quantities during the process of skinning. These antelopes are exceedingly heavy in the hind quarters, short in the legs, and have the most delicate feet imaginable. We both searched high and low for koodoo, which were reported to be plentiful, but without effect, though I found a couple of worm-eaten heads lying in the bush; and for some days we had no luck with sable, although there was much fresh spoor; but eventually I succeeded in bagging a fair bull. No antelope looks grander than an old bull sable, standing like a statue under some tree, his mighty horns sweeping far back over his shoulders. The bristling mane gives a massive appearance to his shoulders; there is something suggestive of the goat about him, both in his lines and carriage: a giant ibex!

One evening some natives came to camp with a wonderful catch of fish, amongst which I noticed four different species. One was a long, eel-shaped fish with a curious bottle snout, and very small teeth. The eye, entirely covered with skin, was almost invisible. There is a closely allied fish in the Nile. Another one resembled a bream with very large fins. A third resembled a carp with enormous scales, and was very poor eating. While the fourth, which I have never seen elsewhere, and which was unknown to Mr. MacDonald, who is a keen naturalist, resembled a heavily-built carp with large scales and prominent fins, and was of a beautiful green colour.

Sharp having decided to go to the north of Nyassa to arrange transport across the plateau, then returned to Chiromo, and I quickly followed. But a few days later I again crossed into Portuguese territory, and marched east along the telegraph line to M'Serrire on the Liadzi, a tributary of the Shiré.

The following morning, quietly strolling through some dense bush, I saw two grand bull sable browsing on the tender shoots of a massive creeper. I fired at the better of the two, and they both galloped away. It was easy to follow their spoor in the soft, peaty soil, and a quarter of a mile away I came on him lying dead. The shot had passed through both lungs. In the evening, when tubbing, I was beset by bees who come in clouds for the moisture, and after an exciting and one-sided conflict I hurriedly withdrew, dashed in a state of nudity through the astonished village, and sought refuge in a hut. The stings induced a severe fever, and the next two days were spent in bed and indignant meditation.

Hearing that some old Cambridge friends of mine had arrived in Chiromo, I marched in and spent a jovial evening with MacDonald, who was entertaining them.

A new detachment of Sikhs arrived under Lieut. Godfrey. It was splendid to see the contrast between the manners of these magnificent men and those of the local negro. The respect shown to all Englishmen by these gentlemen of gentlemen, coupled with their proud carriage and air of self-respecting-respectful independence, contrasted well with the slouching, coarse insolence of the hideous African.

A naïve individual arrived by the same boat for some official post, and asked whether it was usual to leave cards on the converted natives and their wives. He appeared to be a striking example of the appalling ineptitude of many of the officials chosen for the difficult and serious work they undertake.

Tales of rhinoceros and elephant fired me with the desire to make a trip to Chiperoni, a large mountain mass east of the Ruo; but my ignorance of the language made such an undertaking difficult, so that I wasted some days in endeavouring to find a companion. Preparatory to starting, it was necessary to make friends with the Portuguese official. The usual man was away, and his *locum tenens* was the captain of the gunboat, which was moored to the bank opposite MacDonald's house.

From previous experience, I had learnt that with Portuguese and natives everything depended on outward appearance; and, as my wardrobe was little calculated to inspire respect, I went round the town and gathered much gorgeous raiment, the finishing touch being supplied by the doctor in the shape of a red-and-white medal ribbon, torn from a pocket pincushion. Resplendent in such gauds, with a heavy riding-whip, spurs (I had noticed that spurs are indispensable to Portuguese polite society, even at sea), and balancing a No. 6 helmet on a No. 8 head, I was rowed across the river in great pomp by the administration boat, midst the blare of trumpets and waving of flags.

The Portuguese officer, a delightful gentleman, received me with open arms, placed the whole country and all that was therein at my disposal, and gave me a "Viesky-soda," insisting on drinking the same thing himself—a stretch of hospitality that was attended with the direst results.

The following morning, having given up all hopes of finding a companion, I collected a dozen raw natives and a Chinyanja dictionary, and on November 10th crossed the Ruo and marched twelve miles to the Liadzi, a parallel stream to the Ruo, and also flowing into the Shiré. Five miles further I forded the Zitembi, another parallel stream of some volume. This I followed up to a village called Gombi (little bank), which is perched on a small cliff at the junction of the Zitembi with a feeder. I had had considerable difficulty in obtaining guides, the natives being very surly, and absolutely refusing any information of the best means of reaching Chiperoni, or of the probability of sport, and at Gombi things reached a climax, the chief telling me that he wanted no white man in his country, that the Portuguese forced them to work for nothing, and demanded a 5 r. hut tax, that my men would obtain no food, etc., etc., *ad nauseam*. However, seeing that I was not to be trifled with, he changed his tone, and brought me flour and fowls, guides to show me game, and a guide to Chiperoni for the morrow. In the afternoon I took a walk round and shot some meat, seeing plenty of fresh rhino, buffalo, eland, sable, and other buck spoor. The country seemed so promising that I decided, if unsuccessful at Chiperoni, to return for a few days. There was an albino woman in the village; all her children, to the number of five, were also albino, and at several other villages in the vicinity I saw specimens, which would argue a strong hereditary tendency. In many of the villages in the higher valleys there were numerous cases of goitre, some very pronounced, and an extraordinary number of lepers and idiots. This was attributable to the isolating influence of mountainous regions, through difficulty of communication, and the consequent tendency to inbreed. The whole of the next day I followed the Zitembi, till, at its junction with a large feeder, about twenty-four miles from Gombi, there is a village called Chirombo. The stream, which is a series of cascades, and lined with bamboo, is exceedingly beautiful, and, by a reconnaissance on the morrow, I ascertained that it rises on the north of Chiperoni. From here Chiperoni has quite an imposing effect. It is a terraced cone deeply seared by water-courses, and rises from the middle of a basin formed by a circle of less prominent peaks, the most important of which is Makambi to the west. Far away to the north-west were visible the heights of Mlanje, while to the east stretched an unending forest-clad plain that reaches to Mozambique. Woods of mahobahoba (the wild loquat) and many flowering trees covered every rise, and the flat interior of the basin; and the glorious golds, reds, russets, and browns of our autumn, which in these climes beautify the landscape in spring, were at their richest, while a carpet of vivid green and purple flowers lay spread beneath the shade. It was a beautiful country, cool, even at midday, cold at night, free from mosquitoes and flies, and every mile or so an ice-cold stream came tumbling down behind its curtain of ferns and orchids.

Marching round the southern face of Chiperoni for twenty miles, we came to a long ridge or arete which I followed till within 500 ft. of the summit, which is rocky and precipitous, but would offer no difficulty to a man without a load. Here I camped on a small plateau in a glade of mahobahoba. It was a delightful change after the sweltering heat of Chiromo, and I could imagine myself again in Switzerland as I looked out over miles of rolling upland and undulating forest. There were numerous signs of elephant which were feeding on the small sugary loquats, but I failed to find any, though I followed one spoor for many miles. From here we worked round to the east face, till, being short of food, I was obliged to follow one of the numerous streams down to the plain. Here was a considerable but scattered population with a large number of domestic pigeons, pigs, ducks, and cats. The pigs were the ordinary bush-pig, while the pigeons, which were blue rocks, must have been originally introduced by the Portuguese. The stream, which flows into the Misongwe, a tributary of the Shiré, is called the Machingiri, and there are numerous signs of rhino, though few antelopes; however, I managed to bag a good sable. As my boys were following very badly on the paths, I cut straight across to Gombi through the forest, a very long, waterless march, and on arrival found there was not one boy a hundred yards behind; after that I had no further difficulty with them. At Gombi I decided to stop for a few days, and the next morning, after spooring a herd of sable for two hours, I shot a splendid bull.

I had told the chief, who was now most friendly, that I was going to shoot sable, and he came and asked me what I intended to kill the next day, and was much amused when I jokingly replied that I should bring home a rhinoceros.

With this end in view I started early, at 5.30 a.m., and crossing the river, skirted along the foot of the hills, and killed a bull hartebeeste for the Mahomedan boys, who refuse to eat the meat of any beast that has not had its throat cut before death. Although this is a great nuisance (as cutting the throat spoils the head skin), it is right to respect such customs, and I always made a point of killing something else, so that they should not suffer for their belief.

At 7.30 I found fresh rhinoceros spoor which I followed under a blazing sun till 12.30. The country had been very difficult, and I was just beginning to despair when I heard a snort, and looking up, saw the rhino trotting round the corner of an ant-hill, behind which he had been sleeping. On seeing me he stopped, snorting, blowing, and stamping, looking exceedingly nasty. I was carrying my .303, and turning round for my 4-bore, I found that all my boys had bolted up a small thorn tree, from the branch of which they were hanging like a cluster of bees. They had thrown down the gun, and I was compelled to stoop down and grope about for it in the undergrowth. The brute was blowing and snorting only fifteen yards away, and I felt very uncomfortable, as in my position I offered a magnificent target. However, at last I found the gun, and firing past his cheek, hit him full on the edge of the shoulder. Instantly there arose a very hell of sound, squealing, stamping, and crashing of bushes and grass. The smoke hung like a pall around me, and I thought he was charging. Having nowhere to run to, I stayed where I was, and suddenly his huge mass dashed past the edge of the smoke-cloud, and I saw him disappear at a tremendous pace into the grass. We followed hard, but though he bled freely and lay down several times, we did not come up to him again till 3 p.m., when we found him standing at ten yards' distance in a bushy nullah far up in the hills. I fired the 4-bore at his shoulder, knocking him down, but he rose again, and tried to climb the far bank; so I fired the second barrel hurriedly; the cartridge split at the back, and I was knocked over a tree two yards behind. That stopped him, and three solid bullets from the .303 finished him.

I found that the first shot had penetrated about 2 ft., smashing all the shoulder, yet he travelled for two and a half hours, over the steepest hills and through some precipitous water-courses.

In cutting off his head, I found an old iron native bullet in the muscle of his neck.

We were terribly exhausted from the desperate work in a pitiless sun, and hastily grilled a portion of his liver, which was excellent.

A twelve-mile trot brought us back to camp at 7 p.m., and the old chief turned out in state to meet me, and falling upon his knees, rubbed his face in the dust in token of admiration at my powers of prescience.

The natives departed in hundreds there and then to cut up the meat, and arrived early the next morning with the head intact; twenty boys carried it slung on a pole. Skinning it was a fearful business, and occupied me till dark; toil that I have much regretted, since I find that the skull, skin, and many other trophies and curios have been unfortunately lost in transit.

The old chief again came to me and asked me what I was going to kill. I suggested eland for a change; and knowing that there were several herds near where I had killed the rhinoceros, I set off in that direction, my local guides carefully placing a bunch of leaves under a bush on the left-hand side of the path. This, they informed me, ensured success.

The country was full of splendid hunting-grounds; the young grass was sprouting from the black, peaty soil, and the new foliage of the trees afforded grateful shade, beneath which one could walk for hours without encountering any undergrowth.

The spoor of buffalo, rhinoceros, sable, and hartebeeste was plentiful, but nothing would satisfy me except eland, and it was not till midday that I found tracks fresh enough to follow. A six-mile burst brought me in sight of a herd of twenty, and I was creeping round under cover of some trees to obtain a good shot at the leading bull when a boy, who had followed me from the village, let off a dozen ear-piercing whistles to inform me that he too had seen them. Away dashed the eland, and any one who has once followed alarmed eland does not eagerly repeat the mistake. They usually keep up a steady trot till they are clear of the obnoxious neighbourhood, and when they do stand are so wary that approach is impossible. The offending native was an ordinary type of the creatures depicted in books as wonderful hunters and trackers. Personally I have never found a native of Africa who was anything but an abominable nuisance out hunting; and after many trials I strictly confined my hunting attendants to one or two gun-bearers whom I trained to act instantly on a definite set of signs, and never used them for any purpose, except to occasionally follow obvious spoor when I wanted to rest my eyes; even then they needed watching, or they would go wrong. The Bushmen are, of course, an exception to this rule.

On my way back to camp I was startled by a deafening report and the shriek of a bullet past my head. The boy who was carrying my 4-bore had slipped the safety-bolt back, and the trigger had caught in a twig. He was, of course, carrying the gun loosely on his shoulder, and the effect of the explosion of fourteen drams of powder was terrific. It knocked him several feet off the path and stunned him, while the gun described a graceful parabola, and landed, muzzle downwards, on a patch of soft soil, fortunately escaping damage.

A messenger arrived in the evening with a note to the effect that the stray baggage had arrived, and the following day I returned to Chiromo after a most enjoyable trip.

CHAPTER V.

BRITISH CENTRAL AFRICA AND LAKE NYASSA.

At last, on November 28th, I left Chiromo and started up the river once more in the good ship *Scott*, and again realized the feelings of a pea on a drum. Fortunately the skipper was so ill with fever that we took charge of the boat ourselves, and thus contrived to have something to eat.

We had lost six valuable weeks through our kit having been put on the wrong boat at Beira, and as Mohun's expedition had gone on in front we lost eventually six weeks more, through the transport on the Tanganyika plateau being temporarily demoralized. Thus the carelessness of our agent delayed us in all three months. Such is African travel. I no longer fret when my train is ten minutes late. Even after this wait some of our things never turned up at all. Mr. Commissioner Alfred Sharpe, C.B., the greatest and most reticent of African Nimrods, was on board, but we tried in vain to induce him to tell us some of his experiences. However, he gave me a piece of advice that afterwards stood me in good stead: that, when charged by an elephant, the safest course was to remain quite still till the brute was within four yards, and then to blaze in his face. This almost invariably turns the brute or makes him swerve; my experience has certainly proved its efficacy. Mr. Sharpe has the reputation of being the hardest and most daring shikari who ever followed an elephant; and many amusing tales are current of how in the excitement of the chase he would charge cow elephants to make them get out of his way, in order that he might obtain his shot at the leading bull. In view of the success that attends many of the imaginative literary efforts of missionaries and week-end tourists on the subject of Africa, it is a great pity that the few men like Alfred Sharpe and Lawley of Beira railway fame, who have had gigantic experience of Africa past and present, resolutely refuse to record their invaluable data in a book. Sir Harry Johnston and Selous have set an admirable example, and if a few more men of their stamp would write, much of the misleading balderdash that now passes current as representing the Dark Continent would be happily crushed out of existence.

A slight mishap with the machinery delayed us for several hours, and it was not till noon the following day that we reached Makwira's village. Young Makwira, who is quite the young gentleman, in knickers, stockings, spats, collar, and hard hat, provided us with whiskies and milk, and discussed local politics, displaying no little acumen. I believe that it was his father who used to be a terror to all travellers on the Shiré, and that but a few years ago, when the elephant still roamed in thousands on the Elephant Marsh, undisturbed by the shrill whistle of the stern-wheeler or the bark of the playful 4-bore. It was either old Makwira or another genial darky in the vicinity, who for some time kept a tame Portuguese band, and utilized the bandsmen when off duty as machila-carriers.[5]

The Elephant Marsh is a large tract of country lying on the left bank of the Shiré river, north of Chiromo. In days gone by it teemed with elephant, buffalo, and game of all descriptions; but the persistent gunner soon drove the elephant away and decimated the other beasts. And it was due, I believe, to Sir Harry Johnston that it was made into a game reserve. The effect has been most beneficial. Herds of waterbuck and buffalo come to the banks of the river, and lazily watch the steamers pass; and even elephant have been occasionally seen of late playing in their old haunts. A more suitable spot for a reserve could not have been selected. The Shiré and Ruo rivers to the south-west and east, and the highlands to the north, form natural boundaries; there is plenty of water and ample grazing at all times of the year. Every night one may hear the lions roaring. By legislative foresight a game paradise has been saved in the midst of one of the busiest and most progressive of our African possessions.

At Makwira's we reluctantly bade farewell to Mr. H. C. MacDonald, whose dry humour and all-embracing hospitality had made my weary sojourn in Chiromo one of the most delightful stages in our journey. The company on the steamer was rather embarrassed by the extravaganzas of an evangelical madman, who had arrived in the country in a state of destitution, and who is probably by now, under the title D.B.S., a burden on the community. Such men should be caged, or at least prevented from running loose amongst the natives, and adding to the already well-nigh insuperable difficulties of the administration.

A few hours' run brought us to Katunga's, the African Lakes Corporation's port for Blantyre. The Government station is a little distance further up the river. The crocodiles, which were very numerous, had been causing much mortality amongst the natives; one had even seized the station's bucket, which, for greater safety, was lowered into the river to draw water from the end of a long pole.

The Government station is the highest navigable point of the river south of the rapids, and everything has to be unshipped and carried round to the upper river by native porters or wagons. From Katunga's to Blantyre there is a well-constructed road, with a half-way house belonging to the African Lakes Corporation. Captain Rhoades, of the B.C.A. navy, accompanied me in a mule-cart, and we arrived at Blantyre, the commercial centre of B.C.A., about sunset. The road quickly mounts from the Shiré valley on to the plateau of the highlands. Looking back over the valley from the edge of the plateau the view is superb; and much of the scenery through which the road passes is very beautiful. Most of the highlands are covered with woods, which at that season were in the full glory of their vernal tints; the grass was springing up green, and carpeted with millions of beautiful purple flowers resembling crocuses. There were many specimens of the mahobahoba tree, or wild loquat: the timber of this tree is much prized for telegraph poles and similar uses; and the broad dark-green leaves are

---

[5] *Machila*: Portuguese word acclimatized; a hammock slung to a pole and carried by a team of men.

exceedingly handsome. We passed several comfortable-looking homesteads belonging to coffee-planters, and the fields of neatly-planted coffee-shrubs staggering under their burden of snowy blossom made me fancy that I was back in the fruit-farms of Kent.

Coffee is the great industry of British Central Africa, and one that is likely to bring the little protectorate into the vanguard of our new possessions in the near future. The quality is second to none; some of the crops have realized the highest price on the London markets. At present the industry is more or less paralyzed, owing to the majority of the planters having started operations on borrowed capital, and, with one or two exceptions, without previous experience of coffee. But as soon as the plantations are put on a sound business footing the prosperity of the community should be assured, always provided that the administration, by judicious legislation as to rate of pay for labourers, prevents the labour market from being spoilt. The present rate of pay is three shillings a month, and a rise must be prevented at all costs. The labour supply, properly handled, should prove well-nigh inexhaustible, and, owing to the immigration from the Portuguese sphere, is steadily increasing. I was informed by many men that the first crop should pay the expenses of the first three years during which there is no yield. This is a magnificent return, and by judicious combines, capitalization, and concentration, Nyassa coffee should become an important industry. The coffee being of such quality, is only used for blending at present, so that there is little chance of over-production. It is one of the few African countries that has natural easy communication with the coast, and when a light railway has been built, and shipping and agency have been properly organized, the cost of transport will be very small. There is also undoubtedly great scope for subsidiary and supplementary industries, such as cocoa and rubber.

I consider that in British Central Africa there is an excellent opening for British capital—an opening that appears to be as yet practically unknown at home. The fact is that Africa is supinely neglected where it cannot flaunt the magic war-cry, Gold. The Germans, who are ever on the alert, are already alive to its possibilities, and there were rumours of a great coffee combine financed by well-known German East Coast capitalists. It is to be hoped that England will awake to the chance before the ground has been cut from under her feet, as has already been done in so many places that I have visited. The wily Teuton is very much alive to the advantages afforded by British rule, and has already levied heavy toll on the budding possibilities of trade in our African dominions. Our trouble is that, with few exceptions, we do not send out the right men, but consider that any one is good enough for Africa. This is far from being the case, as new business lines have to be adopted to ensure success. Adaptability and enterprise belong to genius and not to mediocrity, and no country requires a more delicately-adjusted combination of dash, tact, and perseverance than Africa.

There is a passable hotel in Blantyre, and many fine buildings in brick. The missionaries have built a large church, and laid out avenues of eucalyptus which have grown wonderfully well. Unfortunately, as in Rhodesia, the white ants attack the roots when the trees attain a certain height. Extensive plantations would unquestionably considerably modify the climate, which is far from good. The worst type of hæmoglobinuric fever is very prevalent, and the death-rate is consequently high. However, as more and more land is brought under cultivation, the country should become healthier. Probably much of the fever that prevails is brought from the lowlands, which must be traversed before arriving in the higher altitudes: an improved service with the coast will obviate this to some extent. At Blantyre I met with much kindness at the hands of Mr. Codrington, the Commissioner of Northern Rhodesia, Major Harding, C.M.G., who had been recruiting Angonis for the B.S.A. Police, and Mr. Wilson of the Trans-Continental Telegraph, an old school and Cambridge friend, whom I was much surprised to find in this out-of-the-way corner of the world. Three days later I left with Mr. Hall of the African Flotilla Company in machilas for Zomba, the administrative capital. We were to spend the night at the Nomasi river, which we reached in a torrential downpour. Our delight, when we discovered that the transport people had sent our tents and provisions by the wrong road, may be imagined. Fortunately we learned that Mr. Harrison, whom we had met on the river, was camped in the vicinity, and he kindly provided us with a shakedown and something to eat. The following day we reached Zomba, having passed through many flourishing coffee estates. Here Mr. C. C. Bowring put us up and plied us with all the obtainable luxuries and comforts, in the intervals of a fight to the death with a swarm of irate bees who had taken possession of the interior of the wall of his house. The view across Lake Shirwa and the forests that clothe the flat plains which surround the lake ranks amongst the finest that I have seen in Africa. Vast purple masses of hills enclose the placid lake and its forest-clad plains, and the eye roams on over an infinity of broken upland and shimmering haze. The Government House is a large picturesque building standing in the midst of a well-planted tropical garden, which had, however, been lately ravaged by a flight of locusts. There was tennis accompanied by a tea-party, presided over by Miss Harrison, who has nursed many a sick man back to life, and it seemed as if I had suddenly dropped back into civilized England. After two pleasant days spent in these unwonted surroundings, I started in a machila for Liwonde on the Upper Shiré, where I arrived at sunset, and was entertained by Mr. Drummond Hay, an old "Herzog" friend. I am much shocked to hear that he has since fallen a victim to the climate.

From Liwonde the S.S. *Monteith* took me to Fort Johnston, which is the port of Lake Nyassa, and is situated a few miles south of the bar at the outlet of the lake. A short distance from Fort Johnston the river opens out and forms the small lake Pamalomba, formerly a great haunt of elephant. The lake is very shallow, and as the steamer passes along, the disturbed mud emits enormous volumes of marsh gas: so great is the quantity that the water has the appearance of violently boiling. There have been several instances of men being blown out of their cabins, owing to their having ignited the gas by absent-mindedly striking a match. When Sharp passed with Mr. Mohun, somebody threw a lighted match overboard. Instantly a sheet of flame passed over the barge that was being towed alongside, and two saddles were seriously burnt.

As we arrived at Fort Johnston late in the evening, I elected to sleep on board, and was much gratified to find that two couples of married German missionaries, not content with having monopolized the only two cabins, had rigged up a large canvas enclosure and were sleeping on deck. Consequently, I was compelled to place my blankets by the wheel and sleep in the wind and dew.

Mr. Wallis, the Vice-Consul, entertained me. He has laid the new town out most admirably, and I could scarcely believe that it had all been done in a few months. The place was alive with rats, who amused themselves all night by tobogganing down my face, rushing along my body, and taking flying leaps from my feet into outer darkness.

Commander Cullen took me over H.M.S. *Gwendoline*, the large new gunboat that had just been launched for patrolling the lake. It is a splendid work to have accomplished, when the difficulties of transporting some of the heavy portions round the rapids are taken into consideration. I was also introduced to a budding diplomatist, who informed me with pride that he had fired a soft-nosed bullet at an elephant at one thousand yards. The elephant escaped.

On December 15th I started on the voyage up the lake in the S.S. *Domira*, and at midday made Monkey Bay. It is a most beautiful little spot, and reminded me forcibly of the South Sea Islands. Bold rocky headlands plunge into the lake and enclose a white strip of sand with straggling villages at the back. The water is clear as crystal, and broken by the heads of hundreds of natives diving, swimming, and splashing about. Ringing peals of laughter echo in the rocks and startle the troops of baboons that sit watching with curious eyes the trim little steamer. Picturesque groups of natives are scattered about the beach, and the little picaninnies are playing on the skeleton of a wrecked Arab dhow, little dreaming what that dhow had meant to their fathers a few years before. In the afternoon I strolled out, hoping to get a shoot at koodoo, for which the place is famous. But the koodoo were not at home; however, I saw several impala, and shot a small buck which I believe to have been the duiker described by Sir Alfred Sharpe as a probable new species. Unfortunately, my natives devoured the skull and the rats ate the skin. It was a small, reddish-brown buck, similar in build to a klipspringer, with wiry hair and thick, high-standing hind quarters.

The next wooding station was Domira Bay, and on the 17th we arrived at Kota-Kota, which used to be the headquarters of the Arab slave traffic across the lake, and the starting-point of the Arab raids towards Mweru. Mr. Swann, the collector, who has had many years' experience of Tanganyika in the old Arab days, entertained me, and gave me two Angoni spears which had been taken in the Mpeseni trouble. There are several missionaries at Kota-Kota. They have started football, and in a rash moment I was induced to play—a freak which I regretted for many days afterwards, as it brought on a sharp attack of fever.

Kota-Kota is exceedingly beautiful, as indeed is all the coast of Lake Nyassa. The hills are heavily wooded, and their bases are broken by the waves into fantastic caves and rocky promontories against which plays the white line of surf. Small rocky islands stand out here and there, and form the resting-place of myriads of cormorants.

Here I first saw the extraordinary "Kungu" fly, which is, I believe, peculiar to Lake Nyassa. They resemble small may-flies, and at certain seasons of the year rise from the water in such stupendous clouds that they blot out the whole horizon. Seen in the distance, they have exactly the appearance of a rainstorm coming across the lake. When they are blown landwards they make every place uninhabitable by the stench which arises from the countless millions that lodge and die on every inch of sheltered ground. I myself have seen them lying a foot deep in a room, and I was told that they are often much worse. The natives sweep them up and make cakes of them. I tasted one, and found it by no means bad. The next morning we reached Bandawe, another important station, where there is a large mission-house with extensive plantations of pineapples and some splendid mango trees. At Nkata Bay, a few miles further up the coast, a native came and begged us to go and see his master, who was very ill. Accordingly we set off in the dark, and found Mr. Broadbridge of the African Trans-Continental Telegraph down with a severe attack of fever; we did what we could for him, and he shortly recovered. After a short stop at Luawi to pick up wood, we steamed into Florence Bay, and at Miss MacCallum's invitation I accompanied her up to the Livingstone Mission at Mount Waller. Mr. Stewart, one of the missionaries, who has been for some time working among the northern Angonis, told me that he had been investigating the history of the Angonis, who are descendants of the Zulus. There were two great treks north of the Zulus in the time of Chaka. One, under Moselikatse, marched to Matabeleland, leaving the ancestors of the present Matabele, and then north across the Zambesi. There they came into conflict with the Barotse, and were driven east, eventually settling in Southern Angoniland of to-day, which lies south-west by west of Lake Nyassa.

The other trek marched north through the Sabi district, leaving the present Shangaans on their way, and then crossed the Zambesi by the Kabrabasa rapids and passed near Lake Rukwa. Here the chief died and the trek split up: one part went north of Tanganyika and settled near the south-west of the Victoria Nyanza, where they were rediscovered by Stanley; another part marched round the northern shore of Lake Nyassa; and yet another returned south and founded Northern Angoniland of to-day.

Dr. Robert and Mrs. Laws treated me with the greatest hospitality; he took me round the mission, and showed me the results of their four years' work since the founding of the station. Dr. Robert Laws was one of the first explorers of Nyassaland, and was in no small way responsible for the checkmating of the Portuguese pretensions to what is now British Central Africa. The station is admirably situated on a plateau surrounded by hills with valleys intervening, and commands extensive views across the lake to Amelia Bay and the Livingstone Mountains, and to the west towards the valley of the Loangwa or Northern Angoniland. There is a large printing-machine which the natives work under the superintendence of Mr. Thomson. Here books and magazines and much work of great merit are produced. The processes of stereotyping and picture-reproducing on zinc are thoroughly understood by the skilled natives. In the workshops are several carpenters, one of whom in a few hours made me a folding camp-chair that accompanied me to Cairo. The farm and the quarry are both managed by natives. Dr. Laws' system is to employ native teaching as much as possible. If ability, whole-hearted earnestness, and hard work can accomplish any good in missionary endeavour, Dr. Laws ought to succeed. Laden with butter and gigantic water-melons, I returned to the boat, and the following day we reached Karonga's, the starting-point for the Stevenson Road.

CHAPTER VI.

KARONGA TO KITUTA ACROSS THE TANGANYIKA PLATEAU.

On arrival at Karonga I was much disappointed to find that Sharp, tired of waiting, had left two days before to try and arrange transport on Tanganyika. As it was the season for sowing their crops, very few carriers were available, and it was evident that I should have to wait some time before I could obtain sufficient men to transport our loads. I commenced operations by repacking all the food-boxes and discarding everything that was not absolutely necessary, as well as the considerable quantity of stuff that had spoilt through being improperly packed. The firm responsible, either as a practical joke or an experiment in the cultivation of fungus, had packed chocolate in paper wrappers and laid them in hay in a leaky wooden box. As a practical joke it was weak, but as a venture in fungi-culture a complete success. In fact, unpacking the boxes reminded me forcibly of the days when, as a youthful disciple of Isaac Walton, I used to dig for worms in the garden manure-heap. A series of remarkable tins of sausages added materially to the excitement of these excavations, one and all having assumed the outward and visible form of a Rugby football; while as to the inward invisible grace, I was careful to throw them down wind, when they exploded on contact with the ground in a manner most satisfactory, to the utter consternation of six Kaffir dogs and a hyæna. They, having followed up the wind of the first (a comparatively mild one), were so overcome by its successors that they clapped their tails between their legs, and, with a dismal howl, fled, convinced of the superiority of the white man, even in what they had hitherto considered the black man's monopoly. Native rumour has it that they are running still.

Having arranged everything and reduced the loads to a minimum, I succumbed to a dose of fever, and spent Christmas Day in bed, on a cup of tea. Dr. Castellote, the medical officer of Mr. Mohun's expedition, was most kind, and when I had sufficiently recovered, we went out together for a few days' shooting on the River Songwe, which, flowing into the extreme north-western point of Lake Nyassa, forms part of the Anglo-German boundary-line.

Before starting, however, I went to a neighbouring village and called for volunteers to accompany us on our long journey north. I informed the people in the guest's resting-place, which is kept apart in every village, that the journey would take many moons; that we should go to Tanganyika, that north of Tanganyika we should find another lake, then mighty mountains that made fire, then another lake, then still mightier mountains so high that the water became as stones; then a fourth lake, out of which flowed a great river which, after several moons, took one to the dwelling-places of the white man—large even as hills—where the white men were even as the sands of the lake-shore; that there we should find the sea—the water without end—and that I would send back in steamers large as villages those who came with me, so that they might return to their homes and tell their brothers of all the wonderful things they had seen. The people were much impressed and evidently considered me a very extra special line in liars. They asked me how I knew what was there—"had I been there to see?" I told them that the white man knew much, and what he did not know he could find in books (showing them one). Then they realized that I must be even a finer liar than they had at first taken me to be. After a little more talking four stalwart Watonga volunteered to come, thinking it a pity not to see more of such a transcendent Ananias. One of them, Makanjira, was a small chief on the lake-shore, and those four men stuck to me through thick and thin, and all arrived safely at Cairo; but I regret to say that I have just heard that one of them, Chacachabo, died during the voyage down the coast. The next day a nude dirty little ruffian came and asked to go too; he, though but a small boy, came through safely, and is now setting up a reputation as a liar on his own account. Later on I obtained twelve more recruits, whom I handed over to Mr. Mohun's sergeant to be drilled: these men, as it will later transpire, deserted *en masse* a few days north of Ujiji. They were Asiska, and a very unwholesome lot of ruffians.

The doctor and I started off along the lake-shore on a couple of donkeys lent to us by Mr. Mohun. We had much trouble in inducing them to cross a large stream that flows into the lake a few miles north of Karonga, and eventually had to take them bodily by the four legs and throw them in.

At Chikopolo's there is a Government station in charge of a few native police; here we stayed for a day, but finding nothing more interesting than waterbuck and reedbuck, moved north and camped on the Songwe, which is a stream of considerable importance, and navigable for several miles from the lake. I was informed that there was a German post on the northern bank of the river at its junction with the lake, and accordingly went across to pay my respects. On arrival I found that the station was in charge of a Goanese native, who promptly endeavoured to annex my rifle, saying that I had brought it into the country without a permit. I called upon Mirambo, a splendid old Arab who used to be a great man in the country. He entertained me with true Arab courtesy, and loaded my boys with magnificent pine-apples and lemons when I went away. It was pitiable to see the poor old man, who a few years ago had commanded thousands, putting on the faded relics of his greatness to do me honour.

On the way back to camp I came upon an enormous native fishing weir: there were two or three natives wading waist-deep in the water above the weir pulling fish out of the baskets, while down-stream, with nothing but the crazy sticks between, the water was being lashed into foam by the gyrations of scores of huge crocodiles. I shot fourteen in as many minutes, averaging fifteen feet in length. The natives flocked in to express their satisfaction, and actually brought me a present of some fish. There were a few pookoo on the plain. They are most beautiful little antelopes and carry themselves exactly like a waterbuck. The hair is reddish, long, and curly, and the hide (as with all the waterbucks) very tough and thick. It has been obtained by comparatively few sportsmen, as it is only found on the Upper Zambesi, Loangwa, Chambesi, and Mweru district.

On the 13th I moved my camp twelve miles up the river to a village called N'kana. Here the hills close in upon the river, but leave a series of delightful little green glades, most likely places for finding roan antelope, which are numerous in the country. But I was unsuccessful, though there was some spoor about. While crossing one of these small glades, a shout of Njoka (snake) from my gun-bearer made me spring to one side. I found that I had put my foot so close to a sleeping puff-adder that it would have been impossible to have slipped a visiting-card between us. The brute still slept; on, till I crushed the life out of it with an enormous log of wood. It rather scared me, as I was hunting with bare legs. All this country is infested with puff-adders, which are the most dangerous snakes in Africa, as they do not dart away like other snakes, but lie sleeping in the dust till they are trodden upon. They differ from other snakes in that they strike backwards. Later on, near the Chambesi, I actually trod upon one; it struck, but missed me, and turned a back somersault in the air, leaving the ground entirely. After that I always wore gaiters or stockings. I have heard of another instance of a puff-adder springing clear of the ground. This is rendered possible by their habit of striking backwards. The natives complained of the hut tax and of being forbidden to kill game: they said that many had crossed over into the German sphere; but they have all come back in a hurry.

Failing to find roan antelope, I marched back to Chikopolo's across the hills, and was much struck by the number of butterflies in the woods; some of them were very beautiful, but so rapid was their flight that it was exceedingly difficult to catch them. Everywhere there was splendid cattle country, but unfortunately very little cattle. Before the rinderpest the whole of the Songwe valley was black with buffalo; now I do not believe there is a single beast, except in some jungle two days' march to the north, which the natives told me was haunted by a few buffalo and elephants. And only a very few head survive of the countless herds of cattle which were characteristic of the Wankonde. The Wankonde are a very pleasant-mannered, intelligent people, who were saved from absolute extinction at the hands of the Angoni, Watonga, and Arabs by the British occupation of the country. Ethnologically they are extremely interesting: their ethnographical position in the races has not yet been satisfactorily ascertained. Their huts, which are very neat and picturesque, are sometimes square, sometimes round, and worked in a pattern of round knobs of clay stuck in between the rush walls. Many are built on a raised clay foundation with a trench to draw off the rain. The roof is worked in fancy patterns. Their metal work is first-class, in fact the most finished that I have seen on the east side of Africa. They have a fair breed of cattle, goats, and sheep, and grow pineapples, bananas, and pumpkins in profusion. Probably owing to Arab influence their villages are well laid out, and the banana palms are planted in carefully aligned avenues. The Arab influence on their music is obvious. And despite Arab influence they are an exceedingly moral race. Being a peaceful, pastoral, and agricultural people, they fell an easy prey to their warlike neighbours and the slave-raiding Arabs. Lugard speaks of them as having been shot down in the most merciless manner by the Arabs in his time.

The natives informed me that Mr. Mohun and Captain Verhellen, the Belgian officer in command of the telegraph escort, were camped on the Songwe, so I marched back and joined them. They were out for a short hunting-trip, and I found them ignominiously slaughtering a goat for meat, although the whole plain was alive with game. On examining Mr. Mohun's rifle, which he had just bought from a local man of God, I found that the barrel was so badly worn that it was almost possible to insert the whole cartridge at the muzzle. That explained his having fired forty shots without effect. In the evening we strolled out together, and after a very difficult stalk I pulled off a long shot of three hundred yards at a good bull pookoo. Captain Verhellen informed me that he had seen four small grey antelopes, one of which he had wounded and lost. I could not imagine what they could be; so on the following morning turned out with his boy to show me where he had seen them. I had only walked about three miles when I saw one standing in a patch of green grass. It appeared to be a reedbuck of a beautiful bright silver-grey colour. There was a small ant-hill between the buck and me which made stalking easy, and I approached without difficulty to within sixty yards. I was just pressing the trigger when an ordinary reedbuck sprang out at my feet and dashed away with a shrill whistle; this started the grey one, and I only got a running snapshot. The bullet struck it in the stern but failed to stop it, and the second barrel only grazed the side. I galloped wildly in pursuit, but the buck kept on its course for nearly two miles before it stopped. The distance between us was fully four hundred yards, but I had to take the shot, as it was watching me, and was evidently prepared to resume its flight. The bullet struck it far back, and it again galloped away, the second barrel going wide. Fortunately the plain was extensive and the grass in most places short, so that I managed to keep it in view for the next four miles. Then it stood again, near some bushes; I endeavoured to approach under cover of these, but was again spotted, and the weary chase recommenced. The country became more broken, and I lost sight of the brute for some time, but eventually saw it lying down a thousand yards away. I approached to a tree, whence I could see if it moved, and waited in the hope that it would get stiff and allow me to come within certain shooting-range. After waiting half an hour I commenced to stalk it, crawling flat on my stomach; there was a convenient bush within fifty yards of where it was lying, and I made for this. After half an hour's desperate crawl through thorns in a blazing sun, I reached the much-desired spot, and peering cautiously round the edge found, to my infinite disgust, that it had moved on. I searched high and low, but could find no trace, and soon lost the spoor which showed but faintly on the grass. As a last effort I made a circuit of two miles, but returned to where I had lost it without result. Then I sat down, waiting for my boys to arrive with my water-bottle. The pace had been so hot that they were completely lost, and I waited in vain. The fever from which I was still suffering made my thirst intolerable, and I rose with the intention of returning to camp. Then a bright idea struck me, and taking the siren whistle which I carried on my belt, I blew a piercing blast. A rustle! and the buck leapt out of some grass which I imagined would not have covered a mouse, and dashed off. To throw down the whistle was the work of a second, and a quick double-barrel brought the little brute at last to grass. I was more than delighted, and realizing that I had obtained a new species of antelope, as the eyes, lips, horns, and hoofs showed no trace of albinoism, skinned it with loving care, and carried it back to camp. Dr. Sclater of the Zoological Society has kindly described it for me. I called it Thomasina's reedbuck (*Cervicapra Thomasinæ*) after the lady who is now my wife.

The following day I slew another good bull pookoo, which took more killing than any buck I have ever shot. The pookoo's tenacity of life is proverbial among those who are acquainted with this most beautiful little antelope. They have a curious gland about 4 in. below the head in the side of the neck.

The Wankonde play a curious little musical instrument resembling in conception a zither: the strings (six or seven in number) are stretched on a back of hollow reeds; it is held under the leg when sitting, and fingered like the Maderia machette with the right hand, the strings being stopped with the left. They also play on a bow with a gourd or cocoanut-shell as a sounder, and a species of guitar.

Having received a note to the effect that porters had at last come in, I returned to Karonga to prepare for my final march of two hundred and ten miles west to Tanganyika.

On the way I stopped for a day with Mr. Fox, who was managing the telegraph construction across the plateau. The line was just opened to Karonga from Salisbury, and Mr. Mohun had put up the first telephone seen on Lake Nyassa between Karonga and Mr. Fox's camp. The work of construction up the west coast of Lake Nyassa had been attended with the greatest possible difficulties from the precipitous and densely-wooded nature of the country, and the pestilential climate. These had, however, by superhuman efforts, been overcome in the stipulated time by the handful of men engaged on the work. A wide track, straight as an arrow, up hill, down dale, across abysmal chasms, and through swamps, had been cleared, and iron posts set in iron shoes supported the wire. No one at home can realize the stupendous difficulties that have been overcome. But I from observation know, and take off my hat in awed admiration of that gallant band who, quietly, relentlessly, and without a murmur, have accomplished the seemingly impossible. It stands out in bold relief as a colossal monument of what the Anglo-Saxon can do, and will ever sigh to the African wind the greatness of that master mind which, in spite of the fossilized apathy of the British Government, has raised a British South Africa to be a dominant factor in the world's history of the future. It was instructive to mark the characteristic distinction between Mr. Rhodes' telegraph expedition and the expedition of the King of the Belgians. On the one hand was an unassuming handful of men (without a single armed man), whose very existence might easily have been overlooked by the casual passer-by. Yet behind them lay many hundreds of miles of perfected work which brought the far interior of Africa within a minute of Cape Town; before them stretched an arrow-like clearing to Tanganyika (two hundred miles long), waiting for the transport service to bring poles and wire. Quiet men, rotten with fever, were being carried to and fro— inspecting, measuring, and trenching. Above their base floated a diminutive Union

Jack; no pomp, no fuss, not even a bugle; yet all worked like clock-work. On the other hand, a huge camp thundering with the tramp of armed men, uninhabitable from the perpetual blare of bugles, a very wilderness of flags. Gorgeous and fussy Belgians strutting about in uniforms, screaming and gesticulating, with a few sad-visaged Englishmen doing the work—piles and piles of loads—and ever those bugles. It resembled the triumphant march of an army through the land, and the cost must have been appalling. Yet months after they had eventually arrived at Mtowa, nothing had been accomplished. The petty jealousy of the local officials proved an impenetrable barrier, and now if anything has been accomplished, the wire has been merely slung on trees. According to the latest reports, there had been trouble with the natives, and the whole expedition had been broken up, with the loss of most of the plant. There is undoubtedly a quiet something about the Anglo-Saxon that gets there somehow.

Fever overcame me once more, and I was confined to my bed for several days; but at last, on January 24th, I made a start, and marched to Mpata, the first camping-place on the Stevenson Road. The Stevenson Road is a clearing through the bush that covers the greater part of the plateau, and barely deserves the title of road, although in some places a few logs have been thrown across the streams, and the more swampy portions have been trenched.

The second stage brings one to Mkongwés, about twenty-seven miles from Karonga. Chumbu, the next halting-place, is fourteen miles further. The country is very hilly, and the scenery not very attractive. At intervals, intersecting the road, the telegraph clearing sweeps on in its relentless line, looking like a gigantic ride, where one expects every minute to see the white tail of a scared bunny or a gorgeous cock-pheasant bowling along as though on wheels. But one looks in vain; no sign of life breaks that monotonous line stretching away over the far hills till the trees at the side merge together, and it is lost in the far distant horizon.

A very long day's march brought us to Fort Hill, the frontier station of Nyassaland, which is in charge of a few black police. It had been very wet, as the rains had broken, and I was exceedingly thankful to take cover in the substantial house which is in the centre of the stockade. I had a bull-calf with me, and gave it in charge of one of my Askaris, who retaliated in the usual annoying way of natives by coming and asking for some string to lead it by. Asking for string is a common and intangible form of insolence, as they make string from the bark of several kinds of trees, very common all over the country. But this time I scored. I had a large coil of Alpine rope weighing about 20 lbs. I gave him this, and told him on pain of death not to cut it. Then he said, "It did not matter, he would make some." But I was relentless. "He had asked for string, and I never refused a reasonable request." That youth never again asked for string. At Nyala the telegraph people have built a substantial house, which is to be a telegraph station and general depository of material; they have selected an admirable position. A large blood-sucking fly made life rather a burden; they settled so quietly that one never felt them till they had driven a proboscis, like a red-hot bodkin, half an inch into one's neck or face. Amazing downpours every morning added to the joys of life, and for several days I had to live in wet clothes and sleep in wet blankets, while it was almost impossible to start a fire. I had a sou'-wester and an oilskin, but they were of no avail. The rain fell like a wave, and with such force that it splashed up underneath, and one was soon drenched to the neck by capillary attraction. Passing through Mpansa we reached Ikawa on the 31st.

Ikawa is the first station of Northern Charterland, on the Tanganyika Plateau. Mr. Mackinnon, the collector, had gone to the Chambesi district to neutralize the political machinations of a fractious missionary.

Nine miles further on is Fife, the A.L.C. station, and the oldest settlement on the plateau. Mr. McCulloch, who has been in charge for several years, tells some delightful stories about his exciting experiences in the old days of Arab predominance. Two members of Lieut. Schleufer's expedition, which was endeavouring to transport a steamer for the German Government to Lake Tanganyika, were camped outside the walls waiting for porters. They had some heavy loads with them on carts, and had taken seven weeks to make the journey from Karonga. Fife is the half-way house between Nyassa and Tanganyika. From the verandah I looked out with longing eyes over the vast Awemba country that lies at the foot of the plateau. The view was superb, and typical of Africa in its misty uncanniness. Mr. McCulloch has planted splendid gardens, and we revelled in green peas, new potatoes, cabbage, lettuce, and many other European vegetables, all of which grow luxuriantly on these altitudes. In the days of overcrowding not far distant there will be a fine country for European settlement on the Tanganyika Plateau. There is much fever at present, but I think most of it is brought from the low countries. The nights were quite cold, and fires necessary for comfort. Mr. McCulloch has a wonderful knowledge of the native; he is considered as a chief by the large village close to the station, and is much respected by the native chiefs for many miles round. I purchased some beautiful wooden snuff-bottles from the Mambwe people, and some extraordinary ear-plugs which are worn by the women in the lobe of the ear; some of them were 2 in. in diameter.

The Anglo-German Boundary Commission had just completed its task, and the new boundary enclosed many of the large labour centres in the German sphere: some of the chiefs, however, availed themselves of the time limit allowed by proclamation, and came across to British territory. But the Germans, contrary to the terms of the agreement, had posted native police to intercept and terrorize them into remaining. The Germans did not behave very well over the boundary settlement, but insisted on retaining a small strip of territory that fell to their share, but which cut across the Stevenson Road, though they were offered a handsome *quid pro quo* elsewhere. However, the British collector set to work at once, and in a few days took the road round the obstructing strip.

At Ikomba, another B.S.A. station, I found that Mr. Forbes had gone home, and promptly looted the excellent new potatoes which I found in his garden. On February 9th I reached Mambwe, and from there made a trip down to the Awemba country, which is described in the next chapter. On our return to Mambwe I was laid up with a very severe attack of fever which did not leave me for two months, till I reached the highlands around Kivu. I was delirious for some time, but improved sufficiently to be carried to Kawimbi, a mission station near Abercorn. Mr. and Mrs. May were most kind to me; the station is very pretty, and looks like an English village with its picturesque little cottages and numerous flower-beds. The following morning I was carried on to Abercorn, although the missionaries kindly pressed me to stay, promising to nurse me and make me well. I was sorely tempted, but felt bound to hurry on. At Abercorn I utterly collapsed for several days, and in the intervals of delirium eked out a precarious existence on Worcester sauce and limes. Here I heard a lion story. The hero of the story (also the author) having been told that a leopard was taking toll of the goats, built a platform in a tree and sat up over a goat. Nothing, however, turned up; but in the morning, tired of doing nothing, he fired an arrow at a venture into a patch of grass, and on going to pick it up, found that it had transfixed the heart of a stupendous black-maned lion. Considering the state of my health, I thought this rather unkind. At last I was sufficiently recovered to move once more, and was carried in a machila, under Mr. Boyd's care, to Kituta, the A.L.C. station at the south-eastern extremity of Tanganyika. The first glimpse of those waters, round which so many dark tragedies have been enacted, cheered me considerably. I had realized another ambition, and had arrived at the real starting-point of our Odyssey.

Kituta is a beautiful but pestilential spot, chiefly remarkable for its abominable smells. It is also the scene of another lion story which deserves perpetuation.

There was once a very nervous agent in charge of the station with a particular horror of lions. One of these brutes commenced eating the natives of the village; so the agent barricaded himself in his room and slept with six native watchmen in case of attack. Hearing, or thinking that he heard, the lion prowling round, he fired out of the window and knocked a hole through the administration boat. The following night he again heard sounds and fired, bagging the collector's donkey at the first shot. A certain well-known sportsman, who was hunting in the vicinity, wrote in and congratulated him on shooting his first lion. He rose to the occasion, and now silences all sceptics by producing the letter, and has acquired quite a reputation as a hunter of big game.

While purchasing trade-cloth for the journey north, the carelessness of the British manufacturer was again brought home to me. All the loads contained different lengths, and as the marks had been rubbed off, the operation lasted several hours instead of ten minutes; and they were so badly packed that after a week's knocking about most of them came undone, and the contents were consequently in part spoiled. I wonder when the British exporter will realize the advisability of studying the requirements of his markets. Kituta was at one time the call-place of many Arab caravans, but now it has sunk into insignificance, although there is a flourishing rubber trade in the country, which is paying very handsomely.

CHAPTER VII.

THE CHAMBESI.

On reaching Mambwe I had the good fortune to find Mr. C. R. Palmer, the assistant-collector, on the point of starting for the Chambesi, with the object of waking up one or two of the chiefs who had been tardy in sending in labour. His offer to take me with him, and his glowing description of the game to be found there, were so tempting that next morning I found myself on the march to Tanzuka, a border village of the Mambwe; and on the following day we entered the country of the Awemba, a very powerful tribe apparently of Zulu origin. The difference between these people and the neighbouring Mambwe is as cheese from chalk: whereas the latter are of the ordinary dirty, stunted, cringing or insolent, ill-fed type of Central Africa, the former are of a very striking caste. Among the upper class are some magnificent specimens of the native, tall men of powerful build, with much of the well-bred carriage of the Zulu; their noses are straight and thin cut, their colour bronze; and their hair, which they wear in grotesque tufts down the middle of their head, is the only conspicuous negro characteristic. Many of the young women, with their regular features, beautiful colour, and small, delicate hands and feet, are quite pleasing. Until the advent of the Chartered Co. they led the rollicking life of the old Zulus; herding cattle and depending for the meaner necessaries of life and the replenishing of their harems on the efforts of their neighbours. Far and wide they used to raid even to the Atonga country on the east coast of Tanganyika, and many and wonderful are the tales told of their stupendous forced marches, when the weaker members used to fall out and die from sheer exhaustion. All the chiefs of any standing maintain bands, composed of singers, drummers, and players on the castanets, in which they take great pride. On the approach of any visitors to whom they wish to do honour, the band is sent forward to meet them; the leading part is usually taken by a man who sings the theme, some of them having remarkably fine voices, while the refrain is taken up by other men, playing drums of hollow wood with lizard or snake skin stretched over the apertures, and a chorus of boys rattling pods containing dry seeds; the whole is accompanied by grotesque dancing, the main object of which appeared to be to go as near falling down as possible without actually doing so. The strain, like most African music, plays on about three notes with untiring repetition, and, though rather pleasing at first, palls after the fourth or fifth hour. Should a chief find any singer of unusual power, he promptly removes his eyes to prevent him from going elsewhere, and many men thus mutilated are to be seen in every district. In fact mutilation in various forms appears to be the chief recreation of these autocrats. Mr. Palmer told me of three youths who came in to him without their eyes, which had been removed by their chief, because he thought his people were getting out of hand; so to teach them that he was still master he had selected haphazard these three unfortunates. I also heard of some women who had had their ears, lips, hands, and breasts cut off, and who actually travelled a distance of about sixty miles immediately afterwards to the collector of the district. I myself saw many men who had similarly lost their ears, lips, hands, or privates, and sometimes all these parts.

Mr. Law, the able collector at Abercorn, who is known to the natives by the appellation of the "Just man" (and who, by the way, charged me £25 for my rhino about six hours before I sailed north), when on some punitive expedition in the Awemba country, captured a delightful example of the grim humour of these pleasing gentry. It consisted of a large sable horn rudely adorned and fitted with a mask, into which the patient's head was fitted, his throat having been previously cut with a ferocious-looking knife, chiefly remarkable for its bluntness; the blood spurting forth into the horn rang a bell, a performance that gave general satisfaction, with, I suppose, one exception. Some of their old kraals are veritable fortresses, consisting of an outer ringed palisade banked with clay and loopholed; inside is a deep trench, and again an inner palisade similarly banked and loopholed, with, in many cases, a third palisade containing the chief's huts. The site is invariably selected on the edge of a dense thicket, into which the women and cattle are driven on the advent of strangers; nearly every respectable member of society has a gun imported by Arab traders from the north and Portuguese from the south, and there must be several thousand in the country. Such is the people who have been changed in half a dozen short years from a cruel, murdering, widespread curse into a quiet agricultural fraternity; and by whom? By a mere handful of men with less than a hundred native police, agents of that oppressor of the native, the Chartered Company; and this without fuss and practically without bloodshed. The chief industries of the country are pombe[6]-drinking and the making of bark cloth, which is a strong fibrous textile of a pleasing reddish-brown colour, made by beating out the bark of the fig-tree with little wooden hammers, till of the required thinness. A curious custom prevails here, and one that I have not noticed elsewhere in Africa, of wearing mourning for dead relatives; bands of cloth being tied round the head.

The following day we arrived at Changala's kraal; he is a large, powerful man, with a face expressive of determination and character. He came out two miles to meet us, carried on the shoulders of one of his men, as is the custom (for the chiefs never walk), with a following of two or three hundred people. He, as in fact did all the Awemba, gave us a very hearty reception. Having amicably settled all outstanding questions with Changala, we visited Makasa, the big man of the country, whose head village lies about twenty-six miles south-east of Changala's. He is a portly old gentleman of unprepossessing countenance, and rather inclined to make trouble—at a distance; however, guessing our intentions, he had made great preparations for our reception. On arrival we found our tents already pitched and grass shelters built above them to keep off the sun; while large crowds of obsequious gentlemen came out to

---

[6] Pombe: an intoxicating drink made from millet.

meet us and insisted on carrying in our machilas at a run, a form of attention that would not be appreciated by Accident Insurance Companies. His village, which cannot contain less than five hundred huts, is of the usual Awemba pattern, and is a great centre of the bark-cloth industry.

Tales of rhino and elephant galore raised our hopes to the highest pitch, and after a day's rest we launched forth into the game country—a triangular patch of country that lies at the junction of the Chambesi, and its main tributary the Chosi—camping near Chipiri, the original site of the French mission. Here we got our first glimpse of the Chambesi, which, flowing with a devious course into Lake Bangweolo, is the real source of the Congo. It rises between Mambwe and Abercorn, and at Chipiri is already a river of some size, flowing through a beautiful grass plain clothed with patches of waving spear-grass. The plain, varying in width from a half to five miles, is hemmed in by forest bush and park land, dotted over with innumerable ant-hills, some 30 ft. in height, and is the haunt of countless herds of pookoo, two of which graced our larder shortly after pitching camp.

The next afternoon we moved further down the river to the Mafunso; and our carriers started a rhino on the path, the spoor of which we followed in thick brush. But, getting our wind, he departed with a derisive squeal, and, though I nearly came up with him again, I was compelled to give up the chase by nightfall, and only found camp with considerable difficulty. Still further down the river we camped in a delightful hunting-country, the Chambesi plain lying to our south, the vast plain of the Chosi to our east, and north, just behind the camp, strips of bush alternating with glades and groves of mahobahoba. The bush was ploughed up with rhino spoor, and that afternoon both Palmer and I unsuccessfully followed spoor of the morning. Never having seen roan antelope, I was very anxious to shoot one, and the following day started out with that intention. I found several fresh spoors, but failed to make anything of them, but on my way home I found recent lion tracks. These I followed for about two hours; at times it was very difficult, their soft pads leaving no impression on the carpets of dead leaves in the patches of bush, but I managed by casting round to pick the track up again when at fault, and eventually, hearing a low growl, I caught a glimpse of four yellow bodies disappearing round the end of a bush-covered ant-hill. I ran as fast as possible to the other side and almost into their midst; they had tried the old, old lion tactics of doubling. At sight of me they stood, and I put in a right and left; off they galloped, I in hot pursuit, following, as I thought, the first, who had got a fair shoulder-shot, and not wishing to lose sight of her, because of the thickness of some of the bush. I could just see her bounding round an ant-hill, and was making a desperate spurt to see if she would double, when I rushed round the corner of a bush right on to the top of a tail. I lost no time in skipping to one side; however, she was at her last gasp, gnawing her forepaw and making that peculiar deep gurgle, once heard, never forgotten, the lion's death-groan. I found she was the recipient of the first barrel, and the one I was following, which had dropped for a moment to my second barrel, must have crossed when I lost sight of them behind an ant-hill. Then to my disgust I remembered that I had had a solid bullet in my second barrel in case of an unexpected rhino. I picked up her spoor and followed her all round the country for about three hours, but she was playing the fool with me, and though several times I must have been very near, I never obtained another sight of her. The other two, which were three parts grown, found her after a while, and their spoor led over the top of all the ant-hills, where they had stopped to watch me till I came too close. To judge by the blood, I had hit her too far back, and the solid bullet going right through would make very little impression. This was the second time I had dropped a right and left and lost one, and I was grievously disappointed. The one I killed was a superb lioness with unusually long hair, and she measured 8 ft. 5-½ in., from tip to tip, in the flesh. Owing to the hot, rainy weather I had much difficulty in curing the skin, but eventually made a complete success of it. I made a raised quadrangular frame, upon which I stretched the skin, with a grass roof to keep off the showers; then, in default of any better preservative, I had wood-ash continually rubbed in by relays of men.

Making short afternoon marches and hunting in the morning, we gradually worked down the river to the Chosi junction, then up the Chosi, which is a fine stream about forty yards wide, with a large body of water, till we arrived at Kalungu, a small isolated village, and the only one between Makasa's village and the Chosi. I made a circuit of the plain, waded some swamps, and emerged on a second plain. Here, in the distance, I saw three huge unwieldy monsters slowly threading their way in and out of the numerous ant-hills, till they vanished behind one larger than the rest. I had left my glasses behind, and owing to the slight mirage could not be sure whether they were rhino or hippo. Having loaded the double 4-bore, I hurried forward, creeping from ant-hill to ant-hill, till at last I arrived in a line with the one behind which the brutes were still hidden. Crawling cautiously up, I climbed to the top, the big gun at the present, then peered over while my heart beat the devil's tattoo. There they were, not fifteen yards off, three of them, neither rhino nor hippo, but camp boys, with three loads of wood by their sides, peacefully smoking a hubble-bubble. I looked at them, then back at the sickly grey face of my gun-bearer, his teeth chattering with fright, and then marched into camp, to find that Palmer had shot a splendid roan on the high road.

Turning out early the next morning I struck the spoor of the herd of roan, and after sixteen miles through water ankle-deep, came up with them; but they saw me first, and I only succeeded in dropping a good cow, which stood on an ant-hill to have a last look at me. I had arranged to join Palmer and the boys at Nondo, which lies at the junction of the Mwenda and Chosi, but found that he had gone further up the Mwenda and camped at Chupi, which lies on the border of Luwala, the *pièce de résistance* of our trip. At Nondo the Chosi forms a wide pool, formerly the abode of numerous hippo till the advent of one of the French priests, who murdered the majority, for the satisfaction, I suppose, of seeing them float down-stream. The same enterprising individual, with other kindred spirits, organized a drive of the herds of pookoo on the plain. Huge fences were built at one end with funnel-shaped openings, where the gallant sportsmen stationed themselves, and, if report speaks true, slaughtered about two hundred. I wonder how many they wounded? By the side of the pool is an enormous pile of old hippo skulls that is regarded with superstitious awe by the natives, and close by is a sacred tree, the burial-place of some old chief, where quite a respectable herd of cattle has accumulated from the native offerings. East of the Chosi there is another Awemba god, who dwells in a thicket decorated by a wonderful collection of horns.

When a big chief dies, they smoke him for a year and then bury him in bark-cloth. The general belief is that his spirit enters into a lion, an animal that they hold in superstitious awe, and refuse to kill.

From Chupi we marched into Luwala, a hitherto unexplored tract of country. During the rains it is under water, and is consequently quite uninhabited, a few natives only camping there for fishing purposes, as the waters begin to leave the plain. On the north and east it is bounded by the Chosi for a distance of about sixty miles, and on the west by a slight ridge covered with bush, through which numerous streams flow and lose themselves in the marshes, eventually draining into the Chosi by the Mwenda.

Unfortunately we were too late in the season, the rains having already broken, and were consequently unable to penetrate far from the west side; even there we were compelled to wade from camp to camp through water from 6 in. to 3 ft. deep. The natives told us that when the rains are drying up, immense numbers of game come out from the bush to feed on the new grass round the rapidly diminishing pools, and that often they could see as many as half a dozen rhino at a time. It is also a favourite haunt of the comparatively few elephant that still roam over this country. On the first day's trek we crossed rhino spoor about four to five hours old, and as Palmer, who was out of form, was unwilling to risk a long chase, I started off in pursuit. After following for about an hour, I passed quite close to a large herd of roan containing three or four magnificent bulls, which stood and watched me at about forty yards. I was sorely tempted, but held to my principle of never leaving a spoor except for something better. For some time the rhino had been travelling very fast, but suddenly the spoor freshened, and from the side of an ant-hill I saw a great pink body in the distance moving slowly through the grass. It is curious how decidedly pink hippo and rhino look at a distance. As there were many large ant-hills about I followed the spoor right out, and coming round the corner of one, suddenly saw him about forty yards off just walking out into the huge bare plain; but the birds, many of which were on his back, saw me and gave the alarm. In turning he gave me my broadside chance, and I fired the 4-bore, burning fourteen drams and throwing a four-ounce spherical ball; then, as he swung round to bolt, I popped in a forward raking second barrel, which quickened his pace considerably. He rushed round in a half-circle to try and get my wind, while I peppered him with .303 solid bullets, which appeared to have about the same effect as hailstones. When he got my wind he stopped short and faced me, then swayed from side to side, staggered, recovered himself, and finally, with a shrill squeal, toppled over, kicking his four fat little legs in the air, and gave up the ghost, or the rhino's equivalent, there being nothing very spectral about these incongruous old survivals of the past. Choleric, dyspeptic, unsociable old fellows with a lordly contempt for, and fixed determination to suppress all such indecent innovations as guns, Cape wagons, and Mombasa railway-trains, they always remind me of those fire-eating, civilian-repressing, cheroot-smoke-belching Bagstocks who frequent Madeira, the Lake of Geneva, and other temperate and economical resorts, and who glare at all newcomers with that peculiar bloodshot ferocity only to be acquired by many years of curry, Bombay duck, and unlimited authority over servile millions. Owing to the difficulty of providing food for the large mob of Mambwe who had accompanied us to see in safety their old masters, the Awemba, the meat was very acceptable. The rhino was a large bull. Being particularly anxious to preserve the head, I took the trouble to cut through the hide all round to be sure of having sufficient neck-skin, and, to avoid any possibility of mistake, I left a boy by the carcase; yet in the evening it arrived in two detachments, having been considerably hacked in two to facilitate carriage.

After floundering about the country for miles and camping on isolated ant-hills, surrounded by sheets of water, and as, owing to the continued rains in the hills, the water was daily rising, we were compelled to retreat north-west. Here we made two more ineffectual efforts to penetrate into the interior. So, cursing the rains, we marched to the Luchewe, the largest of the streams which flow into Luwala, and following its valley, arrived at Kyambi, the mission station of the Pères Blancs. Here, with their usual enterprise and abilities, they have constructed a splendid two-storied building with a large cloister-like verandah, surrounded, as are all their other stations, by a solid, fortified wall; outside they have collected a large village and laid out extensive irrigated gardens well stocked with bananas, limes, lemons, and other fruits. The priests were most charming hosts. Their hospitality is, indeed, famed throughout Central Africa.

From Kyambi we marched straight into Mambwe, where we arrived drenched to the skin; and two days later I was down with an attack of fever which lasted till I reached the highlands of Kivu.

CHAPTER VIII.

TANGANYIKA.

At last, on April 2nd, we sailed from Kituta in the *Good News*.

Mr. Mohun and a large number of his Zanzibaris were with me. Consequently there was not much room. The *Good News* was originally the property of an English Mission on the Lake, and when the Mission moved to find healthier quarters, the steamer was sold at a ridiculously low figure to the African Lakes Corporation, although, I believe, the Administration of Northern Rhodesia offered a larger sum. A large hole had been knocked in her bottom and filled up with cement; and the machinery was tied together with string and strips of sardine-tins. Vast cockroaches were in possession, and night was made hideous by their peregrinations; some of them were almost as large as mice, and it was a great strain on one's mosquito-curtain when they climbed up the sides in droves. Mr. Mohun endured them all night, but I, in a very few minutes, gave up the unequal fight and retired on deck.

Our noble captain, who was quite new to the lake, did not know where he was going, nor did he care. His idea of navigating a boat consisted in sleeping in his bunk until the natives told him we had arrived somewhere; even then, he never inquired what the place was. His only anxiety was lest he should oversleep himself and miss a meal.

In the evening we arrived at the Congo Free State post of M'liro, which is at the south-western corner of the lake, a few miles over the Anglo-Congolese boundary.

On board I discovered two of the boys who had gone up with Sharp, and who had been left at Kituta. At Kituta I had given instructions that they were to be sent back; so the following morning, having crossed the lake to a wooding station, on the eastern shore, I turned them off with their pay and cloth to buy food on the road; but one of them, on adventure bent, slipped on board again. During the night, finding the sleeping-places rather limited, he calmly threw a crate containing twenty-eight fowls, belonging to Mr. Mohun, overboard.

On April 4th we recrossed the lake and arrived at the French Mission Station of M'bala. This station is of several years' standing, and the Fathers, who are seven in number, with several lay brothers, have built themselves a substantial and comfortable home. They have also built a magnificent cathedral, capable of holding many hundred devotees. I am afraid it would need a large expenditure of cloth and medals to fill it. There are also elaborate workshops, and the gardens, which are very extensive, are planted with numbers of flourishing fruit trees. The coffee-shrubs were particularly remarkable for their size and yield. On the walls were many gigantic sable heads. The horns of one that I measured were 46-½ in.; while many others were almost as long. All these antelope had been shot in the immediate vicinity by native hunters employed on the mission station. It was here that the record sable head which Mr. Boyd presented to me was obtained; and it is evident that these sable must be the largest in the world. They also had a few rhino horns, which had been shot in the neighbourhood.

They gave us a tremendous dinner, with a bewildering profusion of courses and some luscious kinds of fruit, amongst which the *ceil-de-boeuf* was particularly soothing; and delicious Algerian wine flowed freely round the festive board. There are two or three white sisters at the station; it was very sad to see how ill they looked.

After dinner, some natives brought in a large catch of fish, amongst which was a splendid kind of white-fleshed salmon. The Fathers informed me that this fish, at that time of the year, runs up the small streams, and jumps up waterfalls of considerable height.

The charming point about these white Fathers is that they never ply one with fantastic accounts of the work which they are doing. When we regretfully took our leave, they presented us with several large baskets of potatoes, tomatoes, pomegranates, and many other fruits and vegetables.

Along this shore there are enormous dug-out canoes, and we were carried to and from the steamer in one very fine specimen, probably 40 ft. in length.

On the run up to M'towa, we encountered a terrific sea, and were for several hours in imminent danger of turning turtle. The wind rushes down the narrow gulleys between the mountains that enclose the lake, and lashes the waters into a very frenzy. The arrival of these squalls is very sudden and impossible to predict; consequently, sailing on Lake Tanganyika is a most dangerous amusement. All the natives were most abominably ill, everything was wet, and the cabin and the captain formed an impossible combination.

Early in the morning the tempest subsided and we made M'towa, which is the chief Congo station on the lake. Here all the officials in the district had collected, having ignominiously fled from the rebels. One gentleman who had retired from a station further up the lake, had thrown all the station ammunition and ivory into the lake, solely on a report that the rebels were within a hundred miles. The rebels, hearing of the action, went to the place and quietly fished up both the ivory and the cartridges, thereby gaining a new lease of life. At M'towa the Belgians had built elaborate defences and had protected all the approaches with barbed wire; and in case the rebels should come they had cut down all the bananas, and were consequently short of food. There were one or two unfortunate Scandinavians in the service, who were being thrown out as pickets. One of these gentlemen came and asked us for some poison, in case he should be caught by the rebels with his totally inadequate force.

This chaotic condition has now lasted for five years, and there appears to be no man capable of grappling with the situation; it seems to me a great pity that they did not allow Commandant Henry, whom I afterwards met on the Nile, to follow up his preliminary successes against the rebels. Had he been given a free hand, in all probability the revolution would have been crushed long since.

Mr. Mohun's expedition was camped on a hill about a mile from the Government station, and they complained of most indifferent treatment at the hands of the local officials. Although they had been ready to start operations for more than six weeks, the officials had failed to provide them with any labour. It was obvious that there was much jealousy and friction between the expedition and the authorities. Fortunately, the King of the Belgians had sent Mr. Mohun a supplementary commission, which would give him the free hand necessary to the successful carrying out of his difficult task.

I was very pleased to again meet Sharp, as we had been separated for nearly three months. He was looking very ill, having only recently been laid up with fever in Ujiji. Dr. Castellote, the medical officer of Mr. Mohun's expedition, and who I am grieved to learn has recently died of fever, hearing of Sharp's sorry plight, crossed the lake and brought him over to the comparatively healthy uplands near M'towa.

Sharp had visited the station of the white Fathers on the east coast of the lake, where we had only put in to obtain wood. He told me that there was an elaborate church of brick with stained-glass windows, where he had attended service. He had been much amused at watching dirty little nigger boys from the village passing in at one door, draped in the usual filthy strip of greasy cloth, and presently emerging from another door clad in scarlet cassocks and lace tippets, waving censers, etc.

Bidding a regretful farewell to our good telegraph friends, and wishing them every luck in their venture, Sharp and I, with a mean temperature of 104°, repaired across the lake to Ujiji.

It was with feelings of curiosity that I looked out for the first time on the one historic spot in Central Africa. A few mango trees and a few white buildings scattered about on the top of the long, gently sloping shore of the lake: such was Ujiji, the meeting-place of Stanley and Livingstone, and the heart of the great slave-raiding ulcer of the past.

After considerable difficulty, we landed all our belongings by means of some unstable dug-out canoes; and having piled them on the beach, left them in charge of our boys, while we rode on donkeys, sent to us by the Greek merchant, through a gruesome array of grinning skulls that still lie scattered about the beach, the last relic of the days of Arab predominance.

We were given beds in an old mission-house which is now tenanted by two Greek traders, who, by their enterprise, richly deserve the success which they are enjoying. The old mission-house is substantially built, and is surrounded by enormous mango and guava trees.

Having fixed up our loads, we crawled up to the Government house to pay our respects to Hauptmann Bethe, the German chief of the station; he is a most delightful specimen of a German officer. He treated us with every kindness and showered the most lavish hospitality upon us. Without his cordial co-operation, we should never have been able to take the route via Kivu, on which we had set our hearts. He strongly advised us to go by the hackneyed route by Tabora and the Victoria Nyanza, the road by which Dècle went from Ujiji to Uganda, and which is the high-road for all the caravans that ply between the Victoria Nyanza and Tabora, and Ujiji and Tabora. He informed us that it would be most risky to take the route which we intended without at least a hundred armed men.

He also told us that the Congolese rebels had sent a deputation to him to tell him that they intended once more to attack the Belgians. They asked whether, in the event of failure, they would be allowed to hand their guns in to him, and to come over and settle in German territory. This is an indication of the natives' feeling towards the Congo Free State Administration.

Unfortunately both Sharp and I were too ill to see much of Ujiji and its interesting people. Many charming old Arabs, clad in gorgeous array, came and paid their respects, and sent us many presents, such as fruit, eggs, and vegetables. It was sad to see these venerable old gentlemen in their then condition, and to think of how, in the good old days gone by, they had held undisputed sway over many, many thousand square miles.

The day after our arrival we lunched with Hauptmann Bethe and his staff. We were plied with the most bewildering succession of drinks; starting with port, then through successive courses of champagne, brandy, beer, Vermouth, and claret, we slowly wended our way, with the temperature 110° in the shade. This diet, the Germans informed us, was absolutely essential to avoid fever. They protested that no teetotaller who had arrived in Ujiji had ever left Ujiji for any other place in this world; and certainly the Germans who were there were living examples of the efficacy of their treatment.

The courtesy, assistance, and confidence which we received in the German sphere shone bright in contrast with much of the treatment which we received under our own flag; and our warmest thanks are due to those whole-hearted Germans who are upholding the honour of the Fatherland on the far distant shore of Tanganyika.

My fever, which had now lasted for more than three weeks, took a decided turn for the worse, and I began to lose the proper control of my hands. Sharp, on the other hand, was slightly better.

We witnessed several dances. It was quite easy to start one, by providing the funds necessary to obtain a considerable quantity of native beer, when the natives would arrive in hundreds in the market-place and perform the wildest and most grotesque dances imaginable. Hauptmann Bethe arranged a most elaborate one for our edification.

At last, on April 12th, we had organized our caravan of one hundred and thirty men, and made a start up the lake. We had been compelled to leave some loads behind, and it was not till four in the afternoon that the last man left the courtyard. We had had no difficulty in recruiting as many men as we wanted, as the Germans afforded us every facility.

We only marched out sufficiently far to get our caravan quite clear of Ujiji; and the Germans kindly sent out a few soldiers to avoid any trouble with the men, the last farewell of the natives being invariably accompanied by much pombe. However, they all turned up, and we got them into some sort of order. I had brought from Nyassa sixteen boys—ten of whom had been drilled for a few days by one of Mr. Mohun's Zanzibari sergeants—two of them were kitchen boys, and the other four gun-bearers and tent-pitchers: this made our caravan one hundred and fifty strong.

Sharp ignored the mosquitoes the first night, and in consequence suffered severely from blood poisoning of the hands. The path led through a fertile country, but as the high grass overhung the narrow track, it was very wet travelling and not conducive to a speedy recovery from fever. The way became gradually worse and we had many sharp rises to face, and many small streams to cross, while satisfactory camping-grounds were hard to find. On the fourth day, after a struggle up an almost perpendicular hill, we camped at an elevation of nearly 6,000 ft., and obtained some lovely views over the country to the east—high, tree-covered hills, with a few native huts and their accompanying gardens in clearings where the ground was not too steep, and, down below, deep valleys covered with dense bush—while to the west we could just catch a glimpse of the lake backed by the rugged and forbidding-looking hills on the Congo side.

A cold white mist came up in the afternoon, and put all thoughts of scenery away, driving us to refuge in tightly-closed tents.

Next day we mounted still higher—about 7,000 ft.—and the scenery amply repaid the exertion. From thence we made a rapid descent by a path so steep and rough that we had to glissade at times with the aid of a strong spear. At the villages here we found the people wearing wooden tweezers on their noses; on inquiry we discovered that they injected snuff mixed with water, and then put the apparatus on to keep the concoction from wasting away at once. A day or two later we reached the lake-shore, and the path, such as it was, came to an end. We now had to make our way along the shingle. The bush overhung the water every few yards, and as it was mostly mimosa, or other equally prickly matter, we had to wade round to avoid it—often up to our middles in the water—while an occasional mountain torrent necessitated our being carried on our boys' shoulders. As the lake was swarming with crocodiles, this was rather exciting. Our Nyassa boys, who had earned the name of the Guinea-fowls, owing to their dress of dark-blue bird's-eye cotton and greeny-blue fezzes, had been a great comfort, pitching our tents and doing all the little odd jobs inseparable from camp life, and we were congratulating ourselves on having some natives of a different race to our Manyema porters.

The heat and continual wetting now began to tell on the fever which we had not been able to shake off, so we hired two big canoes, and putting our deck-chairs in the largest, over which we rigged up an awning, we proceeded by water while our boys plodded through the shingle. On reaching the halting-place after our first day's canoeing, we were horrified to find that our ten Askaris and the cook had bolted, leaving their rifles and bayonets on the path. Though I was bad with fever I got a fresh crew for the big canoe, and made all haste back to our last night's camp. Nothing was to be seen or heard of the fugitives, and though I offered the Sultani (chief) of the village heavy rewards for each captive, we never heard any more of them, but trust that they did not escape their deserts when they reached Ujiji, if the natives on the way let them go free, which is more than doubtful. I had left Sharp to try his 'prentice hand at cooking, and returning wet through, very tired and full of fever, found his attempt at soup had ended in a few bones and a blob of fat at the bottom of the pan! The heat was intense, never a breath of air, and no shade, while the rays of the burning sun were refracted from the face of the water. At every camp one or more of the neighbouring chiefs came to pay his respects, bringing with him a present, according to his standing, of pombe, native beer, bananas, three or four fowls, and in the case of a big "swell," two or three goats or sheep. Each chief was followed by as large a retinue as he could gather, and most of them were dressed in semi-Arab fashion—a long, white shirt or "kanzu," a coloured cloth, and a turban or white head-dress. The natives had many knives of local manufacture, the sheaths of which were ornamented with well-carved patterns, while their spears were very thin and light, and often adorned with brass and copper wire. Of course we had to make return presents of cloth and beads to an equal value. Eggs were rather hard to obtain, and it was still more difficult to make the natives believe that we did not want them for electioneering purposes. My fever was now so bad that I had to depute my baking to Sharp, who was becoming quite a passable cook under my tuition, and retire to bed as soon as I could get my tent pitched. To add to our enjoyment Sharp got a sunstroke and a dose of fever, and we were consequently reduced to the most pitiable plight. My temperature went up to 106.9, and left me too weak to move, while Sharp, ill as he was, made superhuman efforts to look after me. At last, after several days of intolerable misery, we eventually arrived at Usambara, where the German official, Lieutenant von Gravert, took us in hand. Under his care we recovered slightly.

Usambara, with characteristic German thoroughness, has been well laid out. Substantial buildings have been put up, good gardens made, and an immense avenue of pawpaws and bananas planted from the Government House to the lake shore. A small sailing-boat adds materially to the comfort and efficiency of the commanding officer.

Every morning a large market is held, and the natives bring in enormous supplies of fish, bananas, beans, grains of different sort (even rice), and fowls. The German black troops keep splendid order, and the station has the most flourishing air. I am a great believer in the Germans' African methods. Of course they are severely handicapped by having such a poor country to work upon. But their methods are thorough and eminently practical, and not characterized by the stinginess which paralyzes most of our African efforts. The men selected for the work are given a practically free hand, and are not cramped by the ignorant babblings of sentimentalism.

CHAPTER IX.

THE RUSISI VALLEY.

At last, on May 7th, we were sufficiently recovered to move, and bidding farewell to our good friend, Lieutenant von Gravert, we left Usambara and made a short march along the lake shore to Kijaga, a deserted Government station near the most easterly mouth of the Rusisi.

Being still much too weak to walk, I was carried in a hammock slung from a pole by a team of twelve natives of Usige kindly recruited for me by Lieutenant von Gravert, who were to take me to Dr. Kandt's headquarters on Kivu, where the climate of the highlands, it was hoped, would render me sufficiently strong to continue my journey on foot.

After the trained "machila" teams of Nyassaland they were very crude, and many amusing incidents arose from their inexperience. However, they were willing, and served me very well.

The northern shore of the lake is flat and sandy, and for a long distance from land the water is very shallow; even at a distance of two miles hippopotami could walk on the bottom with their heads above water. The natives are great fishermen, and own many dug-out canoes; they fish mainly at night. There was little moon at the time, and we could see scores of canoes punting about, each with a great flaming torch in the bows, and the fishermen with poised spears eagerly scanning the water. The effect of the number of dimly-defined canoes gliding to and fro on the oily water, of the strong reflection of the flaming torches, and of the phosphorescent wash was most picturesque.

The Rusisi, which is the outflow of Lake Kivu, falls into Lake Tanganyika through five mouths, four of which are close together slightly to the east of the centre of the northern shore, while the fifth is on the extreme western point under the gigantic hills that line the western shore. The enclosed deltas are very flat and swampy, and in part covered with forest, the haunt of many elephant, a large portion of which are said by the Arabs to be tuskless.

During many weary days of sickness at Usambara, I had gazed up that mighty valley, the vast flat gently merging into endless vistas of purple hills, behind winch lay the mysterious waters of Kivu and the giant volcanoes (the pulse of Africa), flanked by two massive walls of mountains—the path that led to the yet unknown, the first real stage of the task that we had set ourselves! And for long it seemed as though I had struggled thus far only to die at the very gate. The extraordinary beauty of the scene fascinated me, and with its eddying mists and fading hills, redolent of mystery, it seemed a fitting entry to an unknown land.

At Kijaga we rose to find that our cook and the three boys whom we had engaged at Usambara had bolted in the night, taking with them their month's pay and two months' rations. We immediately sent a note in to Von Gravert, and his police very cleverly caught them two days later, although they tried to go down to Ujiji by a path that leads over the hills at the back of the station. The capture was a very clever one, and reflects great credit on the German administrative organization.

Our cow-boys were a great nuisance; they refused to go near one of the cows which kicked, and they evidently considered that the little milk they succeeded in extracting from the others had been earned by the trouble of extraction, consequently what eventually arrived for us was limited in quantity. A strong protest, backed by mild physical correction, produced a larger quantity, but it was sour, and on inquiry we found that they had drunk our fresh milk, and for a small consideration purchased some sour milk from a neighbouring chief; they foolishly brought it stone cold, ostensibly fresh from the cow. They assured us that all the cows in that country produced sour milk.

For the first fifteen miles the valley is absolutely flat, and deposits of semi-fossilized shells indicate a historically recent upheaval.

There are two streams, the Mpanda and Kazeki, flowing from the east; the former has a considerable volume of water.

The flat, which is about two miles wide, is covered with very short, poor-looking grass, and dotted here and there with magnificent specimens of the candelabra euphorbia, looking in the distance like gigantic cabbages. An occasional palm-tree breaks the desolate monotony, and a very occasional small antelope lends a suggestion of life.

To the west the Rusisi makes a long curve towards the enclosing mountain range, and in places spreads out into swampy lagoons apparently of some extent.

Our carriers had been giving much trouble, lagging behind and not arriving till two or three hours after our arrival, hoping thereby to escape fatigue duties. It was most desirable to have the caravan as compact as possible on the march, in view of possible troubles with the natives.

We allowed them, therefore, half an hour's margin, and every one who arrived after that, without having obtained permission in the morning for sickness or some valid reason, was made to stand with his load on his head in the middle of camp as long as was deemed sufficient for his particular case. We found this much more effectual as a punishment than fines (a system to be deprecated, except in Government stations). The native enjoys his afternoon nap, he likes to stroll into the neighbouring villages, show his best clothes off before the local beauties, and pass the time of day with the village cronies. It jars on him to have to stand doing nothing while he sees his friends chatting and discussing their bananas and the topics of the day. One such punishment usually sufficed for at least a month, and a native must be very much impressed to remember anything for as long as that.

Fifteen miles from Kijaga there is a bunch of large villages. The chief is called Balamata. They are situated on the advance spur of a line of conical peaks which divide the main valley into two sections: the western branch, which trends north-west by north, is the valley of the Rusisi; while the eastern branch, which trends north-east by north, comes from Kirimbi and Imbo. Close to Balamata a small stream flows from the central peaks towards the eastern valley, and as we did not pass any stream of consequence, I imagine that this small stream and the whole of the drainage of the valley loses itself in the swamp which I could plainly see a few miles to the east.

Passing round the western side of Balamata's peaks, we found the country similar to the first stage of the valley, flat and dotted with euphorbia, the mean altitude being slightly higher than the lake level. We passed over two extraordinary ravines dug out of the flat country. One was evidently a dry stream-bed, but the other appeared to have no outlet, and I could find no satisfactory clue to its origin.

The Rusisi here flows under the eastern wall; it is a large body of water flowing through wide expanses of papyrus, and is probably navigable for small steamers to a point forty miles north of the lake.

The population is very scanty. The scattered villages and their cattle-pens are enclosed by artificial hedges of euphorbia.

A large stream, the Kagunozi, flows down from the east a few miles north of Balamata's, and three miles further north is the village of Buvinka, a chief of some importance.

North of Buvinka's, a large stream called the Kabulantwa flows into the Rusisi from the east, which appears to be very broken and mountainous in the distance. We had much difficulty in crossing the stream with our cattle and goats, owing to the power of the current. Several goats were washed away, but with the exception of two, all were eventually rescued by the boys, who were expert swimmers. In places the stream narrowed considerably, forming foaming rapids, and it was splendid to see some of the Manyema shooting down like arrows in pursuit of an old billy-goat, eventually dragging him half drowned on to the bank. Some of the cows refused to enter the water, and had to be forcibly dragged across by ropes.

Opposite the junction of the Kabulantwa and the Rusisi, the western range of hills sends a long spur down into the valley, culminating in a well-defined conical peak, which abuts on the river, and is a splendid landmark for many miles north and south.

The dominant peaks at the back are very striking, and apparently at least 7,000 ft. high; they are very rugged, and in parts heavily wooded.

A few miles north of the Kabulantwa the valley again splits into two; the eastern branch is drained by a small and very rapid stream called the Muhira, which appears to be a highroad for elephant crossing the valley. The western branch is the valley of the Rusisi; it is very flat, and covered with coarse grass with slight thorn-scrub at the sides; part of it is marshy.

We camped in a scattered village of considerable size, thickly planted with bananas. The Rusisi flows close by, cutting its way through a dyke, which crosses the valley. The country here was much more broken, and our camp was about 300 ft. above the lake level.

The natives have a good supply of cattle, and live in scattered villages of considerable size; they are well set up, with good faces, high foreheads, and not prognathous to a conspicuous degree; they all carry long, slight, spears with small heads, and long sword-knives with elaborately-decorated sheaths. They also use a long-bladed axe with a hook on the end for cutting bananas, the handle of which is also elaborately decorated with iron, copper, and brass. On their arms they wear many wire rings and large wooden bracelets of curious shape.

In the evening I discovered an enormous jigger in my small toe, and one of my Watonga boys skilfully removed it; the bag of eggs was the size of a marrowfat pea, and as there was only the bone and top part of my toe left I was afraid that I should lose it; however, after giving me some trouble, it yielded to the persuasive influence of that panacea for all African ills, permanganate of potash, and healed.

During the night a hyæna grabbed one of the goats, and tore the poor brute so badly that it had to be killed. The following morning, after crossing some very broken country, and fording a deep stream called the Nyamgana, we arrived at the first of the three Soudanese forts, established by the Germans on the Rusisi to prevent raids of the Congolese rebels.

The treaty boundary, between the Congo and German East Africa of 1885, runs from the mouth of the Rusisi to cut the 30th degree east longitude, at a point 1° 20' south of the equator. Hence all these three posts are well within the Congo Free State. The Germans have cleverly availed themselves of the Congolese chaos, and having placed these advance posts for the plausible object of defending their country, by occupying the natural line of defence afforded by the river, are now pleading effective occupation. In the meanwhile Dr. Kandt, under the auspices of the German Government, is investigating the possibilities of the country. On his report the Germans will know whether the country is worth a struggle.

The fort is well placed on a flat-topped hill overhanging the river, which here races along between precipitous rocks, and although it is only in charge of a native officer, it is clean and well kept. The troops are Wanyamwesi, officered by Soudanese.

We camped on the north bank of the Nyakagunda, a large stream flowing from the east; here again a line of rounded hills (a long spur of the mass of hills that hems in the north end of the valley) cuts the valley into two branches. The main or Rusisi branch is still flat and grass-covered, and obviously an old lake-bed; while the eastern branch, down which flows the Nyakagunda, is broken by many small hills.

About an hour before sunset some natives rushed in to say that they had seen elephant close to camp; they said that they were travelling, so that there was not a moment to be lost. To put the 4-bore together was a question of seconds, and hurriedly collecting the few necessaries, and ordering my "machila" team to follow, as I was still very weak, I dashed off in the direction indicated. Sharp had, unfortunately, not yet unpacked any of his 10-bore cartridges, and as every minute was precious at that time of day, it would have been useless to wait.

About two miles from camp we found the elephants; they had stopped, and were standing round a clump of euphorbia. Making a detour to catch the wind, I approached them, 4-bore in hand, and with one boy carrying the .303 behind me. There was absolutely no cover, but, to my astonishment, they took not the slightest notice of me. Gathering confidence from this, I went quite close and inspected them. There were twenty-nine in all, mostly cows, some of which, however, had enormously long, thin tusks. Taking care to avoid any sudden movements which would be likely to attract their attention, I passed to leeward of them, so close to some that I could have touched them with my rifle. The three bulls were at the far end, and I at length made up my mind which one to take. The cartridge missed fire, and at the same moment the middle bull, which had appeared small, lifted his head from behind a small euphorbia and showed a pair of very massive tusks, almost black from use. Inwardly blessing the miss-fire, I went up to within six yards of him, when the one I had left caught a puff of my wind and cocked his ears; that was all he did; he never made a sound of any description, yet the whole twenty-nine (many of which had their backs turned, or were completely hidden by the euphorbia) moved off instantly. As the black-tusked male swung round, I gave him the first barrel on the shoulder, and again the second barrel at nine yards; he dropped on to one knee, but never even lost his stride; the others closed round him, and helped him away, and that was the last I saw or heard of my first elephant. I was too weak to follow far, and the next morning I sent out some of our boys with local natives, but they never found him. When hunting elephant and other game, the extraordinary ease with which they pass on the danger-signal has often made me wonder whether they have another sense, which we, by disuse, have practically lost. Perhaps even with us it survives in a rudimentary form, causing the inexplicable phenomena of second sight, mesmerism, etc., etc.

The next morning we followed the eastern branch, and passing many steep hills, crossed a pass 5,500 ft. high, and again descended into the main valley. Numerous small streams intersected the hills, and at each ford clouds of gorgeous butterflies enlivened the scene, attracted apparently by the moisture. On the way we crossed many fresh tracks of elephant, and on the western slope of the valley a large herd had followed the track in the early morning. At the base of the slope we had much difficulty in fording a deep and rapid river, called the Kasilo; several goats and a calf were washed away, and the rest were only saved by the brilliant swimming of the Watonga contingent. Thence two hours' hard travelling brought us to the second German Soudanese fort, situated on a small hill overlooking the Rusisi, where it issues from its broken course through the mountains which dam the south end of Lake Kivu, preparatory to its seventy-five-mile run through the flat valley bed to Lake Tanganyika.

The Soudanese officer in command was most courteous and personally presented all the local potentates, who brought us supplies of bananas, flour, and goats. He also promised to try and trace my lost elephant, but said that if, as was most probable, it had crossed the river it would be impossible to recover ivory from the obstreperous chiefs in the Congo Free State. Here, as during the whole of our journey from Tanganyika, the mosquitoes were appalling; colossal of stature, they arrived in myriads at sunset, and continued their plaintive wail till the cool hour before dawn.

On the morrow we left the Rusisi once more, and passed to the east of many striking conical hills along the flat plain of the Kasilo (which obviously in remote ages was the course of the outlet of Lake Kivu), for a distance of four miles, crossing several small tributaries of the Kasilo on our way. We turned west, and climbing the high plateau through which the Rusisi has now forced its way, camped on a high ridge 2,000 ft. above the plain. There were numerous villages and large herds of cattle, which at night are enclosed in pens strongly stockaded. Here we had entered the terrible Ruanda country, and the paramount chief of the district, Ngenzi, the most powerful satrap of the King of Ruanda, came and paid his respects. From his pleasant manner we little guessed what a source of trouble he was to prove in the near future. Small boys followed us on the march with huge wooden utensils filled with fresh milk, and our welcome was most cordial. Forests of bananas stretched far as the eye could reach to the north, east, and west, and vast fields of peas and beans bore witness to the fertility and prosperity of the country.

To the south lay the mighty valley of the Rusisi, stretching away between its enclosing walls of hills, till, in the far distance, gleamed the waters of Tanganyika.

Bidding a last farewell to those historic waters, we plunged into the wild turmoil of hills which surround Kivu, and after a six hours' tramp, accompanied on the way by Ngenzi and his hundred followers (not forgetting the inevitable cup-bearer with his gourd of pombe and the regal sucking-straw), climbed on to a ridge from which we saw the waters of Kivu lying at our feet.

The mighty sheet of water, dotted with a hundred isles and hemmed in by a thousand imposing hills, was of surpassing beauty; the only one of the vast lakes of Central Africa which had not been first gazed upon by British eyes.

CHAPTER X.

LAKE KIVU.

An abrupt descent led us through many straggling villages and endless banana plantations to the German Soudanese post on the extreme south-west point of the lake.

We camped on a small rise opposite the Government stockade and overlooking the lake; the outlet is a long, thin arm, narrowing to where the Rusisi tumbles over the first cascades, and starts on its broken course through the hills to the point whence it finally issues on its long, long journey by Tanganyika to the sea. The body of water leaving the lake is small, but, with the numerous tributaries from east and west, soon swells to a considerable size; and forty miles from Tanganyika it is of about the same volume as the Thames at Richmond.

The south-western extremity of Kivu is really a small lake in itself, separated as it is from the main body of the lake by a narrow neck, which is again almost blocked by a network of islands.

On all sides long straggling promontories jut out into the water, cutting the coast-line into a multitude of lochs and bays.

They are the spurs of the wild groups of hills which enclose Kivu on the east, south, and west sides, and which, ever increasing in height as they recede from the lake-shore, eventually culminate in the mighty peaks which crown the enclosing walls of this vast Rift Valley, in which Tanganyika, Kivu, the Albert Edward, and the Albert Lakes are but residuary pools.

Miles and miles of banana plantations clothe the lower hills, and vast fields of peas give a touch of green to the purples, reds, and yellows of the luxuriant pastures. There are no trees in all the Kivu region nearer than the summits of the distant peaks and the slopes of the volcanoes, with the exception of a very occasional solitary tree on the extreme summit of some of the conspicuous hills. These latter are left untouched, despite the value of wood, and would appear to be held in reverential awe; they form conspicuous landmarks, which may be the primary cause of the superstitions that attach to them. Their existence points to the country having been at one time more or less wooded; and the trees which served no essential purpose have fallen before the requirements of the enormous population.

This same enormous population, and the pervading air of prosperity, are a striking indication of the possibilities of native races left to work out their own destiny.

The far-famed unity and power of the Ruanda people have deterred the Arabs from making slave-raids into their country, and with the exception of one or two Belgian looting expeditions, which fortunately met with no success, they have been left in peace.

All the southern and eastern coast-line drops abruptly into the lake, and there is no beach or marshland such as are found on the other lakes of Central Africa, but the feeding-streams, at their junction with the lake, become papyrus swamps.

There were only ten soldiers in the fort, and they rolled in the lap of luxury, calmly relieving the neighbouring population of what they (the soldiers) considered superfluities, such as goats, sheep, fowls, etc. This is the invariable result of placing natives in a post of responsibility without constant supervision.

As to their duties, they had none; and it was patent that the sole *raison d'être* of these posts was to be able on the day of reckoning to show a definite asset, a claim to effective occupation—in fine, a fulfilment of the duties imposed upon European powers by the Berlin Conference.

The Soudanese officer in charge was most friendly, and the neighbouring chiefs arrived in long procession and paid their respects. They presented us with several goats and sheep, and when we expressed the wish to purchase more, they brought them along in a ceaseless stream. Subsequently we discovered that the affable Soudanese officer and his brother ruffians, hearing of our approach, had annexed several herds from some villages two days north; these were the beasts that arrived in such bewildering profusion. They had insisted on the owners accepting a handful of beads, thereby establishing a claim to legitimate purchase, and compelled the local natives to bring the beasts in to us as their own property.

There are numerous small villages in the vicinity of the post, and the people, who live in the most wretched huts, thrown up like hayricks, appear to have been very thoroughly bled by their undesirable neighbours.

An extraordinary feature of Kivu, and the rivers and small lakes of the Kivu system, is the absence of hippopotami and crocodiles. As they swarm in Tanganyika and the Rusisi to the south, and in the Rutchuru and Albert Edward Lake to the north, this is very remarkable. Probably the abrupt nature of the shore, the depth of water, and the absence of sandbanks and shelving beaches may account for it. The only possible landing-and-resting-places would be the papyrus swamps that I have mentioned as existing at the mouths of the streams; and the water, hurrying down from high altitudes, and shaded from the sun by the papyrus, is here intensely cold, and therefore unsuited to their requirements.

The natives brought us quantities of fish similar in appearance to bream, and of most delicate flavour. The same fish is common in Tanganyika and the Albert Edward. This was the only species that I saw in Kivu, and the natives told me that there are no large fish, such as are found in the other lakes. A conspicuous feature is the extraordinary number of large otters, which are to be seen in scores swimming and diving in every bay. Lake Ngami in South Africa is also remarkable for the number of otters, the skins of which are obtainable in quantities from the natives.

There are many butterflies on the rich pasture-land, the most common kind being almost identical with our *Coleas edusa.*

After a day's rest we marched to Ishangi, the base of Dr. Kandt, who is making an exhaustive study of all the "district." He was most kind, and gave us much useful information and advice.

His work is being done with characteristic German thoroughness. In a recent surveying expedition, in the course of which he travelled 560 miles, he found his error on rounding up the trip amounted to less than a quarter of a mile. This astounding result was obtained by counting every step, and taking three bearings a minute. It is this amazing attention to detail which makes the Teuton so formidable a competitor. Amongst many most interesting specimens, he had the finest pair of tusks that it has ever been my fortune to see. Unfortunately we had no scales, and it was impossible to judge of their weight. The elephant had been shot in Mushari, the country where I afterwards narrowly escaped being eaten. Hearing from the natives that the beast was in a small gully close to camp, Dr. Kandt sallied forth with four soldiers; only the back of the elephant was visible over the scrub, and they fired a volley at four hundred yards. One lucky shot hit the knee and disabled the beast, when the gallant doctor established a valid claim to having killed an elephant, as he naïvely remarked, by finishing it off. Close to Ishangi is Lubengera, the site of a former Congo Free State station, where a few black troops had been posted to raid cattle from the rich cattle districts of Lubengera and Bugoie.

The mean of my aneroid readings on the lake level was 5,000 ft., and the height of the hills contiguous with the lake ranged between 5,500 and 6,000 ft.

At Ishangi we purchased some spears, amongst others an interesting specimen from Bunyabungu, on the west side of the lake. It was simply a long, coarse spike, and the natives said that the people of Bunyabungu could not manage the final stage of beating it out into a blade. Dr. Kandt warned us about the thieving propensities and light-fingered ability of the Wa Ruanda, and told us how he had suffered from their depredations. One thief had entered his closed tent under the nose of the sentry, and abstracted a pair of trousers from under the pillow on which the doctor was lying. Another had removed the fly of his headman's tent. Consequently, the following night we took the precaution of carefully closing our tents, and of placing all the loads in the third tent, with men sleeping at each end. Notwithstanding, the following morning a tin box weighing 60 lbs. had been taken from my tent, and had completely vanished, while two canvas kit-bags had been abstracted, cut open, and the desirable contents removed. Thus, at one fell swoop, we lost our sextant, artificial horizon, boiling-point thermometers, a bag of one hundred sovereigns, all my trousers, stockings, and socks, and many valuable papers, books, and photographs. On this discovery we summoned the chief, our old friend Ngenzi, who had been hanging on our flanks for about forty miles. He arrived with a supercilious smile and a host of attendants. Having explained the situation, I asked him what he intended to do. "There are many bad men in my country of whom I know nothing," he answered, and again that evil smile flitted over his countenance. It was obvious that bluffing was to be the order of the day; so, taking the same line, we clapped him into the guard-tent, stopped his drinks and smokes, put a guard with fixed bayonets over him, and delivered an ultimatum to the effect that, unless the stolen goods were restored intact by midday, we should take further steps. Of course he protested absolute ignorance, but the sudden and resolute nature of our proceedings took him unawares, and for once the guile of the native failed him. Instead of protesting to a finish, which would have left us powerless to act, he produced by his men a few of the articles that seemed most important to him, such as caps and native shirts. This proved his complicity, and at twelve noon we decided to act. Sharp opened a case of Snider cartridges, issued rounds to the ten men who carried guns, and prepared the camp for defence; while I took my revolver and an old French cutlass purchased in Cornhill, and with my two Watonga carrying my rifles, climbed the hill on which the chief village was situated. Hundreds of natives with spears turned out and showed signs of an intention to resist me.

I harangued them, explained what had happened, and told them that my quarrel was with Ngenzi, and with Ngenzi only; that he had allowed thieves to come and steal the goods of strangers in his country, strangers who had come to see their country, to pass through it on a long journey to far lands, and who had come in peace paying for what they (the natives) brought, receiving and giving presents. I then told them that I was going to take all Ngenzi's cattle, drive it in to the German post, and let the Germans, their overlords, decide between us. I warned them that any man coming to the camp would be shot, but that they might bring food as usual for sale. Eventually, without firing a shot, I collected and drove in to the camp one hundred and ninety head of cattle.

They made a few tentative rushes at me, but were repulsed by the simple expedient of waving the cutlass in the air. Such were the terrible Ruanda people, whose reputation has spread far and wide, and whose country has been left alone for fear of their military organization. At least five thousand men sat on the hill-tops and watched three men with a revolver, cutlass, and two rifles drive off one hundred and ninety head of cattle; and I am inclined to think that most Central African warfare could be settled as easily. Had I had despatches to write I might have acted differently.

The Germans, overestimating the power of the Ruanda kingdom, had weakened the white man's prestige by subsidizing Ngenzi with extravagant gifts of cloth; and he imagined that he could bleed any one who came into his country.

I have always utterly refused to pay "hongo"[7] to any native, and never give presents until I have received one. Then, if the present is a liberal one, I give a yet more liberal present; but if the present is niggardly, I give the exact market value of the goods received, unless, of course, the niggardliness is due to poverty.

We placed a strong guard over the cattle, and removed our camp from the undesirable vicinity of the villages to a round, flat-topped hill half a mile to the south. At one end we pitched our three tents and arranged the boys' tents to complete the circle. Inside we fixed a long rope plaited from banana fibre, and kept in position by spears. Inside this circle we drove all the cattle, and we placed pickets round the side

---

[7] Tax on people passing through chief's territory.

of the hill to guard against surprise or an attempt to stampede the herd. The moon rose about midnight, and during the hours of darkness Sharp and I took it in turns to go the rounds. The noise was appalling, as some of the cows had lost their calves; and one or two attempts were made to break through, but we succeeded in quieting them before the panic became general. Thanks to our precautions, the night passed without incident, and in the morning Sharp drove the whole herd over to Ishangi and gave them into the charge of the Soudanese, whom we had summoned from the post at the tail of Kivu.

Of course, immensely exaggerated accounts of our proceedings spread throughout the land, and the chief near Dr. Kandt went to him and asked him whether he had better fly from the country. He was promptly reassured, and the doctor kindly came over to see if he could be of any assistance, while the Soudanese officer sent his men to scour the outlying villages to see if they could find any of our property, but without avail.

Fortunately the natives did not attack Sharp on the road, and with the exception of some difficulty in crossing bogs, he arrived without mishap.

We sent in an exhaustive report to Lieut. von Gravert, and released Ngenzi with a caution. He promptly made up for lost time in the way of tobacco and pombe, and was most respectful. That sinister smile has for ever faded from his dusky features, and I am sure the lesson has been of inestimable benefit to him.

For many days to come it was curious to see the military appearance of our Manyema: no one stirred from the camp without two spears, a sword-knife, and, if possible, a gun with fixed bayonet.

The smaller fry were delighted at the humiliation of the mighty Mtusi, and many came in to do obeisance and thank us for our action.

Society in Ruanda is divided into two castes, the Watusi and the Wahutu.

The Watusi, who are practically identical with the Wahuma, are the descendants of a great wave of Galla invasion that reached even to Tanganyika. They still retain their pastoral instincts, and refuse to do any work other than the tending of cattle; and so great is their affection for their beasts, that rather than sever company they will become slaves, and do the menial work of their beloved cattle for the benefit of their conquerors. This is all the more remarkable when one takes into consideration their inherent pride of race and contempt for other peoples, even for the white man. They are most jealous of their descent, and no Mtusi woman ever marries any one but a Mtusi. A Mtusi man will take another woman as a working wife, but his true wife is invariably of his own stock, and her children alone can succeed to his position.

The half-castes, and individuals with any trace of Mtusi blood, form a medium between the full-blooded Watusi and the aborigines, whom they call Wahutu, but associate only with the upper class, or are the paramount chiefs of insignificant districts. Many signs of superior civilization, observable in the peoples with whom the Watusi have come into contact, are traceable to this Galla influence.

The hills are terraced, thus increasing the area of cultivation, and obviating the denudation of the fertile slopes by torrential rains. In many places irrigation is carried out on a sufficiently extensive scale, and the swamps are drained by ditches. Artificial reservoirs are built with side troughs for watering cattle. The fields are in many instances fenced in by planted hedges of euphorbia and thorn, and similar fences are planted along the narrow parts of the main cattle tracks, to prevent the beasts from straying or trampling down the cultivation.

There is also an exceptional diversity of plants cultivated, such as hungry rice, maize, red and white millet, several kinds of beans, peas, bananas, and the edible arum. Some of the higher-growing beans are even trained on sticks planted for the purpose. Pumpkins and sweet potatoes are also common; and the Watusi own and tend enormous herds of cattle, goats, and sheep. Owing to the magnificent pasturage, the milk is of excellent quality, and they make large quantities of butter. They are exceedingly clever with their beasts, and have many calls which the cattle understand. At milking-time they light smoke-fires to keep the flies from irritating the beasts.

All the dairy utensils are of wood, and are kept scrupulously clean; but they have an unpleasant method of repairing cracked jars by filling up the crevices with cow-dung, and of using the urine as the cleansing medium.

They are tall, slightly-built men, of graceful, nonchalant carriage, and their features are delicate and refined. I noticed many faces that, bleached and set in a white collar, would have been conspicuous for character in a London drawing-room. The legal type was especially pronounced.

Centuries of undisputed sway have left their mark in the *blasé*, supercilious manner of the majority; and in many ways they are a remarkable and far from unattractive people.

The Wahutu are their absolute antithesis. They are the aborigines of the country, and any pristine originality or character has been effectually stamped out of them. Hewers of wood and drawers of water, they do all the hard work, and unquestioning, in abject servility, give up the proceeds on demand. Their numerical proportion to the Watusi must be at least a hundred to one, yet they defer to them without protest; and in spite of the obvious hatred in which they hold their overlords, there seems to be no friction.

Formerly there was a far-reaching and effective feudal system, which constituted the proverbial strength of the kingdom of Ruanda.

The king was supreme, and the sole owner of all the cattle in the country; the large provinces were administered by prominent Watusi, usually blood-relations of his Majesty, whose power locally was absolute, but who were directly responsible to him for the acts of the subordinate chiefs and for the loss of cattle. Each subordinate, again, had the use of a portion of the cattle, for which he was directly responsible to the satrap of the district. The king's title is "Kigeri;" "Ntwala" is the title of the satraps; and the term "Sultani" is usually applied to the smaller chiefs. The old Kigeri died, and the rule passed to his son Musinga, who appears to have been a mere child.

There is a native superstition against the Kigeri being seen by strangers, and consequently a substitute, an individual known to the natives as Pamba Rugamba, has been presented to the Germans who have visited the Residence. The child appears also to have died, and the power now is divided between Kisunga and Gwamu or Mwami. Mwami was the name told to me by many natives, but it appears to be merely a title, as other natives addressed me as "Mwami." These two men were described as the sons of the old Kigeri, possibly by another wife than the mother of Musinga; but son is such an elastic term with natives that they may have been nephews. This division has materially weakened the strength of the Ruanda kingdom.

In Africa almost every kingdom is divided against itself, as well as against every other, so that unity is indeed strength. And it was this unity which constituted the power of Ruanda and of the Zulus, just as at the present day it constitutes the power of the mighty Dinka and Shilluk tribes of the Nile.

While Sharp was away I purchased several curios from the natives, and amongst others a most curious bracelet that I was informed came from the Nyema district of the Congo. It consisted of a semi-tubular circle of iron, the hollow being filled up with a crude ivory mosaic held in place by rubber.

The Germans, who have a favourable opinion of the possibilities of the Ruanda country, are talking of sending emigrants there. The soil is very rich, but the country is so inaccessible that I fail to see how they could be self-supporting—a desirable condition for emigrants—or how they could cultivate anything for export that would bear the cost of transport.

Amongst the natives who brought produce for sale were two pigmies; they were most curious little fellows, and appeared to be immensely powerful. I fancy they were not quite pure-bred dwarfs, or else they had been enslaved when young, as they had none of the shyness so characteristic of this singular little people, and appeared to be living with the local natives.

To the south-east the enclosing line of hills culminates in four large peaks of 8,000 to 9,000 ft. All four are conspicuous landmarks for many miles.

A favourite device of the Manyema carriers, when in a country of thieves, is to conceal a load of cloth during the night; in the morning they arrive in great distress, and say that a load has been stolen; nothing can be done; the unsuspecting traveller abuses the natives, the land, and other things, and the wily Manyema annexes the lost load on his return home. To obviate this, we informed them that every man in future would be held responsible for his own load, and that he would have to make good, out of his pay, any loss or damage. This was doubly necessary, as Swahilis and Manyema generally contrive to find a boy or starveling who will carry their load for a consideration. Apropos of this point, I find the following in my diary: "Talk about Charles Kingsley's description of sweating as a result of civilization! Here we have porters hiring natives who hire others to the fourth degree, each walking along like a gentleman and pocketing his proportion. There is nothing new in this world."

The difficulty of preventing our Manyema ruffians from swindling the natives was almost insuperable. After the Ngenzi fracas, I discovered that they were making capital out of our action to extort things from the natives; so I insisted that for a time every transaction should be performed before me. If a carrier wished to buy a bunch of bananas from a native, he brought the native with the bananas to my tent, and they bargained, and the price was paid in my presence.

One of the blackest of our villains promptly sent his small boy out into a neighbouring plantation, whence he issued in the scanty garb of a local native with a bunch of bananas. The villain, the boy, and the bananas appeared before me, and they solemnly performed the bargaining and payment. But I had been waiting for that villain, and without appearing to do so, watched the issue. They all repaired to their tent, and the boy resumed his garments, when they fell to on what they fondly believed was a cheap feed—a belief which a ceaseless succession of fatigue-duties soon dispelled.

Three fiords, several miles in length, necessitated a wide detour. The scenery was superb: a lacework of bays, lochs, and inlets with endless choppy waves of hills sweeping away to the great purple surf of the distant ranges; islets galore, and the vast rugged mass of the island of Kwijwi as a background.

For several days we had much trouble in allaying the fears of the natives; terrible accounts had preceded us, and the entire population fled to the hills on our approach. The fact of our carriers being Manyema, a name of terror throughout Central Africa, was not reassuring to the poor creatures, whose only knowledge of Manyema had been gathered from the Congo Free State soldiers, who for a time had been posted on Kivu, and from reports of the atrocities committed by the revolted troops during the past five years. Accounts also of the cannibals who were battering at the gates of Bugoie must have reached them from their northern kinsfolk. Black masses of natives in a silvery sea of glinting spearheads watched us from every hill-top. Fortunately we had several days' food for our men, and when the natives saw that we passed through without touching even a bunch of bananas, they were reassured, and a few were eventually induced to approach and talk. We caught two of our men stealing, and inflicted condign punishment before a small body of natives who were in camp, explaining the circumstances, and telling them, in case of a repetition of the offence, to come and lay a complaint. But it would be easier to stop a monkey from scratching than a Manyema from stealing; and as the state of unrest of the native population was a grave danger, and petty thefts would probably have precipitated an attack, which we were ill prepared to repulse, we confined all our boys to camp, made water-carrying for the whole camp a fatigue-duty, and established a market where the natives might sell their produce under our personal supervision. I explained the expediency of our action, and told them that there were some such abandoned ruffians amongst them that they must all suffer for the misdeeds of the miscreants. They appeared satisfied, but as we were sitting down to lunch, I noticed an unusual stir in the lines. On going out I found that they were all packing up their belongings and preparing to depart; about thirty were already moving off. It was obviously an attempt to bluff us, as the experience of the boys who ran away at Tanganyika had taught them that it would be impossible to avoid detection even if they succeeded in passing through Ngenzi's country, which they knew would be impossible in view of the then state of the natives. It was a critical moment. If the camp broke up, the entire expedition would be inevitably massacred by the Ruanda. I took my rifle and dashed off in pursuit, accompanied by my two Watonga; while Sharp, revolver in one hand and rifle in the other, threatened to shoot the first man who moved. Rushing over a rise, I saw the ringleader, one of our worst villains, and the originator of the idea, leading about two hundred yards away; I fired at him, just as he turned the corner of the hill, fully intending to drop him. The bullet removed his fez. Down he dropped into the grass, and the whole thirty did likewise. After a few shots in the air, to keep up their anxiety, I sent a headman out to order them back to camp, saying that the affair was now ended, and that I should not know who had left camp. As I expected, every one was present at roll-call, half an hour after dark. The position was saved. In the course of a long harangue, I informed them again of the absolute necessity of confining them to camp till the natives should be reassured; explained that I had spared the ringleader this time, and had removed his hat to show him with what ease I could have killed him had I wished to do so (a remark that my gun-bearer, Makanjira, assured them was true); said that it was for their benefit that we desired friendly relations with the population; we had no desire to see a lot of dirty natives, we wished nothing from them; had we not, as they well knew, food for many weeks in boxes? But if the natives refused to come, where would they be able to buy goats, fowls, tobacco, and all the things that rejoiced the stomachs of men?

The bluff was outbluffed, and with ringing cheers the men returned to their fires to jabber and howl with laughter far into the night. From discontent to merry laughter is but a momentary transition with the African.

From the ridge on which we were encamped we looked down upon a perfect spot, a long arm of the lake winding in between striking hills, terminating in a small bay. Banana palms with the tiny villages nestling in their midst fringed the shore. Weird little islands covered with ibis and demoiselle crane were dotted about. A wall of papyrus showed where the tumbling stream that danced down the encircling hills entered the lake, and the glorious colouring and strong shadows brought out the picture into striking relief. Sharp said it reminded him of Japan; there was an air of *dolce far niente* heavy with the lush glamour of the tropics that carried me back to the South Seas.

The following day we succeeded, after much shouting, in inducing a half-bred Mtusi to come to us. We gave him a present, and told him to go and explain that we wanted to buy provisions; and that if the natives would not come we should be compelled, much against our will, to take what was necessary. He departed, promising to do so, but nobody appeared. After waiting several hours, I took ten men out with me, and cut sufficient bananas for the men; and though I tried for two days to induce the chief to come for payment, he never appeared. This was the sole occasion during the whole of my long trip in Africa when I had to commandeer anything from the natives. I quite agree with Colonel Lugard when he says that it is unnecessary. This was the last time that we had any difficulty with the natives. Seeing that we refrained from looting their fields, they plucked up courage, and came in the same numbers as when we first entered the country. The hordes of warriors whom we had seen sitting on the tops of the hills in the distance came and mingled freely with our men, and a brisk trade started in the numerous products of the country. From many of our camps the scenery was most beautiful; as we rounded the south-eastern corner of the lake, the whole expanse of water opened out before us. The track we followed often led over hills 1,500 ft. above the lake; and from many positions we could look down on the vast oily expanse of water, deep set in its basin of innumerable hills, dotted with a thousand islets, stretching far away till it was lost in the shimmering haze of the northern shore, where, crisp and clear, towered the mighty mass of Mount Götzen, whose jet of smoke alone broke the steel-blue dome of sky.

Close to this part are the sources of the Nyavolongo, which are the real sources of the Victoria Nile. At the actual angle of the lake there is an extensive valley, which is the real frontier of Ngenzi's district, Mukinyaga. Every available inch of this extensive fertile valley is covered with luxuriant crops of beans, peas, sweet potatoes, and millet. To the east, up this valley, lies the road to the old Kigeri's residence, which is about five days' march from the lake.

Here there is a district which is divided up amongst many chiefs, and which seems to have no representative name. At the mouth of the stream that flows down this valley, the lake shores, if possible, are still more broken than elsewhere. The hills which cover the country around Kivu appear to have been sprinkled out of a pepper-pot, they are in the main disconnected, and the country seems almost to have boiled. The hollows are in places filled with papyrus swamps, many of which have drained dry, and now form level lawns a few feet above the lake.

The population round this valley is enormous. The northern wall of the valley rises very abruptly, and the path led along precipitous passes. The scenery is most striking. From the top of this plateau we caught our first glimpse of the volcanoes, the sharp outline of the four main peaks standing out clear and crisp above the misty haze that surrounds their base.

One day's march brought us to the district of Lubengera, which is remarkable for the number of Watusi. There seems to be no prominent chief among them. The banana plantations are of amazing extent, and literally clothe many of the hills from top to bottom. In this district especially we remarked the extreme neatness of the fields and the scattered nature of the villages. The Ruanda do not live together in great numbers, but are scattered far and wide over the country; their villages would perhaps be more aptly described as farms.

It is remarkable that throughout the whole of this country, as in the valley of the Rusisi, there were no antelope, and until we arrived near the wooded slopes of the volcanoes, where a few of the natives had bushbuck skins, we never saw any traces of their having been obtained.

All the natives of Ruanda are great smokers; they use small, neatly-made, and sometimes grotesquely-carved, black clay pipes. At this stage we were much troubled by complaints from our boys of petty thefts. On going thoroughly into the question, I found that besides the numerous slave boys whom our Manyema carriers had brought up from Ujiji, they had picked up many more on the road. Some of these had recently bolted, taking everything upon which they could lay their hands. As it was desirable to stop this, we had all the boys' boys brought up, and registered them. All those who could not show that they had come either from Ujiji or Usambara were given twenty-four hours' notice to quit. I also forbade our carriers to hire local natives to carry their loads, and thus rendered our caravan on the march much more compact, and thereby less open to attack.

On the far coast of the lake two striking hills were plainly visible; these are evidently placed on the two promontories which I have suggested as existing in my map. From the numerous observations which I took, I came to the conclusion that the islands to the north of Kwijwi have either risen since Count Götzen's visit, or else that he underestimated their size; which seems scarcely possible, as he actually landed on one or two of them.

As we were approaching the north end of the lake, several attempts were made to raid the camp at night, and at one place in particular the thieves were very resolute, and succeeded in stealing many small things from the boys. The sentry came and woke me up during the night, and told me that persistent attempts were being made to enter the camp; so I went out, and taking up my position outside the lines, under the cover of a small bush, I succeeded in capturing one of the thieves by collaring him low. This form of attack was unexpected, and though he was greased he failed to escape. The following morning he was handed over to the chief, and suffered the usual penalty of convicted thieves, his head being cut off and placed on the path, as a warning to others. This fortunate capture definitely settled the thieving question.

After crossing the Kashale, we entered the populous and fertile district of Bugoie. The chief is variously called Gwamu or Mwami, and is now, as I have before stated, one of the joint kings of Ruanda. All the way up this coast the scenery is exquisite; nowhere, except in the sounds of New Zealand, have I ever seen anything so fine, and the nearer we approached to the mighty volcanoes, the more dazzlingly beautiful and the more imposing it became.

At one of our camps we were besieged by an army of biting and poisonous ants, and I was just turning in when they assaulted my tent. Countless thousands swarmed all over my blankets and into my boxes and my clothes, and over every available inch both of my person and belongings. Calling my boys to my rescue, we endeavoured to save at least a blanket, and fled precipitately. But so thick were they that it was impossible to escape them. However, eventually the main body had moved on to other people's quarters, and I succeeded in rescuing my camp-bed, which I fixed up in another tent with all four legs in basins of water; by this means I managed to pass the night without more than three or four hundred around me. Sharp, who at first had looked upon it as a great joke, became the main object of their attentions during the small hours of the morning.

Here the people became very friendly again, and one chief provided us with two guides and two cattle-men, who undertook to go with us as far as the northern slopes of the volcanoes. One of these guides and one of the cattle-men bolted the following day with a few trifles, but the other two stuck to us well, and found our company so agreeable that they even followed me right through to the Nile, where they met a sad fate.

The Ruanda people are even more superstitious than most Central African natives. They wear medicine (native name *dawa*) to guard them against every conceivable ill, such as pains in the stomach, leopards, death, etc., etc. It is curious that the natives, like the lower animals, seem to be unable to grasp the fact that they will die; such a thing as a natural death they cannot understand, and always attribute the event to some form of violence, which, if not obvious, they describe as the effect of the "evil eye." The tip of a cow's horn, inlaid with ivory, is considered particularly efficacious against a pain in the side; and if a man wears two small leather bottles round his neck, he can never die. A large red bean is a sure preventive against leopards. One native wore an extraordinary bracelet; it was made of wood, and beautifully worked with various metals; the total weight must have been at least two pounds. He promised to come into camp and sell it to me; but, having promised, naturally did not come. Of all the liars in Africa, I believe the people of Ruanda are by far the most thorough. I have pointed to a mountain 13,000 ft. high, at a distance of three miles, and asked my native guide whether there was a mountain there: he would say "No!" On the march, if I asked whether there was water near, and he told me "yes," I knew that it would take at least six hours to find the next stream, and therefore camped where I was; if, however, he said that there was no water, one could be perfectly certain of finding several streams within the course of the next ten minutes. Even amongst themselves they appear to talk in the same way, and many of the instances, such as I have mentioned, are so extraordinary that I cannot help thinking that it is a custom. I believe at one place on the coast there is a form of Swahili which is spoken backwards, or rather the end of the word is put first. It seems to me to be just conceivable that the same train of reasoning may affect the habits of speech of the Wa Ruanda.

The natives assured me that there were many elephant on the north side of the volcanoes and also to the west, in the countries of Mushari and Gishari; for this reason I was sorely tempted to doubt their existence; however, from Dr. Kandt's remarks we thought it would be worth while, later on, to go and see.

We had a lot of trouble with our cattle-folk. The head cattle-man was a most persistent, pertinacious scoundrel, and as soon as he was detected in one villainy he invariably tried another; the result being that, although we had ten cows, there was barely enough milk for two people, and butter was quite out of the question. So we determined to take the thing in hand, and make a big effort to find out where the leakage was. As we had expected, under our personal supervision, there was a quantity of milk, enough for us both, and plenty with which we could make butter.

The method of making butter, a task which was entrusted to the headman's wife, is as follows: The woman squatted down on the ground, and taking an enormous flat gourd, containing milk which had been kept for three days, she proceeded to rock it to and fro, bringing it up short against her thigh. She assured us that, for the purpose of obtaining butter, it was absolutely necessary to insert two small pieces of wood as medicine. Judging from the quantity of butter, I doubted its efficacy; and suspecting that there was some new villainy in hand, as we obtained about a quarter of an ounce of butter from a bucket full of milk, we waited till the process was complete, and then told her to bring the gourd to us. All my doubts as to the efficacy of the two bits of wood were removed when I discovered that they were just large enough to jam in the neck of the gourd, and that, perched on the top of them, was a pound and a half of butter. She was quite unabashed at the discovery, and evidently mentally prayed that she would have better luck next time, which I have no doubt she did, although not in that particular method.

On our last march up the side of the lake the cattle were, owing to the steep nature of the road, left a long way behind; a band of natives attacked them, but the cattle-guard, firing a few rounds, which did more harm to themselves than to anybody else, repulsed the attack. Hearing about it, I sent Makanjira, my gun-bearer, back, and with his help they brought them all in without mishap.

At the north-east corner of the lake there is an abrupt descent, and to the north of the lake the country is flat, gently sloping to the base of the large, active volcano.

CHAPTER XI.

THE VOLCANOES.

At the base of the descent there is a small bay, the resort of many fishermen, and beyond, two small isolated peaks, on the slope of one of which we camped. In the evening I climbed to the top of the one nearest to the lake to take observations of all the promontories down the east coast.

I think the view is the finest I have ever seen. Far to the south stretched the mighty expanse of water; dark promontories of every shape and size jutted far into the lake; Kwijwi stood out in bold outline; and the mighty wall of mountains on the west was dimly visible on the far horizon. Below me stretched a great plain, the eastern part densely covered with fields of millet and banana plantations, dotted with a thousand huts. In all the fields hundreds of women were working, and small herds of cattle and goats were slowly wending their way to the lake. To the west, the plain was covered with young forest. To the north towered the terrific mass of Mount Götzen, vomiting forth a great volume of black smoke. The old volcanoes towered aloft above the clouds, which swirled in constant eddies about their base. Entranced with the view, I waited till the sun declined and dropped like a molten ball behind the bold outline of the hills; then the moon came up, bathing the waters of the lake in silvery light.

The natives visited our camp in hundreds, and brought numerous presents of goats and sheep, and an unlimited quantity of supplies for sale. We told them that we wanted to buy eggs—a request that always astonishes the natives, who are not used to the ways of white men, as they themselves never eat them. One old gentleman rushed away, and shortly returned, bringing a dirty basket with a frowsy old hen and about fifteen small chickens emerging from the eggs, and was surprised because we said they were of no use to us. We tried to explain that we preferred them fresh, and he evidently thought that we were making a fool of him.

Here we were informed that in the pass between the volcanoes there was no water, and that we should have to purchase what we required at great price from the natives, who obtain a purple liquid by tapping the stems of the banana palms.

The large volcanoes, of which there are six, fall naturally under two heads. The two western ones are still active; the highest I have described on my map as Mount Götzen, in honour of Count Götzen, who was the first to discover Kivu, and who made the ascent of the peak which I have named after him. Owing to the impossibility of obtaining representative names to these mountains, I have suggested names for them. On one of the mountains on which I camped, I obtained no less than thirty-six names of the same place. Mount Götzen is a stupendous mass, and has three craters. The central crater, described by Count Götzen, is very extensive; the bottom of the crater is quite flat, and has two cleanly-drilled vent-holes; the northern and the southern craters are now extinct. It is covered with the densest imaginable forest, almost to the summit; and Count Götzen found it absolutely necessary, during his ascent, to fetch all water from the lake.

Slightly to the north-west of this peak another volcano, covering an enormous area, has formed since Count Götzen's passage through the country. He mentions considerable activity at the end of the ridge; and two years before I passed through the country there had been a terrific eruption, in the course of which this volcano formed; its crater is several miles in circumference. I have described it as Mount Sharp, after my fellow-traveller.

The eastern system is still more imposing. The four main peaks have long been extinct, and the form of the highest, which I have described as Mount Eyres, after Mrs. Eyres of Dumbleton Hall, Evesham, is very striking, reminding me forcibly of the Matterhorn, as seen from the Riffelalp. The height of Mount Eyres is over 13,000 ft., and its summit was almost invariably covered with snow in the morning. A dense, impenetrable forest runs up to a height of 11,500 ft., above which there is open woodland. The actual summit, or last 500 ft., is practically bare. The top has the appearance of slightly overhanging, and shows some bold rock faces. The next volcano in the chain I have described as Mount Kandt, after the eminent scientist who is making such exhaustive studies of Ruanda and the north-west territories of the German sphere.

We insisted upon all our boys buying gourds for water, in case of there being any difficulty in obtaining it on the road. The waterless stage to be traversed was a long one, and we therefore only made a short march, and camped at the last watering-place, which was about four miles from the lake. This was the site of Gwamu's village. Gwamu himself, following the traditions of the Ruanda kings, retired to the mountains, but left his headman to receive us with a handsome present of goats and necessaries.

The population here was enormous, every available inch of country was cultivated, and this portion of Bugoie is undoubtedly the most prosperous, the most densely populated, and the most fertile spot that I have seen in Africa.

Fifteen miles to the east, the range that encloses the Rift Valley culminates in a striking peak. It is known to the natives as Hembe è Bugogo. This peak is at a pronounced angle in the range; and northwards the enclosing hills recede towards the east. The volcanoes themselves are a quite distinct system, having risen out of the bed of the Rift Valley.

On the following day we started on our waterless march with many misgivings. Our route lay along the base of the hills, then over a small chain of extinct volcanic craters, then across the flat, swampy plain, which lies to the east of Mount Götzen. In all directions there are isolated, extinct craters, still perfect in form, and invariably terraced and covered with crops of peas and beans.

We camped in the vicinity of three large, straggling villages. The natives were not very friendly at first, although the headman of Gwamu had accompanied us, and about tea-time one of our men rushed in to say that the herds had been attacked and that they had lost thirty goats and sheep, and that one man had been wounded with a spear. I hurried out to the scene, but it was too late to do any good, and I returned, bringing in the remnants of our flocks.

The path then passed over the summit of the pass between Mount Götzen and Mount Eyres. I found the height to be approximately 7,000 feet. Half a mile from our camp I discovered a small cave open at both ends, in which there was a pool of water, which the natives refused to drink; whether from superstition or because the water is poisonous, I could not say.

At the base of Mount Eyres there are several small craters, and on the north side of the base there is a little rugged patch of country, where the path descends into abrupt ravines, and passes through a strip of the most luxuriant tropical forest, on the far side of which the wonderful pastures, characteristic of this country, recommence. Here, we were told, was the elephant country.

Gwamu's headman was still with us, and he brought in many of the surrounding chiefs. At first they were very friendly and brought us plenty of supplies for sale, the article of exchange in greatest request being salt. Judging from their phenomenal mendacity, I can quite understand their need of it.

Here we purchased several bows made by the dwarfs. They are quite distinct from any other bow that I have seen. The arc is in two pieces, an outside sheath of split cane with another piece of wood let in to the groove; both are neatly bound together by reed, and the string is composed of one blade of a very tough reed which grows in the forest. We also procured some strings of beads which the natives said had come from the west; they are very primitive, and appear to have been made of some kind of shell.

The following morning we went out in search of elephant.

The forest was full of traps set by the Pigmies. The ordinary type was a bamboo bent towards the game-path with a string fastened to the ground, where it was tied in a running noose; by this means, I am informed, they catch many pigs and small quadrupeds of the forest. They also fix spears, weighted with heavy blocks of wood, in the trees, and the elephant passing underneath releases the spear by breaking the cord with which it is attached; but I think their usual method of slaying elephant is by firing poisoned arrows into them—having done which, they follow the unfortunate beast for days, until it drops.

The country was so impenetrable that hunting was a practical impossibility, so two days later I started with ten boys to see if I could find an easier hunting-ground. I passed round to the north of Mount Eyres, and pitched my camp on an eminence of 9,000 ft., overlooking the Rutchuru Valley. Here I immediately found fresh elephant-tracks. A herd of ten had passed towards the north, and a solitary old bull had gone towards the forest on the mountain slope. This I elected to follow, and in an hour and a half I could hear him not far away, tearing down branches of trees. His spoor was bigger than any spoor I have ever seen, and the size of the brute, when I first saw him, filled me with astonishment. Unfortunately he was not standing broadside on, and it was impossible for me to go round. From where I stood, I could see the small glade in which he was standing, but could only see a portion of his head and the ridge of his back. I watched him for some time picking the leaves off a tree; then, having eaten all the leaves within reach, without apparent effort he seized the trunk of the tree about 16 ft. from the ground and laid it flat. The tree had a diameter of more than 2 ft. Fearing that he might move into the impenetrable jungle that surrounded us, I took the shot, difficult as it was; he fell, but instantly recovered himself and dashed away, getting the second barrel in his flank as he did so. For several hours I followed him, without getting another shot, though I found where he had again fallen down and lost much blood. A few hundred yards further on I heard him in some very thick bush; my guide, who was following on the spoor, refused to advance, and I had perforce to take the lead. The wind was very shifty, and he suddenly detected our presence, venting his disapproval in a series of unpleasant grunts. Suddenly, hearing a great crashing of bushes, I thought that he was moving away, and hurried forward as fast as the difficult track would allow, in the hopes of catching a glimpse of him. The noise was terrific, and it suddenly dawned upon me that, so far from moving off, he was coming on. I was powerless to move—a fall would have been fatal—so waited; but the forest was so dense that I never saw him till his head was literally above me, when I fired both barrels of the double .500 magnum, which I was carrying, in his face. The whole forest seemed to crumple up, and a second later I found myself 10 ft. above the ground, well home in a thorn-bush, while my gun was lying ten yards away in the opposite direction; and I heard a roar as of thunder disappearing into the distance. A few seconds later, the most daring of my boys, Zowanji, came hurrying along with that sickly green hue which a negro's face assumes in moments of fear, and with his assistance I descended from my spiky perch. I was drenched with blood, which fortunately proved to be not mine, but that of the elephant; my gun, which I recovered, was also covered with his blood, even to the inside of the barrels. The only damage I sustained was a slightly twisted knee. I cannot say whether the elephant actually struck me, or whether I was carried there by the rush of country.

Following on his tracks, I found enormous pools of blood, and half a mile further on I again heard grunts, which showed that he had caught my wind. He rushed about, uttering those strident shrieks that are so terrifying, but, after his last experience, refused to charge. I spent an exceedingly nervous five minutes, while he devastated half an acre of forest. Then he moved on again, and it was not till two hours later that I caught him up. He was standing in a dense bamboo thicket, and I fired the .500 at his head; he fell to the shot, but quickly recovered and went away. Yet another time I caught him up, and approached within ten yards, but the thicket was so dense that I could not see an inch of his body. I might have turned his flank, but in so doing should have given him my wind, and I funked it. He shortly moved on, and after twice falling pulled himself together, and went through the bamboo forest at an increased pace. I followed hard, but never saw him again, and at sunset was compelled to give up the chase.

We were at an altitude of 9,000 ft. and spent the night sitting naked round a fire, while the rain beat out any lingering sentiments for elephant-hunting that had survived the day's work. The old volcanic soil of these forests is so porous that above the valley there are no streams. We had had nothing to eat or drink since 6 a.m., and it was not till 11.30 the following morning that we found a cattle-station in the forest. Here we drank a quantity of milk, and eventually arrived in camp at two in the afternoon. My boys were almost dead with fatigue, and I myself slept for fifteen hours without rocking.

In following elephant through these forests it was necessary to cut one's way with a native axe on the path that the elephant had traversed only five minutes before. At times, for many yards one never touched the ground, but had perforce to climb along the tree-trunks, and the dense vegetable growth, constantly slipping and falling into thorn-bush and nettles, all of which the elephant would take in his stride; while the bush was so solid that, after the elephant had brushed it aside, it flew back to its original position.

This nettle, which, I believe, is peculiar to these volcanoes, is the most appalling creation that I have ever dreamed of. Some were 10 ft. in height, and it was impossible to brush them aside; they were covered with myriads of long, almost invisible, spines, which penetrated khaki, flannel, and everything except leather. The pain produced by contact with them was nearly unbearable, but fortunately subsided in about ten minutes. At times they were so bad that my natives could no longer move, and I had to beat down a track before they could pass. Many times they sat down and howled like babies. Some of the trees that had been torn down by the elephant were of enormous dimensions, and I had never before even guessed at the stupendous power of the African elephant.

I found that the country here was no easier than that which I had just left, and therefore marched north down the long sloping spur that leads into the valley of the Kako.

The district round the base of Mount Eyres is called Bwisha. It is ruled by a powerful chief called Kahanga. His main village was elaborately protected by a palisade, around which trees and creepers had been planted to consolidate the structure, and it was surrounded by many smaller villages. The whole of the adjacent country was densely planted with banana, and all the intervening land was covered with fields of peas, beans, and millet.

My track led down a small stream that flowed into the Mungawo, which is the western head-waters of the Kako, as the southern part of the Rutchuru is called; it is consequently one of the most distant sources of the Albert Nile. The territory between the Mungawo and the Kako is called Shoni; here I made many inquiries about elephant, and, as usual, was informed that there were none actually there, but that there were tremendous quantities elsewhere.

Kahanga was at first rather suspicious, but plucking up courage at the insignificant proportions of my caravan, he eventually became very communicative, and told off some men to guide me round the country.

Leaving this village I marched to the east, along the base of four extinct volcanoes, to find out the real truth of the vexed question of Mfumbiro.

Mfumbiro, as a mountain, is unknown to the natives, but I eventually ascertained that it is merely a native word which means "The place where there is fire." And when I reached the country where Mount Mfumbiro had been supposed by an imaginative treaty-maker to be, I was informed that "Mfumbiro" was used by the natives in that part to represent the district of the active volcanoes.

In reaching my destination I passed through many almost impenetrable forests of bamboo, and crossed the head-waters of the main stream of the Kako. The natives appeared to be rather disturbed, and suspicious of my intentions. With such a weak caravan I did not desire to have any trouble; I therefore hastily retreated to the base of Mount Eyres once more.

Close to Kahanga's village there is a small pool, probably a relic of the lake that once filled this Rift Valley, as there are a few hippopotami therein, and the hilly nature of the country that surrounds this small lake renders it improbable that they have any connection with the outside world.

From here I made my first attempt to cross the great lava streams that fill the trough of the valley, with the intention of inspecting Mushari, which Dr. Kandt had told me teemed with elephant. Inquiries which I made confirmed his report, and the natives appeared particularly anxious for me to go there. It was not till my eventual arrival in Mushari that I really understood the reason of their anxiety.

When I had penetrated a short distance into the tangled scrub that has sprung up on the edge of the lava-stream, my guide mysteriously disappeared; and as it was already late in the day, and I knew that there was no chance of obtaining water till I reached the hills on the far side, I returned. Passing round the base of the terrace which overhangs the lava-stream, I eventually arrived back at our main camp. On the way I traversed a wonderful succession of plantations and villages. The natives bring all their water from a distance of six miles.

I found that Sharp, after losing two stone in frantic efforts to find elephant, had given up the game as a bad job, and together we started to make another attempt to cross into Mushari.

The natives stated that there was a track round Mount Götzen, and it was not until we had actually started that they informed us that it was impossible to take cattle there. One man volunteered to show the way, but at the last moment endeavoured to escape. However, he was caught, and a string was tied round his neck. I explained to him that I could not risk being left without a guide, and had therefore been compelled to take that precaution, promising him, however, a supplementary present when he had completed his task, as compensation for his offended dignity. He then protested that the track was impossible, saying that there was no water for two days, nor any food, and that the path was so bad that it would cut everybody's feet to pieces. Sharp and I accordingly arranged that it would be better to see what the path was like before moving with the whole caravan. For this purpose I started with half a dozen men, carrying my necessaries, while Sharp returned to our camping-place.

I and my boys set out for the slopes of Mount Götzen, and on the way managed to pick up two more guides. After climbing a very steep hill, we arrived on a flat terrace, where there were many signs of elephant; this we crossed and plunged into the dense forest, characteristic of the slopes of these volcanoes. The track was almost indistinguishable, and the recent depredations of elephant had rendered it practically impassable. After eight hours' work we found that it would be impossible to reach a pool of water which, my guide acknowledged, existed at some distance. At this point two of the guides mysteriously vanished, and I sincerely congratulated myself on having tied the third one up.

I waited for my boys to close up, but waited in vain: all except two had lost the track, and though I fired round after round, there was no response. Everything, with the exception of the inside of my tent, was with the boys who had strayed. To afford some shelter we fixed up this part of the tent on some poles, which we cut with a sword-bayonet.

Torrential rains fell all night, but unfortunately we had no means of catching the water, as the roof of foliage above our heads caught the fall and poured it on to us through unexpected channels. It was exceedingly cold, and we had no food. However, the night passed somehow, and the following morning, retracing our steps and firing shots at intervals, we eventually discovered the other boys. The sun was very hot, and selecting an open glade, we sat down and dried ourselves, while making a square meal.

In the midst of my meal I had an idea that somebody from behind was looking at me; and turning round, I saw the hideous, distorted features of a pigmy leering at me in open-mouthed astonishment through the bush against which I was resting. When he saw that he was detected he dashed away at an incredible pace, and my boys failed to catch him. These pigmies are usually described by travellers as implacably hostile to strangers, but I never had any trouble with them, although I came in contact with many.

Having no water or food, I had, for the second time, to abandon the attempt to reach Mushari, and sorrowfully retraced my steps to camp, burning on my way the hut of the guide who had bolted; a punishment that he richly deserved, as he had undertaken to come for payment and had left me, thinking that I should be lost, and taking with him my axe.

In this part of Africa the natives use the word "tanganyika" for any lake or extensive body of water.

On my way into camp I saw another pigmy in one of the villages. He had brought honey to trade with the Ruanda people for grain. The natives informed me that the pigmies have no settled villages, nor do they cultivate anything. They live the life of the brute in the forests, perpetually wandering in search of honey or in pursuit of elephant; when they succeed in killing anything, they throw up a few grass shelters and remain there till all the meat is either eaten or dried. They depend upon the other natives for the necessary grain, which they either steal or barter for elephant-meat or honey. All their knives, spear-heads, and arrow-heads they likewise purchase from other people, but they make their own bows and arrows. So well are these made that they are held in great esteem by the surrounding people. This pigmy fled on my approach, and although the country was perfectly flat, and therefore my boys were on equal terms when they tried to catch him, he easily escaped. The pace at which he ran was extraordinary. It is curious to notice how perfectly adapted they are to the surroundings in which they live; the combination of immense strength necessary for the precarious hunting-life they lead, and of compactness, indispensable to rapid movement in dense forest, where the pig-runs are the only means of passage, is a wonderful example of nature's adaptability.

After a few days' rest I made my third and successful attempt to cross the lava-beds, which I describe in the following chapter on Mushari.

Sharp undertook to take the live stock and the main caravan round the southern slope of Mount Götzen, and to eventually meet me in Mushari. This involved a waterless tramp of twenty-five miles, unless he could find the pool of water spoken of by Count Götzen as existing in a small crater on the lava-bed between Mount Götzen and the lake.

On the road he had to pass near the place where he had lost our thirty sheep and goats, and he determined to recapture them, if possible. Seeing a large flock being driven off across the plain he gave chase, followed by two of his boys, while the main caravan halted. After a sharp dash over the roughest country imaginable, semi-disintegrated lava and scrubby bush, he succeeded in collecting twenty-five goats, and in driving them to his camping-place. The natives meanwhile collected in large numbers and fired volleys of arrows at him, all of which fortunately missed their mark. When he rejoined the main body of his caravan he found that two men had been wounded by arrows. An enormous concourse of natives rapidly gathered on the surrounding hills.

Having pitched his camp and put the place in a position of defence, he was hailed by a deputation from the chief, who said that he wished to pay Sharp "hongo." Sharp promptly informed them that the chief must arrive with wood, water, and thirty-five goats, as compensation for the loss which we had sustained and the trouble which they had caused us. All this the chief undertook to do. He was a fine native, standing over 6 ft. After a long delay he returned with three goats, and without wood or water. So he was promptly bound with his four headmen and placed in the guard-tent. After much prevarication and some little delay the goats were produced, and with them a small tusk of ivory; whereupon the prisoners were released and their hearts made glad by a handsome present of cloth and beads to show that, now that the account was squared, there was no ill-feeling.

The following day he had much difficulty in getting his caravan through the difficult country, and failing to find water, he was compelled to descend to the shore of Kivu, where a sharp attack of fever delayed him for some days.

The boys, who had picked up wild rumours of the existence of bad men in the country to be penetrated, almost mutinied, and Sharp was fortunately relieved of the necessity of risking a mutiny through pushing on by the receipt of a note from me to the effect that he must return at once, as the country was full of cannibals and devastated from end to end.

CHAPTER XII.

MUSHARI AND ITS CANNIBALS.

After these two unsuccessful attempts to reach Mushari—first, north by Kahanga's country, and secondly, by the path that runs round the base of Mount Götzen—I determined to cut straight across the lava-streams, in spite of everything that the natives said to dissuade me. Lies, lies, lies, I was sick to death of them, and resolved to go to Mushari by the direct route, cost what it might, the behaviour of my pagazi,[8] which caused my second attempt to fail, making me only the more determined to show them that their little games were of no use. In vain I sent out to the villages for guides, none were forthcoming; frightened, as I afterwards discovered, by my boys, they obstinately assured me there was no way across; that we should die of thirst, be eaten by lions, and so forth, *ad nauseam*. I gave out orders that all my boys were to make sandals, and prepare food and water for two days. In the morning three-quarters of them hobbled up on sticks, pleading sickness; and when I finally started, half of them burst into tears and swore that they were not slaves, to be led into the wilderness to die. When we reached the edge of the lava-stream, there were no shoes or food or water; but when I once stepped on to the stones, the whole scene changed. Beads were produced, natives with sandals for sale brought forth, guides sprang up in bewildering plenty, and, as I had half suspected, I found there was a well-used track across. There is one thing to be said for the Manyema: they play their game right out to the end.

We went south-west for four hours across the eastern stream, making about half a mile an hour; it is like a very broken glacier such as that which lies under the north-west side of the Aiguille du Dru near Chamounix, huge blocks of lava piled one upon the other, and sharp as razors. The length is about twenty miles, and breadth about two in the narrowest part. Further north it branches off to the east and west, the western branch mingling with the great western stream about fifteen miles from the pass between Mount Götzen and Mount Sharp. The natives say that the lava came down two years ago, and that great numbers of elephants were killed; I myself saw the bones of one in our comparatively short traverse.

Already there are patches of bush several miles in extent where the stream eddied, stayed by some extra strong clump of trees, and so wonderful is the tropical growth produced by the combination of damp and fertile soil, that in another twenty years all obvious trace of the great eruption will have been erased. The trees on all the higher spurs which were above the level of the streams were snapped off short by the wind, and lie in regular rows towards the main centres of disturbance. The eruption must

---

[8] Porters.

have been accompanied by considerable seismic waves, huge rents occurring in the surrounding forests; and very beautiful these rents are, being already converted by a luxuriant nature into exotic ferneries. After leaving the lava the path led west into the bush, and about 4 p.m. we reached a pool of water formed by an old crater. My inquiry as to the death-rate caused much merriment, and the evening passed with howls of joy and those unearthly noises which in Africa pass current for song.

Here we were joined by numbers of natives coming from Mushari with loads of food. On inquiry I found that they were refugees, having been driven out by the Baleka or Bareka, a tribe of cannibals from the Congo who had raided their country. They told me that those who had survived were living in the forest, and that great numbers were dying every day of hunger. On the morrow we skirted along the base of the new volcano for about fourteen miles through the most beautiful glades, coming across several pools of water. Dead natives lined the path, showing that the tales of our last night's companions were only too true. Towards evening we reached the great western stream, and here we met several natives who were living amongst the stones in the most awful misery, hardly daring even to make a fire. They said that they had been living thus for six months. When driven to despair by hunger, they would make a dash for an armful of half-ripe grain, each time losing some of their number by the Baleka, who were watching all the paths. I lined their bellies and warmed their hearts (identical organs, I believe, in the African and perhaps some others) with beans; and in the morning we advanced into the dreaded land. All the paths up the hills that led to the uplands of Mushari were lined with grain and torn skins, relics of those unfortunates who had been caught; and dried pools of blood, gaunt skeletons, grinning skulls, and trampled grass told a truly African tale. On arriving at the top of the ridge a beautiful rolling country opened out before us, dotted with clusters of grass huts and stately trees; russet patches of ripening mtama contrasted with the emerald green of the wild banana, range upon range of purple hills melted into the nether-world of a tropical horizon. But we were not to enjoy the scenery long, for distant howls showed that we had been observed, silhouetted as we were against the sky; and strings of black figures, brandishing spears and howling at the expected feast, came running down from a neighbouring hill. I was still uncertain as to the exact state of affairs. The refugees and the numerous corpses made it obvious that there was something in the wind, but I imagined that it was merely an ordinary case of native fractiousness, some intertribal squabble, such as occurs every day in these remote corners of the Dark Continent, and that the Baleka and their doings were merely a characteristic effort of the African imagination. But the diabolical noise made by the onrushing natives decided me that the matter was serious. I questioned my guide as to their intentions, and was scarcely reassured by his naïve remark: "They are coming to eat us." Accordingly I kept quiet behind a clump of grass till they were quite close and there was no further doubt of their intentions, and opened fire with my light rifle. They disappeared like rabbits into the standing crops.

We then hurried on to the huts from which we had seen these people come; but they were too quick for us, and fled. A cloud of vultures hovering over the spot gave me an inkling of what I was about to see, but the realization defies description; it haunts me in my dreams, at dinner it sits on my leg-of-mutton, it bubbles in my soup—in fine, Watonga would not eat the potatoes that grew in the same country, and went without food for forty-eight hours rather than do so: ask your African friends what that means; negroes have not delicate stomachs. Loathsome, revolting, a hideous nightmare of horrors; and yet I must tell briefly what I saw, for the edification of any disciple of the poor-dear-black-man, down-with-the-Maxim, Africa-for-the-African Creed, who may chance to peruse these pages.

Item.—A bunch of human entrails drying on a stick.

Item.—A howling baby.

Item.—A pot of soup with bright yellow fat.

Item.—A skeleton with the skin on lying in the middle of the huts; apparently been dead about three months.

Item.—A gnawed thigh-bone with shreds of half-cooked meat attached.

Item.—A gnawed forearm, raw.

Item.—Three packets of small joints, evidently prepared for flight, but forgotten at the last moment.

Item.—A head, with a spoon left sticking in the brains.

Item.—A head, one cheek eaten, the other charred; hair burnt, and scalp cut off at top of forehead like the peel of an orange; one eye removed, presumably eaten, the other glaring at you.

Item.—Offal, sewage.

Item.—A stench that passeth all understanding, and, as a fitting accompaniment, a hovering cloud of crows and loathly, scraggy-necked vultures.

Every village had been burnt to the ground, and as I fled from the country I saw skeletons, skeletons everywhere; and such postures, what tales of horror they told! Let this suffice, worse than all this I saw, and that I have not exaggerated one jot or tittle, may God bear me witness! I would not have entered into these revolting details, but that I think it advisable that those who have not the chance of seeing for themselves should know what is going on every day in this country. A beautiful yellow covers this spot on the map, with a fringe of red spots with flags attached, denoting (as the map informs you) stations of the Congo Free State. And yet a peaceful agricultural people can be subjected to horrors like this for months (*without any one knowing*). And why? Because the whole system is bunkum—the so-called partition of Africa. The stations marked do not exist; and read, mark, learn, and inwardly digest this fact: I have to pay a licence *to carry a gun* in the country.

The next day I reached Kishari, and found that this beautiful and well-watered country had been converted into a howling wilderness, Kameronse having suffered to the same extent. Thus a tract of country about 3,000 square miles in extent has been depopulated and devastated. I do not believe that two per cent. of the thousands of inhabitants have survived the massacre and famine: in Kishari and Kameronse there is not one single soul. And all this is directly attributable to the revolted Askaris of the Congo: they led the attack with thirty guns, took all the cattle, and then departed, leaving this horde of hyænas in their wake; and a similar fate has, I suppose, befallen all those tribes between Tanganyika and Albert Edward through whose country they passed.

The partition or occupation of Africa with a view to sound colonization—that is, to fit the country as a future home for surplus population—is the obvious duty of the nations which form the vanguard of civilization. This is the object of our occupation of the various territories under the British flag, and of the Germans in the East and South-west Africa, and, I believe, of the French in the north, to make new markets and open up country for coming generations; to suffer temporary loss for the future benefit of overcrowded humanity. Experience and the suitability of our institutions are the reasons of our success. The predominance of militarism is the reason of the hitherto comparative failure of the two great land powers, and corruption and senile decay are the reasons of the abject failure of the nation that led the van of colonization. However, *experientia docet*, and Germany, at least, is laying a sound foundation for a broader colonial policy, while Portuguese occupation is only a negative failure. But what can be said in favour of permitting a vast tract of country to be run merely as a commercial speculation without more legitimate objective than that of squeezing as much rubber and ivory out of the natives as possible; of arming large numbers of savages and entrusting them to inexperienced men from a land of untravelled commercials to whom expatriation is akin to disgrace; of making the administrators of districts to all intents and purposes farmers of the taxes? However sound the intentions of the fountain-head, there can be no responsible administration without a connection with a definite home government. Men do not take employment in Africa for the joke of the thing. Hopes of preferment or pecuniary profit are what induce them to give up the comforts of civilization, and where the former is lacking the latter must be offered, or only the dregs of other trades will be forthcoming.

Then followed two of the worst days of my life. Rapid movements alone could save us from annihilation, and we travelled from sunrise to sunset, camping in patches of forest, and concealing our route by leaving the paths and forcing our way through the grass. Mummies, skulls, limbs, putrefying carcases washing to and fro in every limpid stream, marked the course of the fiendish horde. An insufferable stench filled the land, concentrating round every defiled homestead. This was the Congo Free State. Fear of being rushed at night made sleep well-nigh impossible, tired as we were. The country was exceedingly beautiful. Wild stretches of undulating hills, streaked with forest and drained by a hundred streams, each with its cargo of bloated corpses, made a terrible combination of heaven and hell. It was a scene that made one wonder if there be a God. To the west I could see two lakes nestling between the hills. A stream connects the two, and empties out at the south end, flowing, I imagined, towards the Congo. Flights of gorgeous butterflies floated here and there, and, settling on the gruesome relics, gave a finishing touch to the horrors of that land.

Leaving Kishari, we passed over the watershed, about 9,500 ft., and descended into Kameronse. Here we were met by the same scenes of desolation; the whole country had been swept clean—not so much as a sweet potato, which grow almost as weeds, was left. As we were skirting along a large papyrus swamp, which absorbs all the neighbouring streams, we came on the fresh spoor of natives. I had only just seized my gun, for which I had to wait about ten minutes, when a woman, girl, and two small boys appeared. These my natives captured; and no sooner did the woman realize that she had fallen into undesirable quarters, than she offered to show us where her relations lay. I followed the direction indicated with great caution, the way leading through very tall and thick grass; and as I turned a corner, my guide flashed past me like a streak of lightning, and I found myself confronted by half a dozen gentlemen of anthropophagic proclivities on supper intent. The unexpected apparition of a white man checked their rush, and dodging a spear, I got my chance and dropped one with a shot through the heart, two others escaping by my magazine failing to feed the barrel. We rushed on in pursuit, and shortly came on their encampment in a banana grove; here were the same ghastly relics as we had seen before. It appeared that they had raided an outlying village of Bugoie the previous night, and had caught two unfortunate wretches, whose remains were baking and stewing in pots. From the number of the rude huts there must have been at least fifty Baleka, but they had disappeared into the grass and papyrus, and we saw no more of them. Some baskets of grain were lying about, and these the Manyema eagerly seized upon; but I could not bring myself to eat any, and my Watonga were equally fastidious, although we had been almost without food for three days. Our captives were terribly thin, and these outlying bands of raiders are evidently leading but a hand-to-mouth existence; and as the Baleka have cut their boats adrift by wiping out the whole country behind them (in their wanton madness they even cut down the banana palms), I am afraid the people of Bugoie will eventually succumb, although hitherto they have held out. As yet they have only had to repel the attacks of small bands, the main mass of the Baleka being still occupied in demolishing the mtama fields of northern Mushari. When the general onslaught begins, I think they will have to give way before the thousands of savages rendered desperate by the impossibility of retreat, and those, too, men of superior courage. Those Baleka that I had the chance of observing at close quarters were well made and pleasant-featured, averaging not more than 5 ft. Their possessions—baskets, shields, knives, etc.—are very crude, and their dress consists of air and an occasional scrap of hide, human or otherwise. Whether they have a definite country or not, I cannot say; some natives told me that they have, many days' journey west of Kivu, while the majority say that they lead a nomadic existence like a flight of locusts, eating up just as effectually whatever they come across. At a rough estimate, there cannot have been less than 5,000 of them in the countries I passed through.

The next morning we came on another small encampment, which, fortunately, had been unable to see our fires, owing to the dense bush, although we were not half a mile away. To my amazement our guide, seeing one gentleman apart from the rest and unarmed, rushed in and speared him. The others turned on me, but were dispersed with a couple of shots. This was the last we saw of the Baleka, as, in the evening, we reached the outskirts of Bugoie, but skulls and charred relics for many miles bore witness to their recent raids. Very glad I was of a night's rest, for although the moral and sometimes physical effect of firearms on these unsophisticated people is very great, still the danger of being rushed at night, or in the dense forest and long grass, made it very anxious work; also the smallness of my caravan—twelve carriers with only two sniders, and such excitable curs at the end of them that I forbade them to fire—made us a tempting prey for any large number of natives we might meet; however, this was balanced by the rapidity of our movements and unexpected appearance, which would have been impossible with a larger caravan.

Such was the country that had been described to me by Dr. Kandt, who had visited it six months before, as a beautiful district teeming with peaceful agricultural folk. The natives informed me that of all that flourishing community but sixty remained. I was very anxious about Sharp, fearing that he might enter the country by a different road to that by which I had just left. Had he arrived hampered by a large caravan and cattle, he must inevitably have been destroyed. Hoping that he was still south of the volcanoes, I hurried east through the forest that is springing up on the great lava-bed thrown out by the last eruption but one. Here too the path was strewn with skulls, showing the desperate efforts that the Baleka had made to force an entry into Bugoie. Late in the afternoon we arrived at an old volcanic cone. This was the outpost of Bugoie, and the few wretched survivors, seeing us approaching through the forest, naturally mistook us for Baleka, and quickly prepared for battle. It was only after an hour's shouting that we allayed their fears. With some difficulty we managed to procure a jar of bad water, which we sadly needed, having had nothing to drink since daybreak, and we endeavoured to appease our ravening hunger with a brace of pumpkins, which was all the poor creatures had to offer us. Their destitution was complete, and filled me with pity, but I was powerless to assist them. It was impossible to obtain any definite information about Sharp, and it was with the direst forebodings that I started the following morning, as I knew that there was now no chance of intercepting him. However, an hour later I met an elderly pigmy in the forest and managed to induce him to talk. He was a splendid little fellow full of self-confidence, and gave me most concise information, stating that the white man with many belongings had passed near by two days before, and had then gone down to the lake-shore, where he was camped at that moment. These people must have a wonderful code of signs and signals, as, despite their isolated and nomadic existence, they always know exactly what is happening everywhere. He was a typical pigmy as found on the volcanoes—squat, gnarled, proud, and easy of carriage. His beard hung down over his chest, and his thighs and chest were covered with wiry hair. He carried the usual pigmy bow made of two pieces of cane spliced together with grass, and with a string made of a single strand of a rush that grows in the forests.

I sent off two of my boys with a note to Sharp, and pushed on as fast as possible to the food districts of Bugoie, where my boys ate so much that I despaired of their surviving. For the next two days I was very ill, owing to my having eaten a number of green bananas in the first banana plantation that I entered. The scarcity of water made it still more difficult to endure the pangs of hunger during the last day of our march.

Having partially recovered, I marched back to my northernmost camp and waited for Sharp. The natives, thinking that I could be imposed upon with my small caravan, ignored my presence, and in face of several requests refused to bring in food for sale. The country was very rich in produce, so I warned the chief that unless he brought in food in the ordinary way for sale I should be obliged to come and take what I wanted, as I could not starve. I was just preparing to carry out my threat, when Sharp arrived, and the chief soon turned up with a diseased sheep and about a quart of flour, which I promptly clapped on to his head, while Sharp roared with laughter at him. He tried hard to maintain his dignity, but with little effect: a little, tub-bellied man, he presented the most ridiculous spectacle imaginable as he stalked out of camp half black, half white, preceded by his awed followers. In the afternoon he returned with plenty of supplies, and after receiving a handsome present in exchange, retired quite satisfied. After making yet two more attempts after elephant, in the course of which I came on many cattle-yards hidden in the deepest recesses of the forest, we gave it up as hopeless, and determined to press on to the Albert Edward Lake. During one of my elephant hunts I came on the skeleton of a gigantic ape, larger than anything I have ever seen in the anthropoids, but I never saw a live specimen, though the natives assured me that they were plentiful, and were a great source of annoyance to the villages, being in the habit of carrying off stray women.

While exploring with a small number of followers, I observed some ape-like creatures leering at me from behind banana-palms, and with considerable difficulty my Ruanda guide induced one of them to come and be inspected. He was a tall man with the long arms, pendent paunch, and short legs of the ape, pronouncedly microcephalous and prognathous. At first he was terribly alarmed, but soon gained confidence, and when I asked him about game and elephant, he gave me most realistic representations of them and of how they should be attacked. I failed to exactly define their status, but from the contempt in which they were held by the Wa Ruanda their local caste must be very low. The stamp of the brute was so strong on them that I should place them lower in the human scale than any other natives I have seen in Africa. Their type is quite distinct from the other people's, and, judging from the twenty to thirty specimens that I saw, very consistent. Their face, body, and limbs are covered with wiry hair, and the hang of the long, powerful arms, the slight stoop of the trunk, and the hunted, vacant expression of the face, made up a *tout ensemble* that was a terrible pictorial proof of Darwinism. Two of them accompanied me to Mushari. On the road they showed me the ease with which they can make fire with their fire-sticks.

CHAPTER XIII.

THE RUTCHURU VALLEY AND THE ALBERT EDWARD LAKE.

On June 26th we started on our march to the Albert Edward Lake, and camped that night near Kahanga's village. Many of the more important men came and paid their respects to us, but Kahanga himself did not turn up. We inquired of his Prime Minister for what reason he had not done so, and were informed that he was ill; but having, as I thought, seen him, as I passed, looking far from ill, I made further inquiries, and discovered that he was afraid of our caravan, and imagined that if he came to our camp we should make him prisoner and demand a big ransom of ivory. I can only imagine that he had heard of other white men behaving in this manner. I tried hard to induce him to come, but in vain. As when I was there before with only a few boys he had been exceedingly friendly, it is obvious under what disadvantages one labours when travelling through Africa with a big caravan.

The following day we crossed the Mungawo, and following the ridge of the spur which runs down to the junction of the Mungawo and the Kako through the Shoni district, we camped on a bluff overlooking the Kako itself.

The Kako, as the southern portion of the Rutchuru is called, is a large body of water, many feet deep, and quite unfordable. Its banks are clothed with dense forests.

The people of Shoni were most friendly, and we purchased a large supply of beans. At this camp I saw a waterbuck, the first antelope that we had seen for many weeks.

We crossed the river by a native bridge formed of trunks of trees thrown across and bound together with fibre. Beneath, the Kako thundered, a mighty torrent, and the cloud of spray had left a saline deposit on the rocks, which was much appreciated by our cattle.

The name of the district into which we had entered was Imukubsu. From here we had a magnificent view of the volcanoes, and having dropped 4,000 ft. we were enabled to see what an imposing mass Mount Eyres is; its form on this side is an exact facsimile of the Matterhorn from the Riffelalp.

Here we purchased some of the curious hippo spears that are used by all the natives on the Albert Edward Lake; they have a large piece of cork or light wood on the end of the haft which floats the spear if they miss their aim. We also purchased some medicine for producing rain; it was a small goat's horn filled with the congealed blood of chickens.

Our Baleka prisoners were most amusing. Their joint clothing when captured consisted of one string of beads, half a dozen wire bracelets, and a human tooth as a pendant to a necklace of elephant hair. They were very hungry, and quite pleased with their quarters. It was a terrible sight to see how they tore and devoured half-raw meat, but apparently they missed the flavour which they had particularly affected, as they could never satisfy themselves. Because of the quantity of food they consumed, our boys viewed them with considerable disfavour. We issued for their use a large block of soap, and insisted on their bathing in every available stream; after that we presented them with some blue cloth and a red blanket, draped in which they appeared quite respectable, although the style of costume did not seem to lend itself to their figures or type of beauty.

The western side of the valley is covered with luxuriant forest, and the eastern side consists of rolling grass land till fifteen miles from the lake, when the country settles down into one vast plain.

The people of Imukubsu appear to be practically independent of the Kigeri, although they are undoubtedly part of the Ruanda stock.

Here four streams flow down from the east, the most important being the Fuko. At the outlet of the Fuko the Kako becomes the Rutchuru, and the district to the east is called Bukoma, and is very sparsely inhabited. Still further to the east lies the district of Ijomba, which centres round two rather prominent peaks. Six miles further north there is again a considerable population, and large plantations of bananas.

The following day we crossed a stream of considerable breadth, filled with papyrus; the water was very deep, and we had great difficulty in the crossing of our goats and sheep. Marching through a desolate country with no population, we arrived at a good stream called the Gwenda. The bed of this stream is very curious; the country drops suddenly 100 ft., forming a broad, flat-bottomed valley, down the middle of which the Gwenda has carved out a deep trough. The valley is so flat that it cannot be due to erosion, and is probably a recently-dried-up arm of the lake.

From there we crossed a vast plateau, covered with short grass; and it was not until three in the afternoon that we reached an insignificant stream, on the banks of which were a few poverty-stricken villages.

The type of native had changed entirely; they informed us that they were Wanyabinga, and that the name of their country was Wataka. They refused cloth or beads, saying that they had no use for such things, their only garment consisting of well-cured skins.

The following morning we marched through similar country, and saw many tracks of elephant. I was leading the caravan that day, and was suddenly stopped by the cry of "Elephant!" I hastily put my big gun together, and saw a herd of fifty elephant cross the path and descend on to the flat plain below; they reminded me forcibly of an old print of the Spanish Armada, as they sailed past through the long grass; their huge ears flapping to and fro gave the impression of sails; and their gliding action over the uneven ground was exactly similar to the motion of a ship. The grass covered their legs, and the peculiar swinging action of the elephant, who moves both the legs on one side at the same time, gives the appearance of the beast being on wheels. Sending a note back to Sharp, I hurried off in pursuit, as they swept into an extensive patch of dense thorn jungle. The track was easy to follow, owing to the number that had passed, and after a sharp burst of half an hour I saw one standing broadside on, about thirty yards ahead. I tried for the brain-shot with my .303. He threw his trunk into the air, and fell like a rock—dead. Two more appeared at the shot, and looked at me; I fired, and the whole herd crashed away; then I remembered that the magazine of my gun had been loaded with expanding bullets. I rushed after them, but failed to catch them up, and I had the greatest difficulty in retracing my steps; the elephant had forced a way through the thornbush, and it was comparatively easy, in the excitement of pursuit, to follow, as I could push the thorns open in front as the elephant had done before me; but on my return journey it was almost impossible to get through, as the thorns, which had swung back in their place, had to be pulled towards one to allow a passage. However, eventually I arrived at my dead elephant, full of thorns, and torn to pieces. It was only a small bull, but it was my first, and as I strolled back to the caravan, the beast's tail in my hand, I was a proud man.

I had some difficulty in getting out of the jungle. In trying to do so I arrived unexpectedly in a village hidden in the thicket. The people, hearing my shots, had put the village in a state of defence. It was surrounded by almost impenetrable jungle, except at two places, where there was an elaborate gate and stockade. The gate had been filled up with a pile of heavy logs, pointing outwards and upwards, which rendered entrance impossible from without, but, to their astonishment, I arrived through the thicket. As I promptly leaned my rifle against a hut and put out my hand to greet them, their suspicions were allayed, and they gave me some water; then one of their number showed me the path out of the jungle, and I rejoined the caravan. Half a mile further on we camped by two muddy pools on the outskirts of the thicket.

The natives became quite friendly, and brought us large quantities of a small kind of bean, and helped us to cut out the tusks. Our carriers came to see the elephant, and forming a ring round it, chanted a song in its honour, and each man threw a handful of grass on its side to show his respect, but, of course, would not eat the meat. Curiously enough, the natives also refused to eat the meat, although they were very poor; they informed us that they would eat hippo meat, but not elephant, which seemed to me a very subtle distinction. We cut off a portion of the trunk and boiled it gently for twelve hours, but did not eat much of it when it came to table; the meat was excellent, but the two unpleasant tubes through the middle, and the wrinkled black skin with its short, stubby bristles, did not give an appetizing, appearance to the *plat*. However, the youthful cannibals devoured it, although there must have been at least ten pounds, in the short space of an hour. The two elderly cannibals disappeared during the night. It was evidently a move on the part of our boys, who resented the proportion of presents that fell to the cannibals' lot.

The reports of the country in front were not encouraging, so we bought up a considerable quantity of beans; and the following morning marched across the plain, and arrived near another village, similar to the one we had left, which was also carefully hidden in the jungle. This village was elaborately stockaded, and the natives absolutely refused to allow me to enter; however, I eventually succeeded in obtaining a guide, and we continued our march till we arrived at a small lagoon, where our guide promptly left us. Here we saw a considerable number of topi-hartebeeste and Uganda kob; these, with the exception of one waterbuck mentioned above, were the only game that we had seen for many long weeks; and it was a great treat to have a change from the inevitable goat.

Here the plain opened out to a tremendous width and had the most desolate appearance, all the short grass being burnt; and the only relieving features were a few patches of thorn-scrub and an occasional candelabra euphorbia. Having no guide and no idea of what was before us, it was rather a risky undertaking to go ahead without reconnoitring; but retreat was impossible, owing to the scarcity of provisions, and the quantity of game rendered actual starvation improbable.

The following morning we launched forth, and after a long march, as I was beginning to get doubtful as to whether we should find water, I sighted the Rutchuru river, which here swings back towards the east. There was a considerable quantity of Uganda kob, topi-hartebeeste, and Chanler's reedbuck, and on the path we saw several traces of lions, while the river teemed with hippopotami. The country is very barren, and there are numerous salt-pans, which at a distance appear like snow.

While the tents were being pitched, we went out and quickly secured a supply of meat. The Manyema, like all tribes that have come under the influence of the Arabs, refused to eat the meat of any animal that had not had its throat cut while still alive; they also refuse to eat hippo, elephant, or pig, but, curiously enough, are not so particular about rhinoceros.

We deemed it advisable to camp here for a day, while we went out in different directions to inspect the country, as we could still, by a forced march, manage to reach food countries if we found it impossible to proceed.

I went down the river, and six miles north came unexpectedly through a belt of reeds on to the lake-shore. Where the Rutchuru enters the lake there is a very extensive swamp, the haunt of thousands of birds (pelicans, geese, and various storks), and many hippo. Here I found a very sparse fishing population; their huts were built in the swamp, and they themselves travelled about in dangerous-looking canoes. They were very shy, and it was only after repeated efforts that I succeeded in inducing two men to come and talk; from them I purchased a few fish, giving them beads in exchange; and I made many inquiries as to the country that we had to traverse. They informed me that there were no villages for many days, and that the few villages that existed at some distance from the lake were reduced to pitiable straits by the drought, and the raids of some tribe from the east.

Hence it was obviously impossible to proceed without laying in a stock of provisions; so we shot several antelope and made our men dry the meat over fires.

I was suffering from slight fever, and consequently Sharp undertook to return with boys and purchase as many loads as possible of beans.

The fever brought on a very bad foot; I had rubbed all the skin off the heel with elephant-hunting, and had been walking on it ever since; and owing to the poisonous influence of the fever, it swelled to a great size, and was in such an unhealthy condition that when I pushed my finger into the swelling it left a cavity which did not swell out again for some minutes. As it was impossible to stop in the country, I had to make arrangements to be carried, and all the time that I was in camp, sat with my foot in a basin filled with a strong solution of permanganate of potash, applying a poultice of Elliman's Embrocation at night.

Here the water of the Rutchuru was almost too salt to drink, and we were not sorry to reach the lake, where, although the water was salt, it was drinkable.

Sharp shot several fine kob and topi, the horns being equal to anything recorded in Rowland Ward's book, *Horns and their Measurement*.

The water at the edge of the lake was very shallow. Two days from the Rutchuru my leg became so bad that we were compelled to stop; and as the supply of food was already running short, we sent some of our boys back to buy a fresh supply.

Here we were visited by some natives who, having heard our shots, came down the lake in canoes to find out who we were; they had a few guns which they had purchased from some Swahili traders; and as they entered the camp they fired a salute in our honour. The chief, who was a most intelligent native, asked us whether we wanted to buy any ivory. We told him to bring it to us, so that we might see whether it was worth purchasing. He brought a small tusk of 30 lbs., and said that he had another very large tusk, which he dared not bring unless we made blood-brotherhood with him. This we did, our headman serving as proxy.

The mode of procedure was as follows: Our headman sat down opposite the native's representative, each party having a sponsor, while the eldest of the natives constituted himself master of the ceremonies. Two small pieces of meat were procured, and each sponsor held one in his hand; the master of the ceremonies then explained that we were to become blood-brothers of the chief, and evoked a series of curses on either party that might not be true to the pledge. The words of his weird incantation were,—

"May hippopotami run against him; may leopards tear him by night; may hunger and thirst gripe him; may his women be barren; may his children wither, even as the grass withers; may crocodiles rend him; may lions howl round his couch by night; may elephants crush him," etc.

Having thus evoked all imaginary curses on the delinquent's head, he made a slight incision on each of the parties' chest. The blood that flowed from the cut having been smeared on the two pieces of raw meat, each party had to devour the piece smeared with the blood of the other.

A loaded gun had been placed between them, and when the ceremony was complete, this was fired into the air; while the chief and his attendants fired another volley. Thereupon I had the 4-bore brought forth, and told off my headman to fire it, while my gun-bearer supported him—an advisable precaution. The tremendous report, the obvious recoil, and the shriek of the huge bullet impressed them mightily.

We then called the chief up and taught him to shake hands, saying that it was the Englishman's method of making blood-brotherhood; and that now that we had performed the rites of both people, the Wanyabinga and the Englishman, there could be no possibility of the compact ever being broken. And we pointed out our flag,[9] which was flying over the camp, and told him that wherever in future he saw that flag, he might know that he would be well received and treated with justice.

They then filed off with a handsome present of cloth, delighted with the result of their visit; and the following morning they arrived with the tusk, which was a large one, weighing about 80 lbs. But we did not purchase it, explaining to them that we had only come there to see the country, and to hunt elephant for our own amusement, and that we were not like the Swahili traders whom they had met. We allowed them to bring the tusk, so that they might see that they could repose absolute confidence in us. With the tusk they brought several loads of sweet potatoes, and we gave them a present in exchange.

The chief was a very pleasant and intelligent native, and during the next two days Sharp made several short trips with him. One day the chief and all his men showed us how they hunted antelope with dogs. The dogs were well trained; they rounded the beast and drove it within reach of the hunters, who succeeded in spearing it.

The whole of the southern coast of the Albert Edward is the home of hundreds of hippopotami, and the beach is lined with masses of their dung; all night they kept up a tremendous concert of bellowing and grunts, which rendered sleep well-nigh impossible.

My foot having meanwhile sufficiently healed to allow me to be carried, we advanced along the shore of the lake, and camped at the edge of the extensive swamp at the mouth of the three main streams which flow into the lake from the south-east. Here it was obvious that there had been a recent and abrupt rise in the country, the old lake-bed being sharply defined.

From this point I perceived that my observations would materially diminish the area of the lake; the suggested coast-line on extant maps practically corresponds with the last lake level. Judging from the comparatively insignificant size of the vegetation on the recently-exposed lake-bed, the last rise and level must have been historically recent and quite sudden; in fact, a remarkable point was that this vegetation corresponds in age to the vegetation found on the lava-beds that had been poured out by the volcanoes immediately prior to the late terrific eruption.

Owing to the swampy nature of the country, we were compelled to again march south-east; and after crossing a flat table-land, again descended on to the last level of the lake, where we crossed the first of the south-eastern streams, called the Sasa. Here an arm of the late lake level runs five miles inland, and is three miles broad. Then we again climbed on to the table-land, which is the last lake-level but two, and camped on the site of two deserted villages.

---

[9] This flag was accepted by her late Majesty the Queen.

102

Our blood-brother was still with us, and he informed us that these villages had been raided by a tribe from the east, and that the surviving inhabitants had retired to the impenetrable thorn-jungle, or had fled to the Rutchuru valley.

From this camp we looked down on a great swampy plain which absorbs the waters of these three south-eastern streams. In many places geysers were shooting vast jets of steam into the air, and the course of the rivers was defined by dense strips of luxuriant jungle.

The surrounding country must be rising very rapidly, and the geysers are an indication of considerable volcanic activity. By the last rise the lake has lost a hundred and twenty square miles; and the loss occasioned by the last rise but one must have amounted to several hundreds of square miles.

The map of this lake-shore emphasizes the extraordinary similarity of form in all the great lakes of Central Africa, with the one exception of the Victoria Nyanza. A glance at the map will show that the angular inclination and general form of Lake Nyassa, Lake Tanganyika, Lake Albert Edward, and Lake Albert have a wonderful resemblance to one another.

The next day we again descended on to the last lake level, and crossed the Ntungwe river. This river we crossed by means of an ingenious native bridge, which would suggest that the country at some time not very remote was much more densely populated. After passing through one or two insignificant villages, we camped by a small lagoon. The following morning we crossed the third stream which feeds these swamps, but I could not ascertain its name; and we were compelled to make a detour to the east to avoid some very dense strips of jungle, in which we found some carefully-hidden villages, strongly fortified by stockades. The natives had carefully closed the entrance, but appeared to be quite friendly; and here, with great regret, we said farewell to our Wanyabinga brother.

Our day's march brought us once more to the lake-shore, which was still swampy; and as reed was growing at a distance of one mile from the shore, it was evident that the lake was still very shallow, and in all probability the next few years will see another very considerable change in its area.

A few miles further on there is a small bay, where are two insignificant villages close to the lake. Here the natives cultivate dwarf banana-plants, and eke out a precarious existence by trapping hippopotami. They build a stout scaffold of logs and fasten thereto a booby-trap, consisting of a heavily-weighted spear-head.

These villages were on the frontier of Visegwe's country, who is one of Kaihura's chiefs. Here my fever assumed a serious form; my temperature at one time rose to 108.4, but the motherly attentions of Sharp pulled me through; and when I was sufficiently recovered to be moved, he procured a gigantic dug-out canoe, in which I was paddled to Katwe, the frontier post of the Uganda Protectorate.

Sharp marched up the lake-shore, and with the assistance of Kazinga, ferried all the loads and boys across the narrow neck of Lake Ruisamba. The ferry is not more than four hundred yards wide, and with considerable trouble the cattle were induced to swim the distance. Two natives seized each beast by the horns, and, swimming by its side, assisted it across. Fortunately there were no crocodiles in the vicinity. The canoes were of extraordinary structure, and are peculiar to Lake Albert Edward, although they approximate to the type of canoe to be found on the Victoria Nyanza; some of them are very large. They are made of axe-hewn boards, sewn together with banana fibre.

CHAPTER XIV.

KATWE TO TORO.

As we had never heard that the boundary between the Uganda Protectorate and the Congo Free State had been definitely settled, we were surprised to find the Congo flag flying almost within shooting distance of the fort; and on our sending over to buy fish, we found that the natives across the border were not allowed to sell to us. Furthermore, the Soudanese officer in charge told us that the trade in salt had almost died out, as the Congo officials stopped their natives from bringing ivory or food to barter. It is hard to understand why the hard-and-fast line of the thirtieth parallel has been adhered to, when there is the natural boundary of the Semliki. With that boundary there would be no severance of the possessions of a chief, whereas now some of the land of Kaihura is Belgian and some English, and an uneducated native cannot be expected to serve two masters with different laws and widely-separated methods of treating him.

In the fort we were also shown the bullet-marks of the rebel Congo troops, who had attacked the fort because the Effendi refused to give up the fugitive Belgian lieutenant who had taken refuge there. As Colonel Lugard remarks in his *Rise of our East African Empire*, the fort stands in a very strong position; but there was no Congo fort in his time.

We here enjoyed the shelter of a roof for the first time for many months, despite the uncomfortable accessories of thousands of mosquitoes and armies of rats.

The Effendi kindly revictualled our forces, as we were not allowed to trade on our own account, and we gladly turned our backs on the bare ridges of the fort, and the curiously-coloured salt lake, and started on the eighty-mile march to Fort Gerry.

Elephant were reported as numerous throughout the country, and we looked forward to a little sport as a change, more especially as an Askari had shot a fine bull two days before, when he was out bathing in one of the streams we had to cross. We started on an excellent cleared road, myself in a machila, as the fever had left me too weak to walk, and passing several volcanic lakes and extinct craters, camped close by a large salt lake round the edge of which the spoor of many antelope was visible, and in which a few hippo snorted and splashed.

Hundreds of reedbuck dashed wildly about the plains, and a few kobus and waterbuck were seen in the distance, but, the grass being very short, there was no chance of a stalk.

Every day we crossed one or more beautiful clear streams, running down gullies from Mount Ruwenzori, the principal one being the Wimi; but nowhere did we ever get more than a glimpse of the outlying shoulders of the mountain, the higher peaks being always hidden in mist.

Elephant spoor was plentiful, but grass fires had cleared the whole of the plain and driven all the game to the foot-hills or swamps, and day after day our hopes of elephant were doomed to disappointment.

We met a Congo official—a Belgian—returning from a visit to Fort Gerry to his station, Fort Mbeni on the Semliki, whence there is a rapid and easy route or high-road to the Congo, of which the missionary, Mr. Lloyd, has lately given a startling account in *The Graphic.*

On July 27th we camped within sight of the hills, where Kasagama reigns by favour of the British Government, happy in the knowledge of the final extinction of his old enemy, Kabbarega; and on the morrow we gathered that we were nearing the end of our journey, by the amount of "Amerikani"[10] and the quantity of crucifixes, the hall-marks of the Protestant and Catholic sects. Next we saw a large church in a walled enclosure, and two Pères Blancs came out to welcome us, and insist on our trying their excellent Algerian wine. They were much interested on hearing that we had come up from Tanganyika, and asked many questions about the brethren of their order down south. Hospitably they accompanied us a short way till we reached the boundaries of the Church of England mission, whose territory they would not pass, except on urgent business, to the Government station.

Kasagama's hill, on the left, is a magnificent situation for a palace (or fort), dominating as it does the missions nestling below it, and the Boma on an adjacent hill. The king received us a day or two later under the escort of the English missionaries.

The high-road led past the English mission, where extensive building operations in brick were going on, down a steep hill and across a primitive and dangerous bridge, built by the 11th Company of Soudanese, under the late Colonel Sitwell, to keep them quiet during the mutiny, and up a steep hill to the fort, where we were most hospitably received by Mr. S. S. Bagge, one of the founders of the Uganda Protectorate, who has spent nearly nine years in the country, having acquired the pioneering mania in that hot-bed of pioneers, the Western States of America. Captain J. A. Meldon was in charge of the troops. English newspapers and books were most welcome, after being separated from them for many months. Our own literature consisted of Whitaker, Shakespeare, and Keats.

Two days after our arrival at Fort Gerry, our boys began to get troublesome, as they had nothing to do, and pombe (native beer) was plentiful; and one evening they raided the milk belonging to the Soudanese officer, and beat his boys, for which the culprits were duly admonished. Next day they all declared a desire to go home again to Ujiji. We were anxious to take them on to Wadelai, there being no hopes of getting local porters to go anywhere except to Kampala; and at length, after much parleying, arranged that thirty of them should go to Wadelai with me, and the rest to Kampala with Sharp, to lay in supplies for the Nile journey, and then the whole lot could return

---

[10] White trade cloth.

by the Victoria Nyanza to Mwanza in German territory, and thence home in safety, *via* Tabora.

Meantime stories of enormous tuskers were dinned into our ears, and Captain Meldon having very kindly offered to accompany us, we determined to go and have a fortnight's elephant-hunting, as a little relaxation after our arduous march. On inquiry as to licences, we were horrified to find a £25 licence necessary, which entitled the payer to kill two elephant only. Permission might be obtained from the Commissioner of a district to kill others at £12 each—truly a preposterous regulation, in view of our subsequent experiences; however, having come so far, more or less with the objective of elephant-shooting, we paid up like men, and started off on the main road to Kampala.

The country, as usual in Toro, consisted of undulating hills intersected by papyrus swamps, with a few banana plantations, very sparsely populated, and showing no signs of game except some old elephant spoor.

The second march brought us to a very likely country, and the natives said there were many elephant in the vicinity. Sharp went out, but did not see any, the grass and thorn-scrub being almost impassable. Thence a four hours' walk brought us to the top of a small range of hills, from the crest of which I saw an elephant standing in the thick cane-brake on the opposite slope. The main part of the caravan, with Sharp and Meldon, was some distance in front, as the difficulty of carrying my machila through the swamps made my progress slow. Praying that the wind would hold, I was carried as near as the brake would allow, and after a short walk, in the course of which I fell into an elephant-pit, found the unsuspecting old gentleman under a tree, and killed him with a single .303 bullet in the brain. He was a stupendous old bull, 11 ft. 6 in. at the shoulder, with a 64-in. foot (dry), and his teeth, 5 ft. 10 and 6 ft. 2, weighed 86 and 85 lbs. This success filled the others with envy, and a native coming in during lunch with news of a herd of forty, not very far off, Meldon and Sharp rushed off, only to return at sundown hot and tired, having hit and lost a decent bull, while I had gone out to inspect an old gentleman who came and waved his ears at me from a neighbouring hill, but which I spared, not being satisfied with his ivories.

Leaving a few boys to bring the ivory and one foot, we trekked early next day to the ridge overlooking the river, passing fresh spoor and elephant tracks almost every minute, and, while looking for a likely camping-ground, saw a small herd of elephant in the valley. Sharp immediately went in pursuit, and unfortunately for him the Soudanese officer followed, and by cutting the line of elephant, gave the leaders the wind, and thus spoilt an excellent chance. From our camp on the hill we had a splendid view of ten miles or so of the Msisi valley and the hills opposite, and all day long, elephant, singly, in small herds, and, eventually in the afternoon, in large herds of two hundred or more, perambulated up and down, giving us the most magnificent chance of making their acquaintance.

Sharp returned at lunch, hot and miserable, having shot a cow elephant—the grass being so high that it was impossible to judge beforehand what he fired at. The whole of the morning we heard shots from the far side of the river fired by Waganda or Wanyoro hunters, and presently, in a great cloud of dust, a herd of at least a hundred elephant crossed the river and wandered towards our camp. It was a most impressive sight, as they swept the long grass down in front of them as flat as if a steam-roller had passed over it. They stopped for a time about half a mile below us, blowing water and dust over their backs, while we tried to pick out the biggest bull with our glasses. We must have seen a thousand to fifteen hundred elephant that day, and heard thirty or forty shots from native guns across the Msisi.

Next day there wasn't an elephant in sight, but we could hear the natives banging away up-river, and as the elephant near camp began to smell we trekked up the valley. Here the downtrodden grass showed that the big herd had moved off south.

Having exceeded our time-limit, we decided to return to Fort Gerry and start for the north. Taking all the ivory into Fort Gerry for registration, I left Sharp on the road with a few boys to hunt, intending to make the necessary arrangements at the station, and then to send out the boys to him for the march to Kampala; but the evening of my return was celebrated by a pombe revel amongst my boys, and when I went down to see what the noise was about, I was attacked by twenty or thirty of them with spears, and was obliged to fire my revolver at the ringleader. This scared them, and the whole hundred broke out of camp, scattering the Soudanese guards, who were supposed to keep them in order. Next day all the boys came in a body and demanded to be sent home; so, to avoid trouble, we rounded them by strategy into a cattle-kraal, and put a strong guard over them; and after giving them posho (cloth to buy food), and obtaining a guard from Kasagama to see them out of the country, I packed them off to Katwe. Sharp arrived next day, having done the fifty miles in two marches. Ten of our boys were in chain-gang for behaving badly during our absence, and these and Sharp's lot I persuaded to go with me to Wadelai, and thence by high-road to Kampala, and by Victoria Nyanza back to Tabora and Ujiji.

Out of our fourteen calves two alone had survived, and we had been obliged to kill two cows, as they could not travel further. Six cows we exchanged with Kasagama for a tusk of 138 lbs., and six others I sold for 180 r., giving the other cow and calf to Mr. Bagge. During our absence elephant-hunting, four of King Kasagama's cows died, so I rescinded the bargain, and gave two of my tusks and a present of cloth for the big one, and handed the surviving cattle over to Mr. Bagge. Curiously enough, the six I sold to the Soudanese Effendi were still well, while Mr. Bagge's cow and calf had both died. Too good food and too much time to eat it, after a march of two hundred and fifty miles, had evidently overpowered them.

At this stage of my journey, Mr. Sharp, to my great regret, was forced by the ties of urgent business to return home. The Nile was such an uncertain quantity that he was unable to risk the possibility of being buried in the wilds for another two years. He therefore marched through Toro and Uganda to the Mombasa rail-head, and took passage to England via the Red Sea.

CHAPTER XV.

TORO TO MBOGA.

Leaving Fort Gerry and all its hospitalities on August 28th, I skirted along the northern spur of Ruwenzori, passing between the little volcanic lakes Vijongo, and after three hours' walking, arrived at the edge of the first escarpment. Here there is a sheer drop of 1,500 ft. from the undulating table-land of Toro proper to the scrub-clad terrace about eight miles wide, which in its turn overlooks the Semliki valley, a further drop of 500 ft. From the edge of the first escarpment the view is truly magnificent; to the south looms the mighty bulk of Ruwenzori, a purple mass, peak piled upon peak, black-streaked with forest, scored with ravine, and ever mounting till her castellated crags shoot their gleaming tips far into the violet heavens. But it is only for a brief hour at sunset or sunrise: then again the mists swirl up her thousand gorges, again the storm-cloud lowers and broods grumbling round her virgin snows as though jealous of the future—a future of Cook's tours, funicular railways, personally-conducted ascents (with a sermon and ginger-beer thrown in). Well! thank God I have seen her first— seen her as she has stood for countless ages, wrapped in impenetrable mystery, undesecrated by human tread since the awful travail that gave her birth. "The Mountains of the Moon"—the very name breathes mystery and romance, and fitly have romance and the myths of the ancients played round her crest, for is she not part mother of the Nile? Alas! even as we gaze she fades away, a murky glow lights up the evening sky, again she starts into bold relief, 'tis her last farewell! The mists eddy round those frowning crags, creeping here, drifting there, and the curtain drops, hiding all but the great black base. Such is Ruwenzori, when she deigns to show herself; and only when there is rain in the air is she thus condescending.

Scarcely less striking is the outlook to the north. Deep shade is already on the terrific slope at our feet, while the setting sun still lights up the vast basin of the Semliki and the Albert Lake. We seem to be standing on the brink of a new world, ourselves in shade cast by the western spur, and the eye wanders on over sunlit plain picked out with silver streaks, where in places we catch a glimpse of the Semliki, and on till the lake lies gleaming like a sea of quicksilver, and yet on and on, ever-fading steel-blue to grey, till we can just see the black outlines of the hills against the blue-green sky, flecked with the gauzy pink of the after-glow. Then like a flash all is grey, for we are very near the equator, and we turn in to "kuku"[11] stew and the luxury of new potatoes and tomatoes. Those kukus! They are like Sinbad's old man of the sea, you cannot shake them off, for they are really indispensable. Their only resemblance to their English namesake is in name, for neither are they fine birds nor do they fly; nor, if they did fly, would they confine their vocal efforts to the period of their flight,

---

[11] *Kuku:* native word for fowl.

but would, I am sure, still retain that inimitable faculty of producing at all, and more especially unseasonable, times, the most startling and by-no-means-(not-even-by-death)-repressible cries that have justly made them so beloved of African travellers. As I have had so many opportunities of observing the African variety of this world-wide domestic nuisance, less favoured observers may find a few remarks not out of place.

First, they are essentially gregarious. I have often seen large flocks collecting on any strange piece of clothing or blanket, especially if such blanket be placed out to dry after rain.

Secondly, they are capable of feeling and showing great affection for man. In fact, the united efforts of three servants have often failed to prevent them coming into my tent during the heat of the day, and, just out of respect, leaving a few superfluous inhabitants behind.

Thirdly, like the nightingale, they sing at night, taking especial delight in those ditties that have a good, full chorus.

Fourthly, they never lay fresh eggs—only eggs that have qualified for the seventh heaven. Presumably, as the native likes a good, full egg, it is the old tale of the survival of the fittest, and the hen who can lay a real Blondin has been spared. If so, this must dislodge all geological estimates of the date of the creation, as nothing short of incalculable ages could have brought the breed to its present state of perfection. For a long time I considered this elegant bird exempt from the natural process of decay, as no reasonable period after decease produced any modification in its adamantine structure, but a certain incident not unconnected with soup dispelled this excusable illusion.

And lastly, but not leastly, this diabolical fowl, although it can hang head downwards in a temperature of 140° for many hours without showing any signs of inconvenience other than a slightly intensified complexion, and although it greets with contumely blows inflicted with the various missiles to be found at a moment's notice in an average tent, yet, should it be left with natives other than its rightful owner for one short hour, it is so overcome with modesty that it reverts rapidly and without perceptible residue into its original invisible components.

The extent to which the kuku enters into one's very existence in Africa is, I feel sure, a sufficient excuse for this digression. In fact, I believe that, were it not for the counter-irritation produced by the camp goats, I should have "kuku" on the brain.

Having successfully wrestled with the athletic cause of this digression, and unsuccessfully with a prehistoric gun that a neighbouring chief brought me for medical treatment, and dreamt that a rooster with 10 ft. tusks was dancing the double shuffle on my chest, I descended into the valley, and after two hours' walking reached the Semliki, a fine river, here sixty to seventy yards wide, with a current of about five miles an hour. When I had, with the greatest difficulty, wedged myself in a very long, very unstable, and appallingly leaky piece of firewood (called by courtesy a canoe), and had with still greater difficulty dissuaded fifteen gentlemen from risking the voyage in my company, in the lucid intervals of the amazement with which I viewed the frantic efforts of my Charon (for such he was like to prove) to keep the stick's head upstream, I gathered from a benevolent philanthropist on shore that a woman had been taken that morning by a crocodile from the very spot where we came to land, and that on no account must I permit my boys to go to the water's edge, as the crocodiles were very numerous and very daring. However, suitably cheered by this information, and in defiance of all such paltry laws of nature as gravity, we eventually did succeed in landing safely on the other side; how or why I cannot say, as only the two ends of the canoe were in the water, the middle, where I sat, being slightly raised above the surface. I suppose the whole concern had warped. Whatever the cause, I did not fancy trusting my baggage in her, so I sent up the river, and after much yelling and more delay, another more serviceable concern was produced. Having fixed on a place for my tent, I left the boys to attend to the passage of my belongings, and went out in search of dinner.

The plain, which here is about six miles wide, is covered with short grass and dotted with clumps of euphorbia and thorn-bush, and is the home of countless reedbuck and herds of Uganda kob. During the rains it is the playground of troops of elephant and of the few survivors of the teeming herds of buffalo that formerly roamed over all this country. I had no difficulty in bringing two bucks to grass, as the country offered magnificent stalking-ground, and the meat made a very agreeable change after the everlasting mutton. The Uganda kob (*Cobus Thomasi*) very closely resembles the pookoo (*Cobus Vardoni*), though its coat, which is of a beautiful reddish colour, is less foxy and not so long in the hair as that of the pookoo. They both have the regular gait of the waterbuck, that so forcibly reminds one of our own red deer. But whereas the pookoo never seems to run in herds of more than twenty or thirty, I have seen as many as three hundred Thomasi together. The leading buck of this herd, which I shot, had horns 20 in. in length.

Here, as elsewhere, I was much impressed by the two different types of native, the sharp, intelligent, almost delicate features and the lithe limbs of the aristocrats (of Galla origin) contrasting very forcibly with the coarse, squat, ape-like appearance of the rabble. Some of the lower class have really no ostensible claims to being human, beyond the ability to produce fire. Covering even of the most rudimentary description is totally ignored by both sexes. Leaving the Semliki, we travelled west to the hills of Mboga, and shortly left the plain below, rising into a country of miniature cañons, intersected by numerous ravines full of elephant-grass. Here we camped and sent out scouts in all directions to search for njojo (the local name for elephant). I had just made myself comfortable when news was brought of elephant to the south, so I set off without delay, only to find a herd of small cows. On my return to camp my boys told me that there was an elephant quite close, and pointed him out, standing under a tree in the middle of the elephant-grass in the ravine at our feet. As the sun was very hot, I concluded that he was likely to stop where he was, and setting a boy on an ant-hill to watch him, I sat down to lunch. He did stop where he was till I had finished lunch, and then moved on, and as it was useless to go into the grass, 15 to 25 ft. high, without a definite landmark such as the tree would have proved, I was fain to dodge about, watching him, when I could get an occasional glimpse, and to wait for another chance. Several times I lost sight of him altogether, and then again would see an ear. At last, as he appeared to be coming near the stream, which here ran close underneath the bank on which I was standing, I went down through the thorns and grass and waited, but in vain. Again I mounted the bank, but could see no signs of him till I was turning campwards in despair, when my boy saw the grass move, and this time quite close to the stream. Down we scrambled once more and stood in the bed of the stream listening. Then the crack of a twig and the waving of the tops of the grass showed that he was coming, and he glided past a slight gap in the thicket like some spectre, but I could not get a shot, although within twenty yards. I never can understand how they manage to glide through the most tangled jungles almost without sound unless they are alarmed, when it seems as if all hell were loosed. I followed quickly down the stream, the grass now completely hiding him, and suddenly came on him drinking in a small mud-hole, at about fifteen yards distance. He gave me a half side-shot, and I fired at his head, giving him a second as he swung round. Down he came like an avalanche, and lay thrashing the reeds with his trunk. Fearing that he might get up again, I approached to give him the *coup de grâce*. I was already within six yards, but still unable to see him, when a cold puff on the back of my neck gave me warning of a chance in the wind. I stepped back as he struggled to his feet, and his great trunk came quivering forward within two yards of my face. Again the wind steadied, and as I stood motionless as a rock, he failed to see me, swung round, and made off. Three shots I poured into him, then waited, sick at heart, listening to the crash-crash as he went away, till again I heard that welcome roar of rending tree and rush. He was down: a long gurgle and a sob, and all was over. Although a small elephant, he carried beautiful teeth, 7 ft. 9 in. and 7 ft. (tip broken), and weighing 72 lbs. and 69 lbs.

I reached camp just at dusk, and found that Changera, one of the Mboga chiefs, had come in to see me. His country lies between Tavara's and Kavalli's, and stretches from the top of the Congo Semliki watershed to the Semliju. The following morning I went down to see how they were cutting out the tusks, and found that hordes of Balegga had swarmed down from the hills for the meat. A weird sight it was: stark naked savages with long greased hair (in some cases hanging down on their shoulders) were perched on every available inch of the carcase, hacking away with knives and spears, yelling, snarling, whooping, wrestling, cursing, and munching, covered with blood and entrails; the new arrivals tearing off lumps of meat and swallowing them raw, the earlier birds defending their worms in the form of great lumps of fat paunch and other delicacies; while others were crawling in and out of the intestines lake so many prairie marmots. Old men, young men, prehistoric hags, babies, one and all gorging or gorged; pools of blood, strips of hide, vast bones, blocks of meat, individuals who had not dined wisely but too well, lay around in bewildering profusion; and in two short hours all was finished. Nothing remained but the gaunt ribs like the skeleton of a shipwreck, and a few disconsolate-looking vultures perched thereon.

The Balegga live in the hills to the north of Mboga proper, though many of them are now under Changera, having fled south from the Belgians. They are good specimens of the real Central African savage, rather short, but well-set-up, innocent of clothing as a babe unborn, and blessed with an inordinate and insatiable craving for meat, which at that time was, if possible, intensified by the failure of their crops, owing to the drought. They wear their hair in long thin plaits, liberally smeared with grease, which gives them a very wild appearance, especially when, as I noticed in some cases, it hangs down over their face. In the intervals of gorging and hacking, they amused themselves by smearing the caked blood over their hair and bodies—a proceeding that gave general satisfaction. I gathered from them that many had lately come south to Mboga (which is at present administered from Fort Gerry) to avoid the persecution of the Belgians, who had killed, as they said, great numbers both of them and their neighbouring tribes to the north. They indignantly denied my soft impeachment of cannibalism, but from extraneous sources I gathered that any lightly grilled portion of my anatomy that might happen to wander round their way would be, so to speak, a "gone coon."

The neighbouring chief, Tabara by name, apparently suffering from that troublesome complaint known to the faculty as "swelled head," amused himself for the next two days by sending in an intermittent fusillade of insolence; "it was not his business to come and see every white man who came into the country," etc., etc., *ad nauseam*. As I had never sent for him, being unaware even of the gentleman's existence, and as I found on inquiry that he was a chief independent of Kasagama, and owing allegiance to the official at Fort Gerry only, I concluded that my mubaka[12] provided by Kasagama was the cause of the trouble, or that he imagined I was Belgian. I therefore sent a message to him to the effect that I had no doubt he was a most admirable individual, but, strange to relate, till the arrival of his message I had been unaware of his existence; that my object in coming to the country was to shoot elephant, and not to interview obscure natives. The effect was remarkable: the following morning he turned up with a numerous following, carrying an umbrella and a very dangerous camp-stool, and presented me with sundry goats, fowls, and other edibles.

The prevailing type of elephant in these parts differs so essentially from that of Toro, that I have been forced to the conclusion that there are two distinct varieties; a theory in which the natives universally concur.

When in Toro I saw more than a thousand elephant, and without exception they carried a thick, heavy type of tusk, the elephant themselves being unusually large and solid.

In Mboga, on the other hand, the prevailing type was a much smaller elephant, with very long thin tusks. Two cows shot by Mr. Bagge carried tusks about 4 ft., and no thicker than the butt-end of a billiard-cue.

---

[12] A sort of courier.

The average height of old bulls in Mboga is about 9 ft., while the only two that I shot in Toro were 11 ft. and upwards, and several others that I had a chance of observing closely must have been about the same size. The Indian notion of twice the circumference of the foot equalling the height does not hold with the African species; I generally found that it fell short of the height by about 8 or 10 in. In a subsequent chapter I have dealt fully with this question.

A few days later, answering to the call of elephant, I came on a herd of cows, one of which I shot, hoping to be able to send the calf into Fort Gerry. The little fellow stood about 3 ft. high, and stalked towards us in the most majestic manner, rumbling and grunting on a 12 ft. scale at least. So confident was his advance that my boys, guns and all, fled without more ado, and it was only when I had caught him by the tail that they ventured back. His strength was amazing, and it needed the united efforts of myself and four boys to throw him. However, we eventually managed to tie his legs together, and laid him under a tree squealing and shrieking like a steam-engine. Whether in his vocal efforts he broke a blood-vessel, or whether owing to the heat of the sun, the sad fact remains that after I had made all arrangements for his transport to Fort Gerry he left the earthly trials of pitfalls and 4-bores at sunset. I was very much disappointed, as I had hoped that if he had survived he might have been of service in the future, should a progressive Government, departing from the usual practice of thinking of the matter when it is too late, endeavour to make use of the vast transport treasure that is now roaming the papyrus swamps of Toro. In the greater part of Africa the elephant is now a thing of the past; and the rate at which they have disappeared is appalling. Ten years ago elephant swarmed in places like B.C.A., where now you will not find one. Still, there is yet an accessible stronghold of the pachyderm in Toro, where at the lowest possible estimate there must be fifteen thousand elephant. Why is not an effort made, and that at once (for in a few years' time it will be too late), to secure this vast means of transport to posterity? What an inestimable boon to the country, and what an easy solution of half the labour problem that is already such a thorn in the side of the southern administrations! I suppose it is on the same principle on which a paternal Government sends its servants out to a pestilential spot where the sole recreation is shooting, and then forbids them that recreation, while allowing every native who can command a gas-pipe and a handful of powder to sally forth and slay a tithe of what he wounds, regardless of sex and age; or on which the same paternal Government allows the aforesaid servants to take out and pay for a licence permitting them to shoot two elephant, and then confidentially informs them that all ivory shot by servants of the Protectorate, either within or without the Protectorate's dominions, is the property of the Government; however (note the wild, unreasoning generosity), servants returning home may, with the permission of the Commissioner, be allowed to take a pair of tusks as a trophy. Upon what possible theory this preposterous claim is based I fail to conceive, unless the Government assumes that the leisure of their servants is included in their salary, in which case they may claim the pictures of an amateur artist who may be in their service, or his letters home, or anything else equally reasonable. It is the spirit of the thing that is so pitiable, and it seems so unnecessary, for nobody doubts but that the Exchequer can manage to stagger along somehow, even though deprived of the support that the miserable dozen tusks or so would afford; and, after all, the right to shoot and keep a couple of elephant is not an extravagant recompense for two years' isolation in a wilderness devoid of recreation.

I then moved my camp some miles to the west, on a hill overlooking a large patch of very dense elephant-grass.

The next morning I went south to a deep gorge filled with dense forest, where some elephant were reported. We descended a steep grass slope into the gorge itself, which was cut up in all directions by elephant and buffalo spoor. Suddenly, with much puffing, pawing, and snorting, some buffalo rushed past at about forty yards, at the same time starting some elephant, which we heard crashing up the slope. Leaving the buffalo to puff and snort, we struck the elephant spoor and cautiously approached to where we could hear them grunting and rumbling. By stooping low it was possible to follow the path with comparative ease, but the bush was so thick that we could not see two yards ahead. Having approached within ten yards, I stood, hoping that some movement would show me their exact whereabouts; but though they quickly recovered from their fright and started feeding, I could see nothing but the occasional waving of the leaves above where they were standing. After a quarter of an hour of this amusement, during which I was balancing myself on a slippery bank of clay, I descended again, and coming dead up-wind succeeded in getting within two yards of one. A thick tangle of lianas alone separated us, and although I could hear him breathing, and felt sure he must hear my heart thumping, I could see nothing. I know nothing in the world more exciting than hunting elephant in this description of country. One approaches so close, and yet can see nothing; the only thing to do is to wait, in hopes of some movement bringing them into view. Then they make such extraordinary noises, and at every crash of a branch torn down one thinks they are stampeding or coming towards one. Again, the wind is so shifty in cover, and one puff will set them all off, very possibly in the least desirable direction. A dropping shot is almost out of the question, and when wounded they have a nasty knack of looking to see who did it; a whole regiment of lions cannot produce the same moral effect as one elephant when he cocks his ears, draws himself up to his full height, and looks at you, letting off at the same time a blood-curdling scream, while in all probability others invisible are stampeding on all sides with the din of an earthquake. They are so vast (one I measured was actually 15 ft. from edge of ear to edge of ear) that they seem to block out the whole horizon; one seems to shrivel, and the very gun to dwindle into a pea-shooter; try as I will, I can never quite stomach it, and always feel inclined to throw down my rifle and run till I drop.

At last the elephant, having an idea that something was amiss, moved, and showing his head, received a mate to that idea in the shape of a .303 bullet. Down the bank he rushed, taking the bark off one side of a tree, while I stepped round the other. I got another shot home as he passed, and head over heels he went like a bolting rabbit. Trees, bush, blocks of earth, vanished like chaff, till a mighty old veteran trunk pulled him up short about fifty yards below. There he lay, his legs in the air, screaming and vainly struggling to regain his feet, a path like the sea-wall at Brighton leading down to him. A few more shots finished him.

The next day I was again in this gorge, and after vainly floundering about on the spoor of a small elephant, and complimenting in suitable terms a swarm of biting ants which eventually left me indistinguishable from a splash of pickled cabbage, I saw a fine old tusker grazing in the short grass on the top of the further bank. To cross was a matter of minutes, as I knew that at any moment he might descend into the gorge, and on emerging I saw him still in the same place. Walking up quite close, I dropped the poor old brute with one shot. He had very long teeth for their weight, 8 ft. 4 in. (tip slightly broken), and 7 ft. 4 in. (tip broken), and weighing 76 and 73 lbs. respectively. Standing on his ribs—that is, about 6 ft. from the ground—I saw some more grazing on the other side of a branch gully, so I set off in pursuit; but some of the half-starved natives, who would follow me about the country, and had been lurking behind some bushes, spoilt my chance of a shot by darting out up-wind of the herd, presumably to catch any elephant that might drop.

For several days matters were very quiet, and though I ranged far and wide, one day following buffalo spoor for several hours, I saw nothing; till again I was wakened by the welcome cry of "njojo," and snatching a hasty breakfast, set off, this time backed by the double 10-bore paradox which had been sent out after me, and had arrived the previous day; and very thankful I felt for its support. My double 4-bore had gone home with Sharp, who had left his paradox in its stead as the more useful all-round gun. And though I had my double .500 magnum, the firm that provided my cartridges had sent out all expanding bullets, despite the fact of my having ordered half with solids; just to humour me, however, they labelled the packets "solid bullets," so that I never found out till north of Tanganyika. Two other firms distinguished themselves in a similar manner, one by shipping my double .303 in a case, without so much as a cleaning-rod, much less a screwdriver or spare pin, and the other by providing me at the trifling cost of 2s. 6d. each with damaged cartridge-cases for my 4-bore; the majority of them were badly split at the rim, sufficiently split to fill rapidly when held in water, and though they had been carefully repolished, on close inspection the old firing marks were quite obvious. The consequent result was that the first shot I fired I was knocked over a fallen tree two yards behind me.

Our native took us across the marsh lying below the camp by a path that in its various intricacies led into a pit of water 20 ft. deep, into which they fondly hoped some elephant would walk; then through numerous villages where the banana-groves, owing to the depredations of elephant, looked more like street barricades, till we eventually emerged from the odoriferous fog of drying elephant meat on to the ridge where I had last camped. He then told us that two elephant had come into the bananas during the night and had retired up the gorge. Skirting along the edge of the plateau, we soon saw them in the elephant-grass below, and descending with difficulty through the tangled mat of grass, I took up my position behind a tree and waited, hoping that when they moved I might have a favourable chance. One was standing under a small tree about four hundred yards away; and the other, at a distance of two hundred yards, was up to his belly in mud, his stern alone showing round a tuft of grass. Previous experience had taught me that it was useless to go down into the grass, so I had perforce to stay where I was and possess my soul in patience. After some time the one under the tree moved, and in a leisurely manner strolled up to his companion. As he emerged from the long grass round the mud-hole I had one glimpse of his tusks, and, quite satisfied, I took the only chance I was likely to obtain, and fired a half-side head shot. He drew himself up into a bunch of indignant protest, as much as to say, "Who the devil did that?" But a second shot failing to elucidate the matter, he swung round and crashed away across the gully, while number two bolted straight ahead. I rained shot into him while he swerved round and followed in the wake of his companion. Then I dashed along the side of the slope, stumbling, tripping, rolling, and diving over grass that I could not force my way through, till a sudden drop of 10 ft. landed me face first on the bed of a stream, invisible above through the grass, but painfully tangible below. Fortunately my rifle did not suffer proportionately, and scrambling out I reached a small ridge from which I could see my elephant standing about three hundred yards off. Again I fusilladed him till out of range, and then followed, falling twice to the elephant's once. He was nearly spent, but managed to reach some extra long grass, where I lost sight of him for some time, till at length he crawled out into the shade of a tree under the opposite bank. The gorge was narrow at this point, so that he was not more than one hundred yards off when I reopened the bombardment. For a long time he took the phut-phut of the bullets without showing the slightest emotion. Then suddenly over he went like a tree under the axe. He struggled to his feet once more, only to fall for the last time under the continued hail. Cutting across the dip, I climbed on to the bank about twenty yards above him; but the grass was so dense that I could not see him, although considerably above the level of the tangle where he was lying. His great sobs told me that all was over, and anxious to put him out of his misery, I went down, having to approach within two yards before I could see him, and finished him off with the 10-bore, his head being invisible. To my amazement he had only one tusk, 7 ft. 9 in., and 98 lbs.; and as I was sure that I had seen two tusks, I came to the conclusion that this must be number two, and that number one had dropped at the same time that I did. So following back on the spoor, I came on the other elephant, lying four hundred yards from where I had first hit him, but, lo and behold! he also had only one tusk, 7 ft. 7 in., and 86 lbs. So certain was I of having seen two tusks that I followed his spoor back, thinking that possibly there might have been a third hidden by the grass, but it was not so, and to this day I believe he took the other tusk off and threw it away, as a sort of Jonah! On arriving at camp I found that letters and tomatoes had arrived from Toro. Our pagasi had attempted their old games about three days' journey south of the Albert Edward and had been attacked with the loss of twenty men, amongst them Sulimani, the root of all the disturbances. His successor in office, who, like other gentlemen of his kidney, combined loudness of talk in times of peace with extraordinary fleetness of foot in times of danger, was the first to bring the news to Toro.

CHAPTER XVI.

SEMLIKI VALLEY AND KAVALLI'S COUNTRY.

Leaving this country with regret, I descended into the valley once more and marched north, crossing the Semliki to avoid the swamps mentioned by Colonel Lugard at the westerly bend of the river, and recrossed about six miles from where the river enters the lake. For some distance the mournful monotony of aloe and euphorbia is broken by groves of the stately borassus palm. The few miserable Wanyoro, who are sparsely scattered over the plain, were absolutely destitute. The prolonged drought had dried up the maize and millet, and the beans, which form their main food supply, were finished, so that three hippo that I killed for them raised me to a giddy pinnacle of fame; my tent became, for the time being, a second Lourdes, droves of pilgrims pouring in to pay homage to my .303. Their astonishment, when I showed them the size of the bullet and how the magazine worked, was most ludicrous. They had heard how it would drop a huge elephant without a wriggle of his trunk, and they had heard the three shots and could see the three hippo tied to the bank, and had imagined, I suppose, that it was a sort of 7-pounder; so that when they held a cartridge with its pencil-like bullet in their hand, and the truth gradually dawned on them, they would drop it like a hot potato. Some, when I started the mechanism, fairly took to their heels. A native's estimate of a gun varies proportionately with the size of the bore, and his idea of killing range is ten yards, or, if the sportsman is something of a marksman, perhaps twenty. I was fortunate in bringing off several shots at about four hundred to five hundred yards at nsunu,[13] and natives, having no unit of distance, consider everything from two hundred yards to about five miles as the same thing. I have several times heard my gun-bearer, Makanjira, who is a great admirer of the gun, solemnly explaining to an open-mouthed audience how he had seen me kill beasts at such a distance, pointing to a hill some three or four miles away. Consequently, its powers were magnified to the most prodigious proportions, and on the march excited natives would point to mere specks on the horizon, inform me they were buck, and expect me to kill them on the instant; they never gave me any of the credit—it was the gun, the wonderful gun, and I only obtained a reflected glory as its possessor. After crossing the river, I found the natives very nervous and suspicious, and though I visited the village near which I camped, and induced the chief to come to the river-bank to see one of the hippo, which I told him he might have, the following morning, on sending for a guide, I found that they had "shot the moon," carrying off their half-dozen miserable goats, and fled into the bush.

As the guide promised me by the chief on the other side was not forthcoming, and not wishing to delay any longer, as the sun was terrible on these arid plains, I

---

[13] Nsunu: *Cobus Thomasi.*

started without one, and, after two hours' walking, found that I had penetrated well into the marshes at the south end of the lake. In trying to skirt round the arm of water and sudd that stretches to the south, we soon found ourselves in an apparently boundless sea of one of Nature's truly African inventions, a tall grass, 8 to 10 ft. high, the roots forming a hopeless tangle of matted whipcord reaching 2 ft. from the ground, and effectually hiding the honeycomb of old hippo and elephant-holes 2 ft. deep below, while the stems and leaves are covered with myriads of invisible spines, which detach themselves in one's skin and clothes, and set up the most intense irritation.

After floundering through this sea of misery for a couple of hours, we were extricated by the promised guide, who had followed on our tracks, and eventually arrived at a miserable patch of huts; we came so unexpectedly on the people that they had not time to fly, and a few explanations soon put them at their ease. I found that they were Wanyabuga, the same people who were so friendly to Lugard and belonged to Katonzi, a nominal vassal of Kasagama's, and who is now the sole survivor of Lugard's three blood brothers, Katonzi, Kavalli, and Mugenzi. They do not cultivate, but depend on the Balegga and Wakoba for grain, which they barter for fish and salt. They are quite distinct in appearance from the surrounding tribes. The type is a tall (5 ft. 8 in.), large-limbed, square-shouldered negro, bull-necked, bullet-headed, with a very low forehead and coarse features; colour very dark; but they have a jolly expression, and were some of the pleasantest natives I ever dealt with. It was curious to see even amongst these people, who live a life apart from their surroundings, the occasional delicate features, gazelle-like eyes, light colour, lithe limbs, and genteel nonchalance of the Galla influence.

At the south end of the Albert Edward, where the Rutchuru flows into the lake, forming similar marshes to those of the Semliki, there is a people living exactly the same life. Unfortunately, owing to their extreme shyness, I could find out very little about them, but from their mode of life, methods of fishing, and general appearance, I have no doubt that they are closely allied; probably survivors of former inhabitants who have found a last refuge in these intricate waterways and impenetrable marshes. The similarity in the names of these two peoples is significant.

It is a strange amphibious existence in these simmering wastes of weed and water, the stillness of which is only broken by the occasional blow of a hippo, the splash of a fish or crocodile, the wild cry of the numerous flights of wild-fowl, and the everlasting plaint of the fish-eagle. A perpetual mirage hovering over the scene adds to the general mystery; groups of huts suddenly appear where all was shimmering light, and as suddenly vanish; a canoe with its two upright punters glides past apparently in the sky, a goose suddenly assumes the proportions of an elephant, and an elephant evolves out of what one took to be a goose; and thus the scene is ever changing, till the grey of evening and the crisp light of the rising sun bring out in strong relief the placid sheets of water, the long brown bands of weeds, the tiny islands with their little huts perched among the waving reeds, the thin strips of sand with their occasional waddling hippo, the little black canoes slowly gliding in and out amongst the weed-beds and tufts of grass, and the continual flight of flocks of white ibis.

I never tired of sitting on the shore and watching the long string of little black canoes slowly wending their way towards me, bringing in fish and salt, to trade with the group of Balegga who were waiting with loads of beans and millet flour.

The small stretch of country lying between the Semliki, the Albert Lake, and the hills is called Kitwakimbi, and is distinct from Bukande, which begins at the foot of the hills and reaches back to the watershed.

My Wanyabuga friends provided me with two guides, who, after wasting two hours in visiting obscure villages, all of which were deserted, and answering my protests at our zigzag route by ambiguous allusions to marshes, eventually landed me within four hundred yards of where I had started, and suggested that I should camp. Having with difficulty persuaded them that I was annoyed, which they evidently considered unreasonable on my part, they smilingly explained that it was far from their homes, and they had hoped to find me other guides. However, vague allusions to the presence of a "kiboko"[14] convinced them of the inexpediency, not to say positive danger, of further nonsense, and they gaily proceeded on their way, chortling hugely at the success of what they thought a very merry prank. They led me to a deserted village opposite Kasenyi, a small island about a mile from the mainland, and the present headquarters of Katonzi. The Wanyabuga-Balegga market was in full swing, but vanished like mist at my sudden appearance, and it was only by going down to the beach stripped to the waist, and a happy allusion to brothership with "Kapelli," that I induced them to bring their canoes to the shore again. "Kapelli" is the native name of that gallant officer Colonel Lugard, and to have left a name in Africa that opens all doors and all hearts is the finest monument to his exploits that a man can have. They flocked in to see me under Tunja, Katonzi's eldest son, who brought several loads of food, and informed me that Katonzi had left two days before for Toro. They asked all kinds of questions about "Kapelli" and Mr. Grant, who was with Lugard in his expedition to release the Soudanese, and wanted to know why he had never come back, and had the English deserted their country after promising to protect them? I answered all their questions to the best of my ability, and when I showed them Lugard's book and the photograph of Grant, which, to my surprise, they immediately recognized, their delight knew no bounds.

The mosquitoes here defy description; even at mid-day I had to eat my food walking about, and my evening and morning toilet, combined as it was with a Dan Lenoesque extravaganza, if performed on the Empire stage would assuredly have brought down the house. I crawled into my mosquito-net with the greatest caution, disposed all my weighty belongings, such as boots and cartridge-bags, in a circle round my bed to keep down the edges of the net, exhausted all my candle-ends in exploding the odd hundred or two that had crawled in with me, and was quickly lulled to sleep

---

[14] *Kiboko*: whip made of hippo hide.

by the dismal drone of myriads, happy in the knowledge that they were outside; sleep, gentle sleep, during which I evolved in one short hour from my own insignificant self through the alarming stages of Daniel in the lion's den, and a cold bread poultice, to the stern reality that they were inside; and they were, hundred and hundreds of them. In vain I searched for some hole or possible inlet, and eventually had to resign myself to the inevitable, buoyed up by the meagre consolation that I had discovered that, like the light of the glow-worm, the mosquito is possessed of the properties of the Röntgen rays.

Early the next morning Tunja came to tell me that Katonzi was coming back, and at midday he arrived in person. He is a dismal old nigger, and though somewhat rapacious, not a bad fellow. His first request was to see the wonderful book, and then how I struck a match, an accomplishment that tickled him immensely. He then naïvely asked me to give him my guns, saying that Lugard had given them two guns, but that the Belgians had taken them away. I asked him why all the people were so frightened, and where they had all gone; whereupon he proceeded to recount the same tales of misery and oppression that I had heard the day before, from which I gathered that a Congo Free State official rejoicing in the name of "Billygee" had suddenly swooped down on the country a year ago, and after shooting down numbers of the natives had returned west, carrying off forty young women, numerous children, and all the cattle and goats, and putting a finishing touch to the proceedings by a grand pyrotechnic display, during which they bound the old women, threw them into the huts, and then fired the roofs. Several absolutely independent witnesses informed me that this had been done actually in the presence of Billygee and the gentlemen who accompanied him. Katonzi's two sons, Tunja and Kutaru, were bound and taken away, but released after two months. Kavalli's eldest son is now in their hands, while a younger one escaped to the Balegga. As I have mentioned before, when in Mboga the Balegga told me similar tales; here I was repeatedly given accounts that tallied in all essentials, and further north the Wakoba made the same piteous complaints; and I saw myself that a country apparently well populated and responsive to just treatment in Lugard's time (and that under very trying conditions, owing to the numbers of destitute aliens in the country—to wit, the Soudanese) is now practically a howling wilderness; the scattered inhabitants, terrified even of one another, and living almost without cultivation in the marshes, thickets, and reeds, madly flee even from their own shadows. Chaos—hopeless, abysmal chaos—from Mweru to the Nile; in the south, tales of cruelty of undoubted veracity, but which I could not repeat without actual investigation on the spot; on Tanganyika, absolute impotence, revolted Askaris ranging at their own sweet will, while the white men are throwing their ivory and cartridges into the lake, and cutting down their bananas for fear the rebels should take them; on Kivu, a hideous wave of cannibalism raging unchecked through the land, while in the north the very white men who should be keeping peace where chaos now reigns supreme, are spending thousands in making of peace a chaos of their own. I have no hesitation in condemning the whole State as a vampire growth, intended to suck the country dry, and to provide a happy hunting-ground for a pack of unprincipled outcasts and untutored scoundrels. The few sound men in the country are powerless to stem the tide of oppression.

The departure of my mubaka provided by King Kasagama had taken a great load off my mind; he was too heavy a swell for me to keep pace with, dressed in white breeks, yellow putties, red fez, and three fancy cloths, to say nothing of a red and yellow belt; and his terrible anxiety lest he should miss a chance of putting up a large white umbrella with a green lining was so infectious that finally I found myself watching the clouds with one eye and the mubaka with the other, knowing that at the first ray of sunshine he would emerge from his hut and perform for my edification. In the cloudy intervals he devoured such masses of solid food that even with my experience of native capacity I became quite alarmed, and between the struttings and bursting-point tests, he had very little time to devote to my affairs, so that I was very glad to see the last of him.

Katonzi, after relating his own troubles, and thinking, I suppose, that it was my turn to have a few, proceeded to paint the most gruesome pictures of what was in front. With tears in his eyes he begged me to turn back, saying that if I died the white men would blame him; he informed me that all was wilderness beyond—no food, no paths, all the people dead. Putting his hand to his head, he explained how they had all just done so, lain down and expired.[15] Pressed as to the reason of this general collapse, he eagerly shook his head and murmured "Muungu" (Kismet). Though summing up the majority of these perils as "nigger gibberish," I was rather alarmed at the sudden death business, thinking that perhaps it was smallpox or the Bombay plague; but this, like the rest, was simply imagination. It is strange how natives get these ideas into their heads. I do not think it was gratuitous lying, as all his people, as far as I could see without any other reason than belief in the sudden death, were afraid even to hunt in the direction indicated; and he certainly had nothing to gain by stopping me from going forward, since he had no interest in the country. However, I thought it advisable to buy several days' provisions, and to do this it was necessary to draw the Balegga from the hills; all my overtures had failed so far, and I saw that the only way to start was to lay ground-bait for them by killing elephant or buffalo. With this object in view I sallied forth with a guide who was to take me to the elephant country. He wandered about for two or three hours in country that an elephant would not look at through a telescope, and whenever I said that I wanted elephant, he nodded his head and said, "Oh yes, elephant." Then suddenly, as if a bright idea had struck him, he said, "Oh yes, *elephant*!" and promptly walked back through camp to a narrow spit jutting out into the lake and about a quarter of a mile distant. As I could see water on both sides and short grass in front, I thought he meant hippo, or was mad, inclining to the latter belief; but no, he was quite confident, and stalked along muttering to himself, "Yes, elephant! Yes, elephant!" (as much as to say, "Who would have thought it?"); and sure enough there were nine elephant in the reeds in the lake at the end of the spit. The

---

[15] I have since realized that he was referring to the sleeping sickness which entered this district at that time.

place was a mass of vegetation and honeycombed with elephant-holes. I dropped one with a single shot.

As I had expected, after a day of very hot sun, the odour was too tempting, and the Balegga swarmed down from the hills and brought me what food I wanted. I went for a stroll in the evening, and came on a small herd of buffalo; they were very small compared with the South African species, and amongst them were three light brown ones, a bull, cow, and three-parts-grown calf. They were very beautiful animals, with a black ridge of hair running along the neck and the top of the shoulders. I shot the bull, and as my pagasi had as much as they could carry, I told the natives to cure the hide and send it with the head into Toro, so I hope to be able to have it described. When I first saw them I thought they were eland, and it was with the greatest surprise that I found they had a buffalo's head attached. The small one was as light in colour as a reedbuck, and the other two a similar colour round the rump and the belly.[16] I could gather no information from the natives as to whether they had seen others; all they knew was that the buffalo was an evil beast, had once been very numerous, but was now finished.

---

[16] I have since found, on reference to the British Museum, that they were the Congo buffalo. This proves that their distribution is further East than was imagined. The fact that they were running in the same herd as the black Eastern variety is of considerable scientific interest.

CHAPTER XVII.

ALBERT LAKE AND UPPER NILE TO WADELAI.

An hour's walk into the valley of death brought us to a cluster of villages with a large population, which was in a state of utter destitution. The people, who were very nervous at first, eventually gathered round in numbers with the same tale of rapine and murder, and the chief gave me a guide to take me to the foot of the hills. Another hour brought us to Nsabe, which, though generally depicted on maps in large letters, consists of about five dirty little muck-heaps, only recognizable as human habitations by the filthy smell that emanated from them. All the inhabitants fled, leaving their spears, bows, and beer in their hurry, and no amount of shouting and yelling would induce them to return. Our guide promptly made a bundle of the spears and other movables, with a view to appropriation, which when complete I placed against a tree, accompanying the movement by a vigorous application of my boot to the toughest portion of his anatomy. Incorrigible, bullying, thieving curs, one is often tempted to think that the Boer method of treating natives is, after all, the only one they deserve. Their Mark Tapleyism is their sole redeeming feature, and that is attributable to the incapacity of their intellect to hold anything but the impression of the moment. Although of the same tribe and close neighbours, I expect he would have thoroughly enjoyed seeing me burn and loot the place; it is the same everywhere—a guide amongst his own people is a worse thief even than a Manyema porter. He then took us by a devious route to the shore of the lake, and seemed greatly astonished to find that the village he had mentioned did not exist; nor had it left any trace behind. I could see by the way he was behaving that he intended to bolt, and knowing that without a native of the country there was very little chance of inducing the people, in their frightened state, to remain in their villages, I kept a close eye on him. As I expected, when I sat down on the shore to wait for the boys to close up, he began edging off towards the jungle; but when he looked round to see if it was all clear, he found himself covered by my .303. I had him brought back, and explained to him that his chief had sent him to show the way to the foot of the hills, that he had led me into the wilderness and could now lead me out, the two alternatives being villages, another guide, and a present, or a race with a .303 bullet. He chose the former, and seeing that fooling was a glut in the market, promptly took us to a village of the Wakoba called Kahoma, and in Kahuma's country. Here all the people fled, but he followed, and persuaded them to bring food to trade. They, too, had been raided, and had lost two women and two children captured. They could not tell me how many white men or Askaris there were, as they had not waited to see. The majority of them are fine, well-made men, and intensely black. One in particular took my fancy. He was a tremendous swell, with anything from 15 to 20 lbs. of red clay on his head, an enormous ivory bracelet, and multitudes of iron rings. The Wakoba live all along the lake-shore and in the fringe of the hills, and, curiously enough, their villages are mixed indiscriminately with those of the Balegga, with whom they seem to be on the best of terms, although the two peoples are quite distinct, the Balegga being real out-and-out bestial little savages, while the Wakoba are much above the Central African average of intelligence, with quite a wide knowledge of local affairs. They are both in a state of parallel expansion, the Balegga working to the north into the Lendu country, and the Wakoba in the opposite direction encroaching on the Wanyabuga.

Two miles north of Kahoma the hills come down to the water's edge, leaving only a narrow shingly beach, and thenceforward our progress became painfully slow; at intervals the headlands jut out into the water, and the work of transporting the loads round these obstructions with only two or three small and very unstable canoes was one of considerable difficulty, even the latitude of Doctor Johnson's dictionary proving insufficient on occasions; scores of little streams come tumbling down into the lake, each one forming a small delta, on many of which there are Wakoba villages with a few banana palms, and signs of scratching on the hillside, where I presume something was intended to grow, but had turned dizzy and given up the attempt. After Kahanama's, which is in Kahuma's sphere, Mpigwa is the big man, and I passed through many of his villages, some of the largest being Kabora, Zingi (?), Bordo, Nsessi, and Kiboko. Most of the scenery is very fine, the little white cascades gleaming in the shadow of immense trees, many of which are covered with scarlet and yellow blossoms, and in the midst of luxuriant tangles of vegetation the great gaunt slabs of slimy rock deep-set in their snow-white bed of sand, over which the little waves come tumbling in, gurgling and splashing round their feet and moaning and sobbing into a thousand miniature caves; while great apes and little brown-eyed monkeys drop from branch to branch and sit leering and gibbering at us as we paddle past.

The continual wetting and rock-climbing had the most disastrous effect on my already attenuated wardrobe, and for two or three days I was compelled to disport myself clad in a simple shirt, which, thanks to a classical education and consequent ignorance of the art of washing, had contracted to the modest and insufficient dimensions of a chest-preserver, while assuming the durable but inappropriate consistency of a piece of oil-cloth. The roseate hues of early dawn "weren't in it" with my nether limbs after the first day's exposure to a pitiless sun, and I became a sort of perambulating three-tiered Neapolitan ice, coffee, vanilla and raspberry, a phenomenon that greatly astonished a savage who surprised me in my bath, and who immediately fetched all his kith and kin to see; on the second day, however, the alarming desertion of a third of my epidermis so pained me mentally and physically, that after a great effort I produced a double-barrelled garment that in the absence of Poole-bred critics served its turn.

Of the various arts and crafts that one is called upon to undertake in Africa, such as cooking, shoe-mending, washer-womaning, doctoring, butchering, taxiderming, armoury work, carpentering, etc., *ad infinitum*, I think perhaps tailoring is the most trying; the cotton will *not* go into the eye of the needle, and the needle *will* go into one's fingers, and then when you think it is all over, you find you have sewn the back of your shirt to the front, or accomplished something equally unexpected and equally difficult to undo.

At Nsessi, two miles south of Kiboko, there is a superb waterfall; it has a drop of about 500 ft., and is divided into three stages, all at a different angle to one another, falling 100 ft., then swirling round at an angle, plunging into the next pool, and then a last long slide to the level of the lake. Stupendous silver-trunked trees, with foliage the colour of the ilex and brilliant splashes of scarlet bloom, crowd round on either side of the gorge wherever the wild rocks afford a footing; above towers a pointed peak showing bright above the dense gloom of the gorge, and a white stripe of sand fringes the little village, nestling in its banana grove, at the base.

These natives lead a curious existence, shut in between precipitous hills and the lake, their sole means of communication with one another being their leaky little 10 ft. dug-outs. They are wonderfully clever at handling them, and perform the extraordinary feat of crossing the lake, dodging in and out between the waves in the most marvellous manner. As a means of transport they are not to be recommended; the shape of a cross-section being that of an egg with its top off, one slides in with comparative ease like a pickle into a pickle-jar: once in, as with the pickle, extrication is a matter of time and patience. It needs one of Lear's Jumblies to feel thoroughly at home, as they leak like a sieve, and only perpetual bailing will keep them afloat.

The first day, in the sweet innocence of youth, I set off to round a headland with my guns and a tin box containing my indispensables on board, fearing to trust them to a native. All went smoothly at first, till I had arrived well off the rocks with a slight swell on and no landing-place near, and then she began slowly to heel over, while water seemed to be rushing in through the wood itself. After prodigious efforts I succeeded in running into the rocks, the water being then within an inch of the gunwale. I saved my guns and box, but smashed the canoe, and after that turned passenger. It looks so easy when they come dancing along, each with a native kneeling in the stern and plying a huge curved-bladed paddle; but it is a very different thing when one is wedged in oneself; physically incapable of squatting in a kneeling posture, as a native does, one finds bailing out an impossibility; the whole of the bottom of the canoe seems to be covered with boots, and the incurved edges catch the wooden bailing-dish and jerk the contents into one's lap.

Although the lake teems with fish, many of large size, the Wakoba make no attempt to catch them, trusting to the occasional chance of purchasing from the natives on the other shore or from Kasenyi.

One day I shot a baboon at the natives' request, a performance, by the way, that I shall not repeat, nor would I recommend it to any one but the most hardened villain. A frantic scramble took place for the flesh, and when I asked them what it tasted like, they "smole a smile." Amongst the countless troops of monkeys that are for ever coughing and dancing amongst the rocks and trees, I saw a small family of very beautiful little fellows with bright fox-red fringes down their sides, but I could not bring myself to shoot at them after seeing that unfortunate baboon, although I have never seen them described, or elsewhere in Africa.

At Viboko I was compelled to wait, the shore in front being impracticable and the heights behind unscaleable, till Mswa sent down the canoes, which I had requested by numerous envoys. My boys were badly in need of a rest, the work having been very trying since Kahanama's, and the fever from which I was suffering made it equally acceptable to me. In the afternoon two natives arrived, saying that a muzungu[17] was coming down to meet me with ten canoes. After inquiries as to what kind of Askaris he had, etc., etc., I gathered that it must be a Belgian official, so killed the fatted calf in the guise of a skinny sheep and sundry osseous frames masquerading as dorkings, and then plunged for the second time into the turgid flow of Zola's *Rome*, to cleanse my French of probable Swahili trespassers. I even exhumed a tie, and having produced a menu that exhausted all the possible combinations and permutations of an African larder, awaited anxiously his arrival, picturing to myself the joys of a little talkee-talkee once more. A stiff southerly breeze evidently was delaying them, and it was not till after dark that we heard the wild canoe-song of the flotilla, which had rounded the point and caught sight of our camp-fires. Giving a last twirl to my moustache and a nautical hitch to the Poolesque garment aforesaid, and composing my features to the iron-clad smirk indispensable to such occasions, I advanced to do the honours, and grasped the hand of a dirty, greasy little negro clad in, or rather smeared over with, a prehistoric piece of cloth! Here was my muzungu! here my gallant Belgian staggering under the gold braid of a hat of that peculiarly unbecoming shape affected by French guards and German tourists, and majestically trailing the orthodox 30-franc sword! Inquiries elicited the fact that the parasitic relic of Manchester above mentioned established a valid claim to the title of muzungu in these parts. However, he had brought the canoes, so I readily forgave him, and next day we arrived at the old Soudanese station, Mswa. Mswa is the name of the chief, who is a vassal of Tukenda, and Mahagi is the name of the country itself. He is an intelligent old native, and remembered seeing that ubiquitous officer, Bt.-Major Vandeleur, D.S.O., when he crossed from Kibero, and was delighted at the photograph which forms the frontispiece to his book entitled *Campaigns on the Nile and Niger*. Here let me recommend travellers to take out photographs of men who have gone before them; the effect is wonderful on those natives who can grasp the idea, though, of course, to many natives a picture is merely a piece of paper. It convinces those who can understand it that you are speaking the truth—a possibility so utterly foreign to the native mind. After exchanging presents he retired, promising to bring more boys in the morning to work the canoes; but in the morning none were forthcoming, and after waiting some time while Mswa rushed frantically round the country, shouting to his people, who walked off into the grass and laughed at him, I concluded that he was either incompetent or trying to make a fool of me, and, to his consternation, manned

---

[17] *Muzungu:* white man.

the canoes with my own men and started. As I expected, enough men were immediately forthcoming, but too late, and I held on my way.

We did not reach Mahagi till after dark. Here the hills again recede from the lake-shore, leaving an alluvial plain from one to two miles wide, which is densely populated by Lures, while in the hills there are numerous villages of Balegga. Tukenda is the big man, whose influence reaches from south of Mswa to Boki; he has a small herd of cattle and large flocks of goats, and his people are evidently flourishing and very friendly. So dense is the population that the natives have been emigrating down the lake, and have started new villages on the unoccupied sand-spits. At Boki a grand old tusker came sailing by the camp, and after a stern chase and much expenditure of powder, condescended to strike his colours. He was a perfect specimen of the Toro type above described, standing 11 ft. 1 in. at the shoulder, with a forefoot of 62 in., and measuring 5 ft. 6 in. round the elbow, while his tusks were 6 ft. 10 in. and 7 ft 1 in. long, weighing respectively 72 lbs. and 76 lbs. A small patch of forest about two miles by one mile comes down from the hills to the lake-shore, and as my boys had heard elephant there when cutting wood, I went for a stroll after the midday heat of the sun. Never have I seen a more delightful or interesting scene; countless herds of elephant had trampled down the undergrowth, leaving vast shady chambers joined in all directions by galleries. Some of these chambers were fully an acre in extent, and every vestige of vegetation underfoot had been crushed into a level carpet, upon which it was a pleasure to walk. As one entered these delightful retreats, troops and troops of monkeys lined the branches and gazed on us with fearless curiosity; while two or three hundred of the beautiful black-and-white colobus monkey performed the most amazing acrobatic feats overhead. Emerging on the far side I saw a herd of ten elephant. They were standing in long grass, but fortunately there was a small ant-hill close by; climbing up this I found them all with ears widespread advancing in line towards me, and had it not been for the fortuitous existence of this point of vantage they would have walked right on top of us, the grass being about 8 ft. high. They presented a glorious spectacle as they came sailing along, all canvas set (I can find no other word to express the motion of an elephant in grass), ten old tuskers, their ivory now and again gleaming white above the grass; on they came till, when within thirty yards, one turned and gave me a chance. He dropped to the shot, but quickly recovered; succumbing, however, after two more. I damaged three more considerably before exhausting the magazine, and then dashed off in pursuit, passing one which had dropped about five hundred yards off, and reached an ant-hill from which I could see number three evidently very sick. I dropped him with a forehead shot, but he recovered, and eventually reached the forest carrying another ten bullets. Here I followed again, but it was impossible to keep his spoor owing to the perfect maze of tracks, and after wandering around for some time, I climbed up an ant-hill with a large funnel down the middle. From this elevation I saw him standing not more than fifteen yards away. I fired the 10-bore, which staggered him, and knocked me down the funnel, but I scrambled out again just in time to give him the second barrel, which brought him down at the same time that I once more retired into my Stygian retreat; a

3 in. ridge of crumbling earth 15 ft. from the ground is not the most advisable basis from which to fire a 10-bore paradox. All these elephant were of the same type, huge solid beasts with shortish, thick tusks; 6 ft. 10 in., 7 ft. 3 in., 5 ft. 6 in., 5 ft. 6 in., 6 ft. 4 in., 6 ft. 5 in., and weighing 76 lbs., 78 lbs., 56 lbs., 56 lbs., 60 lbs., and 61 lbs. respectively.

The next day I found the fourth that I had hit very hard. He had fallen within two hundred yards of the other two, but owing to the long grass I had not seen him. His tusks weighed 49 lbs., and measured 6 ft. and 5 ft. 10 in., making a total of 633 lbs. for the day.

Between Boki and Munyagora there is a ten-mile stretch of inhospitable scrub covered with a species of acacia, with huge white thorns springing in pairs from hard bulbous excrescences. Formerly there was a settlement named Mjamori about half way, but the chief Akem has fled with his people to Munyagora; he told me that he had fled from the Belgians. I here made the discovery that "Billygee" is a generic term for the Congo officials, and not, as I had previously imagined, the name of an individual. From Munyagora to Igara, which lies at the bend of the river, the country is thickly populated. The Lures build very primitive shelters and surround each village with a scherm of thorn-tree; they do not appear to cultivate the soil, but breed large numbers of goats, which look very sleek and comely. The country, which is very barren and parched, is admirably adapted to that abominable quadruped, which is never so happy as when confined to a little sand and the rancid smell of its own kind.

I was an object of the greatest curiosity, especially to the ladies of these communities, who came in large numbers to inspect me (front seats at bath time being in great request), and who, whether from a ridiculous sense of modesty or a laudable desire to do honour to the occasion, donned over and above the national costume of a small piece of string tied round the waist, a hopelessly inadequate apron of dried grass: a garment that, from the simplicity of its cut and the small quantity of material employed in its composition, I should have no hesitation in classing with the species of female extravagance known, I believe, to the fair sex as tailor-made. The men, who seem to be of a hopeful disposition, spend much time in making wicker baskets resembling two lobster-pots fastened together like a cottage loaf; these they leave in the river tied to sticks and without bait. I saw many hundreds of these, and large numbers of natives visiting them, but only one fish, though my olfactory sense warned me of the vicinity of at least one more. They have a pretty little myth about buying food from the Balegga for fish, and as they do not kill their goats and certainly had not been buying lately, I cannot imagine what they live on; but I do know that in six hours they removed every scrap of five large bull elephant, hides, bones, and all; a small trifle of about twenty tons; so conclude they live a kind of boa-constrictor's existence. Many of the young men aggravate the natural ugliness of their faces by inserting pieces of glass about 5 in. long in their under-lip. One and all carry small bows, with reed arrows tipped with long thin spikes of iron neither barbed nor feathered. Most of the chiefs and elders are obviously of different race, some having the Galla features more or less pronounced. Here at the north end of the lake one emerges quite suddenly from the "Bantu" peoples to the Nilotic, and the line of division is wonderfully sharply defined. There are numbers of reedbuck and nsunu, and in the bush a small very red oribi of which I failed to procure a specimen. I also saw a herd of hartebeeste, and shot a cow; they closely resembled the Lichtenstein, though the rump was not so white, and the horns lie closer together and stand more erect than those of Lichtenstein. Mr. Cape tells me that Jackson's hartebeeste, which it appears to resemble in other respects, is a considerably larger beast; so that it is to be hoped that he will be able to take a skull and hide home for identification.

CHAPTER XVIII.

WADELAI TO KERO.

I arrived at Wadelai on October 1st, and found Lieut. Cape, R.A., in command; the boma is built on a small hill overlooking the miniature lake, and is slightly south of Emin's old site. Here, as elsewhere, the drought had been very serious, and the country consequently looked bare and uninviting. After Rhodesia, B.C.A., and Northern Rhodesia, it was difficult to believe that this land of administrative chaos had been occupied for six years. The mail arrived three weeks overdue, and some loads which had or ought to have been already a month on the road, were three weeks afterwards still untraceable, although the whole distance is only a fortnight's march, while station loads sent off yet three weeks earlier were still unheard of. Nowhere has the Government made any effort to introduce even bananas, much less fruit-trees, vegetables, wheat, or rice; no system of mail service has been organized, and no regulations as to import, duties, etc., had been issued. At Toro I asked for information about the transit dues, naturally objecting to pay the ordinary export duty of 15 per cent. on ivory which I had obtained outside the Protectorate. My request was ignored, and at Wadelai I was met by a demand for duties based on regulations apparently issued for our benefit, but by an error of judgment bearing a date subsequent to our crossing the frontier. From this I can only gather, either that the possibility of the country becoming a trade-route (one of the *raisons d'être*, I presume, of the railway) had never been entertained, or that it was part of the penny-wise, pound-foolish policy that robs officials of their hunting trophies, and maintains, at the preposterous figure of 14 rupees 8 annas a month, a large number of Waganda boatmen on the Nile, where they die like flies of dysentery brought on by unsuitable food. The country is quite unsuited to these Waganda, who are all banana-eaters, millet being the staple food; and this, coupled with the great difference in altitude, is killing them by dozens, while the banks of the Nile itself are lined with capable canoemen, who could be engaged at 3s. a month; 14 r. 8 a. a month to raw natives, many of whom are mere boys, is sufficient in itself to damn any country's future which will be dependent on its agriculture. Where would B.C.A. be with wages for raw labour at £1 a month? It is an uphill fight now at 3s. rate; 8 r. a load from Kampala to Fajao, a fourteen days' march, what produce will bear transport rates like this? Similarly the pay of the Soudanese is absurd; they actually do not know what to do with their money; and the only result of the late rise in their pay is that they no longer cultivate on their own account, but buy everything at exorbitant rates from the natives. They would have been equally contented and equally well off with half the sum, the effect of the other half being increased drunkenness and a general rise in the price of native produce. The Government should have its own plantations or make allotments to the station natives, instead of the present system of money rations, as it will be very difficult to induce the natives to work while they can sell enough produce at exorbitant rates to obtain their few luxuries, and in the near future to pay their hut-tax. Another gross piece of folly was the introduction of the rupee instead of the English currency.

It was very pleasant to find some one to talk to again; in six weeks one finds out what a terribly uninteresting fellow one is. After a rest of three or four days spent in waiting for the overdue mails and the arrival of the Waganda canoe fiasco, Lieutenant Cape took me out to see the Shuli country and for a general trot round, the *pièce de résistance* to be an old bull giraffe that Sheikh Ali, the local potentate, reported to be in his neighbourhood. My host was fortunate enough to be able to leave the station for a few days, though we were hampered in our movements by his having to keep within a day's march. This, I believe, was the second time he had succeeded in getting away for a day or two in his year's residence. The really important work of inspecting the country and winning the confidence of the natives had to give way to the soldierly occupation of sorting mails, and retailing beads and yards of cloth, which could be equally well done by an Indian at 10 or 15 r. a month. This playing at shop is, as far as I could judge, the sole *raison d'être* of these stations, and perhaps a desire on the part of the Government to show the unfortunate officer who has been inveigled into this Downing Street-warranted paradise what an insignificant thing he and his wants (at home we should say necessaries of life) are compared with a Dinka's boots or a Baluchi's ginger. The whole transport of the Protectorate has been paralyzed to supply a miserable mob of Baluchis with rations which their white officers would gladly have bought at their weight in gold, and who have been, are, and will be utterly useless in the country. Heaven knows what they have cost, and Heaven, I presume, knows why they were brought, for I am sure no one else does. There was not one single pound of flour in any station that I passed through, and no white man had been able to obtain a load of the common necessaries of life for months, because what little transport there was had been monopolized to hurry through the Soudanese belts, blankets, comic opera uniforms, and boots, which they take off and give to their boys to carry when they walk. One gallant officer amused me much by telling me that the one touch of civilization of the past year had been a ginger-pudding made from a surplus ounce of the Indians' rations.

We had a delightful trip, killing a good elephant, 71 lbs. and 61 lbs. (broken tusks); but the giraffe turned out to be an unsociable old gentleman and not on view; we were always nearly coming on him, but never quite came. The country was full of rhino, the difficulty being to avoid them. One day natives came in to report an elephant in the Shuli country, and we hurried off to the spot. Here we found that he had killed a woman who had met him unexpectedly on the path. Unfortunately we failed to avenge her, as, after following for some hours, we lost the spoor owing to the hardness of the ground. The following morning they brought us news of buffalo, which turned out to be three rhino lying under a tree. They started off, making a great variety of strange sounds, and after a stern chase we slew the old bull, which stood 5 ft. 5 in. at the shoulder, and measured 12 ft. in length. Unfortunately we had also wounded one of the cows during the bombardment, and so had a long tramp to finish her. On the morrow we again had news of buffalo, and this time found, but they escaped without a shot, Cape's .303 missing fire. For some reason or other they travelled hard, and just as we were coming close again, a confounded old cow rhino, which was evidently sleeping close to their track, charged Cape most viciously. Fortunately he turned her at three yards with a double barrel from the .303, and she rushed past me with a youngster, tail and nose in air and squealing like a steam-whistle, in hot pursuit. I dropped her with a spine-shot from my .303, but to our annoyance she recovered after dragging her hind quarters for fifty yards, and led us a long and exhausting dance in a desperate sun. She was a saucy old lady, but our battery was too much for her, and she never charged again, although after the first burst she made no frantic efforts to go away. A very long shot from Cape's 8-smoothbore glanced off her shoulder. Curiously enough, I had an exactly similar experience with my rhino on the Chambesi: the first shot from my 4-bore glanced off the shoulder, although a broadside shot at thirty yards and striking 18 in. below the ridge. Of course both these guns fired spherical balls. In Cape's case I distinctly heard the bullet strike, and then again strike the trees far away. I regret to say we never caught the calf; he stayed behind in the grass at an early stage of the fracas; he was the funniest-looking little chap imaginable, and reminded me of the mock turtle; if taught to follow, he would have made quite a sensation in the Park. The elephant, which measured 11 ft. 6 in. at the shoulder, 58 in. round the fore foot, 18 ft. round the edge of the ear, 4-½ ft. from the earhole to the outside edge, was chiefly remarkable for the complacent way in which he received a really extraordinary sequence of lead; we kept up a running bombardment over about half a mile; and it was not till Cape put an experimental shot into his leg that we could induce him to take any notice of us. This brought him round sharp, and I popped a shot in, in front of the eye, which knocked him down. Even then he made desperate efforts to get up again, and would have succeeded had it not been for the slope on which he was lying, and the fact that his legs were up-hill.

About this time life became rather a burden, owing to the terrific storms that broke over us nightly. The first one removed my tent as you would a candle-extinguisher, and left me exposed to a torrent of ice-cold water (one can hardly call it rain, as it comes in one solid mass, like an inverted bath). This experience—and a more awful one I cannot conceive—made us both rather nervous, and the greater portion of the succeeding three nights was spent in anxious wakefulness, desperate hammerings at pegs and holding of poles, to the accompaniment of a running and not too polite commentary on Nature and her ways, sustained in a high falsetto to keep up one another's courage. But this became rather wearying, and we consequently returned to Wadelai. The Shulis, whose country lies to the east of the Lures, and extends from the Somerset Nile to about 48 north, are similar in appearance to their Lure neighbours. They hunt game by means of nets and regularly organized battues, and seem to be fair shikaris compared to the other people in this part of Africa. They appear to be braver than the Lures, who are the most abject curs. Near Mahagi I have seen elephant's droppings on the roofs of the huts, and the fields trodden flat, and this in spite of there being a number of guns in the country, while we did succeed in inducing some Shulis to follow the spoor of the murderous elephant above-mentioned, but at the chatter of a monkey they hurriedly disappeared, and it needed ten minutes to collect them again. They build very neat villages, laid out on a definite plan, and very superior to the primitive hayricks of the Lures. An outer ring of huts, with the spaces between stoutly palisaded, encloses alternate rings of grain-stores and huts, while the centre is occupied by a dining and "jabbering" place, formed by piling stout poles in tiers; these, like most of their other possessions, being stained with a kind of red clay. In some central position a large pigeon-loft is built, in which all the small babies are stowed and shut up for the night; a very excellent idea, and one that might be introduced at home. Many of the young bloods wear neat head-dresses made of human hair, with an outer layer of beads and culminating in a peak in front, which is tipped with an old cartridge-case or other gaudy object. They paint their bodies in gruesome patterns with red-and-white clay, and do not distress themselves about the proprieties. They still own considerable herds of cattle and enormous flocks of goats and sheep, and their cultivations are very extensive. Numbers of chiefs came to pay their respects, glad of the opportunity of doing so without passing through Lure country, which they must do to visit Wadelai. One old gentleman arrived with a cane-bottomed chair, which he said had once belonged to Emin; he also distinctly remembered Sir Samuel Baker. His two chief wives came and called on us; they were pleasant-featured women, and scrupulously clean, but their appearance was much spoilt by the inevitable piece of glass and enormous earrings. This wearing of a piece of glass in the lower lip is very curious, and peculiar, I believe, to the Shulis and Lures.

On October 22nd, giving up all hopes of my loads, I sent back my Manyema *via* Kampala, and embarking in my man-of-war with five trusty Watonga, my small boy from Ujiji, and my two Wa Ruanda, I started down stream once more, and profiting by a strong current, made considerable progress, and encamped on the left bank by one of the first villages of the Madi. The Madi are a fine race, closely allied to the Lures; they surround their villages with a dense thorn hedge, and the only means of ingress is through small holes 2 ft. high. They make beautiful arrows with barbs of a great variety of patterns.

Here the mosquitoes were terrible, and as they were small enough to penetrate the mesh of my net, sleep was out of the question, while my wretched natives spent the night in reminiscences of the happy lands flowing with milk and honey now left far behind. On the following day the river widened considerably, in some places resembling a lake rather than a river. In the vicinity of Bora, the old Egyptian station, it must be at least four miles broad, and the current is almost imperceptible, except where the sudd is so extensive as to leave only one or two small channels. There are enormous numbers of hippopotami in these reaches, and they constitute a very real danger to navigation. One of the Uganda canoes, in emerging from the Unyama, a river opposite Dufilé, was attacked, and only escaped by running into the sudd. Captain Delmé Radcliffe, the officer commanding this district, was attacked in the steel boat; and an infuriated old bull chased me for fully half a mile, at one time being within five yards of the stern, but a well-placed shot from my revolver eventually induced him to desist from the pursuit. The Madi attack them with a harpoon-head, fastened to the end of a shaft by a twist of the rope to which it is attached, and so arranged as to detach itself after the delivery of the stroke from the shaft, which remains in the hand of the hunter, while the rope is free to run out until the float, which is tied to the other end, can be thrown overboard. The ridge of hills that commences at Wadelai gradually increases in height, till at Bora the hills become quite imposing; then they rapidly diminish, and a few miles south of Dufilé vanish completely, giving place after a few miles of level ground to some isolated kopjes. On the left bank a range of hills runs parallel to the Nile, opposite Wadelai, but at a distance of about twenty miles from the river; then they bend to the east and merge into the formidable peaks that dominate Dufilé and the Karas rapids. On the bank of the river, and even in mid-stream, there are some picturesque kopjes black with cormorants. In the vast wastes of weed and water through which one passes it is easy to trace the formation of the formidable barriers which further north render navigation almost impossible. There is a small plant, similar in form to our well-known London Pride, which grows in the water, and is entirely independent of the soil, deriving its sustenance from the water by means of a tangle of roots resembling seaweed, and which descend to a depth of 1 ft. 6 in. to 2 ft. This plant grows in enormous quantities at the mouth of the Semliki, and in the placid reaches of the Victoria Nile, and single plants and even large masses are carried by the wind and current, and eventually are caught by a snag, a bed of water-lilies, or a bank of sand; they are soon followed by others, and by degrees the mass becomes enormous. Then grass-seeds are dropped by birds or driven by the wind, and the mass is quickly matted by the grass; driftwood, plants, and refuse of all sorts soon accumulate, and the rotting remains and mud that settles from the stream form a solid bottom. Then come the papyrus and the dense reeds, and what was originally a stick or a water-lily has in a few months become a solid island. There are numbers of Uganda kob and hartebeeste on the banks, but remarkably few ducks or geese. The neighbourhood of old Dufilé appears to be very densely populated, and at my camp, near the old site, I was visited by numbers of natives, who told me that the Belgian post was further down, below the commencement of the rapids, and that the Belgians had been recently fighting a tribe living in the hills.

The following morning, after narrowly escaping shooting the rapids, owing to a mistake in Bt.-Major Vandeleur's map, which transposes the river Unyama and the stream which flows in farther north, I reached Afuddu, a post built in the bottom of a crater several miles from anywhere, and surrounded by dense bush. A more concise summing up of Uganda methods than that afforded by the placing of Afuddu would be difficult to conceive. Subsequent inquiries elicited the monstrous fact that the site had been chosen because of a magnificent shady tree which serves as an open-air dining-room: in fine, two white men and a hundred odd Soudanese are condemned to live in a mosquito-bush situated in a hollow surrounded by hills, two hours from the river and off the main road to Fort Berkeley, for the shade afforded by a tree during meal-times. Naturally the site is now to be changed, which means the loss of a year's work. I was much distressed to find Lieut. Langton of the 21st Lancers, the O.C., in bed with black-water fever. Fortunately two days later Dr. Walker arrived from Lamogi, and when I left all danger was past. The Commandant of new Dufilé sent over wine and other luxuries for the invalid, and sent me a most pressing invitation to go and shoot with him, which, owing to my anxiety to arrive at Fort Berkeley, and obtain the latest news, I was unable to accept.

After three days' wallowing in the unheard-of luxury of glass, china, silver, milk and butter galore, for which Afuddu is justly famous, I set off with thirty Madi porters provided by a neighbouring chief, and crossing the line of hills north of the Unyama, camped on the Asua, which in the rains is a very formidable river. On the road I saw my first herd of giraffe, but owing to the necessity of avoiding delay, the country being uninhabited, and consequently foodless, I had to rest content with a long look through my binoculars. I was much impressed with their immense height and extraordinary action. The road to Fort Berkeley crosses the plateau several miles east of the Nile, and passes through a stony, inhospitable country, the haunt of numerous rhinoceros, antelope, and elephant. Scores of rocky streams flow west to the Nile. In the neighbourhood of the large hills, four days from Afuddu, their banks are clothed with dense masses of bamboo. The third day out we passed through the deserted fields and villages of a chief, Krefi, who, owing to some difference as to the porterage of food with the authorities at Fort Berkeley, has moved with all his people from the road towards the interior. This has been a sad blow to the transport of the region, as formerly a relay of porters and food were to be obtained, whereas now the porters from Afuddu have to do the whole five days to Alimadi's villages, and that without being able to obtain food on the road, an innovation which they naturally resent. At Alimadi's I found a detachment of Soudanese from Fort Berkeley buying food. Alimadi himself is a decent old chief, and still owns a few head of cattle; I believe the only herd in the vicinity that has survived the depredations of the Dervishes. Between here and Fort Berkeley the road traverses the sites of numerous villages, the inhabitants of which have either fled or been slain. Fort Berkeley is quite in keeping with the other stations on the Nile, having been carefully placed under a brow which commands the interior of the zariba. A swamp to the west between the fort and the river, and an extensive swamp to the south, add to the general salubrity of the situation. The nearest food-centres are two days' march, with the consequent result that half the garrison is constantly away buying food. The Maxim has been mounted behind a large acacia tree, which effectively screens it from an imaginary enemy, but at the same time confines its firing area to the inside of the fort, and gives a general finish-off to the situation. The station has been provided with an Egyptian clerk, who can only write Arabic, which is not required, and whose duties are consequently limited to holding a tape-yard at the Stores issue, for which herculean task he receives the very respectable sum of a hundred rupees a month.

Captain Dugmore, D.S.O., the officer in command, received me with every kindness, and nearly broke my heart by assuring me that I should spend Christmas with him. I had counted on being home by Christmas; a vain hope, as it afterwards transpired, and his prediction came near being fulfilled. He was engaged in completing a magnificent water-wheel à la Chinoîse, compounded of broken-up chop-boxes and empty tins. The extraordinary relics employed in its construction and the ingenuity displayed filled me with amazement. But, alas! its life was short, for after three days of service it collapsed in a high wind, which, considering that the only elements available for the construction of its axle were some green wood and a sardine-tin, was not remarkable. Here, as elsewhere, all the crops had failed, owing to the drought, and Captain Dugmore's wheat, though cherished with loving care, was gradually disappearing before the ubiquitous termite. As the launch was away, we were in the ignominious position of being dependent on the Belgians for a ferry across the river. Shabby! shabby! is the only word for our methods in Africa. At present on the Nile we have one steel boat refloated off Mahagi, and below the cataracts one steam-tub. Add to this a few useless Waganda canoes, one of which, after an initial cost of, say, £100, carries one load, and all of which are warranted to spoil half their contents owing to the enormous leakage inevitable in canoes consisting of planks sewn together by fibre, and you have our Upper Nile fleet; while the Belgians, whose transport difficulties are at least equal to ours, have a large steamer and a dozen fine steel whale-boats, with several more in construction and on the road. The majority of the Belgians (there are about twenty on the Nile) are well lodged in burnt-brick houses, while, with the exception of a weird construction in sun-dried brick at Fort Berkeley, all our officers are housed, like the natives, in grass and mud huts. The sum of the situation is this. The Belgians under Chaltin reached the Nile, drove out the Dervishes from Redjaf after some stiff fighting, followed them up, and eventually, by repeated activity and the effective occupation and fortification of Kero on the 5-½° parallel, compelled them in self-defence to evacuate Bohr. They then put their steamer on the river, and by a reconnaissance towards the Bahr-el-Ghazal, ascertained that the Dervishes had left the country, presumably to join the Khalifa in Kordofan. In the meanwhile Colonel Martyr's expedition arrives on the scene, and after establishing four posts—Wadelai, Lamoji, Afuddu, and Fort Berkeley—in the most unsuitable positions, succeeds in launching a small steam-tub capable of holding about ten men, and in which it is impossible to put both wood and supplies at the same time. Everybody, the officers of the expedition included, imagined that an effort was to be made to effect a junction with the Egyptian forces—an excellent opportunity of acquiring a maximum of "kudos" at a minimum of cost, a chance that does not come to all men—and the chance slid by.

From Bohr to Gaba Shambeh there is an excellent waterway, and at the same time that we were bolting from the mosquitoes and imaginary difficulties, some Senegalese with a French officer were flying the tri-colour at Gaba Shambeh, and were advancing their interests via Abu-kuka towards Bohr. After such dismal failures, and in view of the prevailing chaos, it is hardly to be wondered at that the Commissioner found it advisable to issue general orders to the effect that any officials writing home to their friends, and mentioning abuses in letters which should appear in the Press, would be held responsible. At Fort Berkeley I seemed to have come to a full stop. The steam-tub, with Dr. Milne and Capt. Gage, who had suddenly started with Commandant Henry and the Belgian steamer on a reconnaissance towards Khartoum, was still away, and though they had been absent more than two months there was no reliable news. But the arrival of Inspector Chaltin, the victor of the Dervishes at Redjaf, opened up new possibilities. In response to his cordial invitation Captain Dugmore and I repaired to Redjaf in a Belgian whale-boat, and in the intervals of an amazing sequence of various wines and spirituous liquors, Inspector Chaltin kindly invited me to join him at Kero, adding that he would make inquiries about the possibility of going from Bohr overland, and offering me every assistance in his power.

Accordingly, a few days later I found myself again at Redjaf, the guest of the charming commanding officer of the station, Commandant Colin. Here I learnt that I was to proceed slowly down river in the company of M. Beaupain, the judge, a most ardent sportsman, and to whom I am indebted for many kindnesses. The mushroom-stone mentioned by Baker in *Ismailia* is still extant, though hardly of the dimensions depicted. The Dervishes had thrown up enormous earthworks, and the outline of the old station and the foundations of the houses are still visible; while, as at Bedden, lime-trees and oil-seed acacia imported by Emin are flourishing. A few hours' paddling brought us to Lado, which is a howling waste in a wilderness of swamps. Here the river is already of considerable breadth and a network of enormous islands, many of which were covered with crops of red millet, which looked very promising despite the drought. The agricultural possibilities of these thousands of isles and islets immediately after flood as a rule are very great; at highest river most are inundated, but sowings after the first fall give enormous crops, the soil, which is composed of alluvium and decaying vegetation, being of extraordinary richness. The formation of many is very curious, resembling nothing so much as a coral island, a solid bank of varying thickness enclosing a lagoon, with the stream flowing all round. Lieut. Engh received me with the greatest hospitality, and we spent several delightful days in this historic waste. There is here a fine herd of cattle looted from the Dervishes. The earthworks of the old station are enormous, and need a garrison of fully one thousand men. At present there is a small palisaded enclosure in one corner which contains the station, and the approaches are commanded by two Krupp guns and a Maxim posted on a brick tower. But Inspector Chaltin talks of removing the main station from Kero to Lado, owing to its greater agricultural possibilities, in which case the whole extent of the earthworks will be utilized. Between here and Redjaf are enormous swamps, which further north on the Kero road become still more extensive, in places opening out into vast lagoons. The lagoon immediately to the south of Kero is about fifteen miles in circumference, though not more than half a mile wide at the river neck. To the east lie the hills of Gondokoro, and beyond them other ranges of hills with a large population and many cattle. These are the last eminences till we reach the hills of Kordofan, and the country settles down into one vast dismal flat, a wilderness of water, weed, and scrub; the haunt of thousands of hippo, elephant, and dismal marabout storks; the paradise of malaria, misery, and mosquitoes.

Six hours' paddling brought us to Kero, the frontier station of the Congo Free State, on the 5-½° parallel, which is their temporary limit as arranged by treaty with the French. The station is a marvellous example of energy, although only in existence for one year. A large and well-built brick house for the inspector has been completed, and the majority of the whites, to the number of about ten, are housed in baked-brick cottages. There are several large whale-boats, and more in course of erection. At one time there were a thousand Askaris, a number which has been reduced since the reconnaissance of Commandant Henry towards the north, which ascertained that the Dervishes had retreated *via* Rumbek and Mashra er Rek towards Kordofan. The high bank on which the station stands being the promontory at a sharp bend of the river, is being rapidly eaten away by the stream, and the water-edge is now thirty yards further back than a year ago. This shows to what an extent and with what marvellous rapidity the Nile changes its course. The quantity of fish is prodigious, and an Anzande fisherman keeps the station daily supplied with fish of the best quality. Some attain to a weight of 200 lbs., and several enormous specimens have been obtained by dynamite explosions which are the evening amusement. The Anzande method is very ingenious. The fisherman selects a shallow spot, and with a clever knack throws a funnel-shaped net weighted round the rim, and attached by the apex to a cord, by means of which he feels if any fish have been covered; he then slowly draws in, and the weights, thus closing together, form a bag with the fish struggling in the meshes. Several times I saw him take a dozen large fish at a time, and half an hour's work in almost the same spot sufficed to provide fish for all the white men, and many to spare. The food question is one of considerable difficulty, grain being only obtainable at a distance of several days, which necessitates the continued absence of half the garrison. However, the natives managed to eke out their daily ration of one small cup of red millet with fish, an occasional hippo or antelope, and a kind of plum which grows in profusion in the district; it has a hard outer shell, then one-tenth of an inch of sweet fibre which leaves an after-taste of quinine, and finally a hard stone containing a kernel that cooked tastes like a mixture of prussic acid and quintessence of quinine; however, the natives devour them with avidity, and also extract an oil which I am told is quite tasteless—a fact that, after tasting one of the kernels, I am prepared to take on trust. There is also a small berry tasting like an old apple, from which they make a form of bread, which at first sight I pardonably mistook for clay. There was plenty of snap about the Congo State soldiers, who paraded daily with drums and bugles, and it was easy to see by the general efficiency and the progress made in a short time that the country was under a strong man, the whole Nile district forming a very agreeable contrast to the Tanganyika chaos.

CHAPTER XIX.

KERO TO ABU-KUKA AND BACK TO BOHR.

As considerable anxiety was felt as to the fate of the steamer, which had been now three months absent without sending news, Inspector Chaltin decided to send Commandant Renier with a whale-boat to Shambeh to endeavour to obtain information, and very kindly offered me the opportunity of accompanying him, with orders to assist me forward in every possible way. As I was suffering from congestion of the liver, which prevented me from standing up straight, and from a remittent fever which showed no inclination to disappear, I gladly availed myself of the chance, knowing that activity alone would keep the fever in check, and that it was advisable to reach the sea as soon as possible. The camp was beaten up for volunteers to go with me overland either from Bohr or Shambeh, as circumstances might dictate, with the result that one small boy, a Dinka, and a mad criminal in chains, were forthcoming, with which formidable recruits on December 20th, I, an old Egyptian Dervish prisoner with a broken leg, a dozen soldiers, and sundry nondescripts, departed in one of the large whale-boats. I carried away with me many pleasing souvenirs of Inspector Chaltin's hospitality, and everybody's kindness and welcome, and also the sincere hope that never should I set eyes on Kero or any other spot on the Upper Nile again.

For several miles the stream follows the bank, then branches off to the east, and for miles and miles loses itself in a labyrinth of isles of weed. In vain we searched for a landing-place, and it was not till 5 p.m. that we found a small plantation of millet with a few wretched Baris stifling in a fog of mosquitoes on a mud-bank. The following day we paddled for hours, seeing nothing but tall reeds, hippo, and sand-spits, and eventually reached the left bank again at a spot called Semsem, owing to the immense plantations of that grain which existed here in the time of the Dervishes. Here there is a bank nearly 6 ft. high, with a large tree tenanted by hundreds of marabouts; to the south-west and north are swamps, and to the east, beyond the river, stretches one vast howling melancholy—reach upon reach of reed and rush, strips of lagoon, and again rush and reed, till on the far horizon a thin purple haze shows the line of the right bank.

The few Baris that we met on the islands informed us that they had come thither because they had been worsted in an encounter with the Dinkas to the north-west. Their villages were very scattered, the huts being dotted in ones and twos throughout their fields of millet. They beat the ground immediately surrounding their huts into a hard concrete, which they kept well swept, and upon which they dry the seeds of the nenuphar preparatory to pounding it into flour. As most of their huts were covered with strings of drying meat and strips of hippo hide, they would appear to be expert hippopotamus hunters. All their canoes are very tiny, and they work them with consummate skill. The amount of fish that they spear is wonderful. It is very sad to think how the Baris have been wiped out by the Dervishes. It will be remembered what a formidable people they were in Sir Samuel Baker's time; putting thousands of warriors into the field, and owning vast herds of cattle. Now, with the exception of those who took refuge in the Gondokoro hills, they are to all intents and purposes extinct. A few scattered settlements of miserable fisher-folk alone show the extent of the former Bari kingdom. The whole road from Krefi's kraal to Fort Berkeley is lined with the stone foundations of former Bari villages, and the country is strewn with discarded stones, used for grinding the corn. There is still, according to report, plenty of cattle in the Gondokoro hills, but with that exception and the exception of the few beasts owned by Ali-madi, all those vast herds spoken of by Baker have been looted and destroyed. Fortunately the Dervish wave did not reach further than Dufilé, so that the southern Nile above the rapids was left untouched. The country east of the Nile, except on the actual river-banks, was also practically untouched, hence the Eastern Dinkas escaped their depredations, and still own enormous heads of cattle. The Western Dinkas were less fortunate, as the Dervishes from the Bahr-el-Djebel and the Bahr-el-Ghazal penetrated far into the Niam-Niam country, and were at one time a serious menace to the Congo Free State. This is the only valid excuse for the Belgian occupation of the Nile; but I think the result could have been equally well accomplished by protecting the Congo Nile watershed. Still, the Belgians carried out their expedition with consummate ability, and all honour is due to Inspector Chaltin for his able leadership. It was a gross error of statesmanship that ever permitted them to obtain a footing on the Nile. For, however good their intentions, their methods are not ours; and their presence cannot but tend to unsettle the natives.

The key to the difference between their methods and ours lies in the fundamentally distinct objects for which we acquire territory. We acquire territory for generations yet unborn, trusting thereby to find an outlet for surplus population in the congested days to come. It is to the future benefit of the race that we look. We expect no immediate return. It is as with a man who starts farming, and with an eye to the future buys the call on the surrounding country. But with the Belgians it is quite different. They expect immediate returns. They say this country is no good, we can get no ivory or rubber, why do we stay here? And they are advising the evacuation of the Nile stations. It is as with a man who leases a vast tract of country and cuts down all the timber for sale, hoping thereby to obtain a large and immediate return on his money, ignoring the future, or believing his lease to be merely temporary. The greatest difficulty with which the Belgians have to contend—one that paralyzes all their efforts, however genuine—is the character of the tribes from whom they recruit their soldiers. I myself, having had experience of Manyema, can fully appreciate their difficulties in this respect. The majority of the tribes drawn upon are cannibals, and they are so low in the scale of civilization, and in many cases so vice-sodden from their association with Arabs of the Tippoo Tib fraternity, that it is impossible to make any impression upon them. Most natives can be touched in their pride or sense of the responsibility of a soldier's position. But these brutes are mere brutes, feeling the whip if it is laid on sufficiently thoroughly, and nothing else. As I pointed out to Inspector Chaltin, if the

Congo State would draw its soldiers mainly from the northern tribes, such as the Makrakas and Niam-Niams, they would obtain the raw material that could be trained to a sense of responsibility and self-esteem. The ruffians that they employ at present cannot be trusted for one hour away from the superintendence of a white man. Cases of outrages committed by the mail-carriers on even the natives on the British side of the river are of daily occurrence. I can bear witness to the distress that they caused Inspector Chaltin, but they are inevitable with the existing state of the Free State forces. Another potent factor is the inadequacy of the commissariat arrangements; the Belgians are at present endeavouring to maintain about one thousand five hundred men in a country destitute of supplies. They have to make expeditions ten days' march into the interior to obtain any supplies at all. And I am convinced by the frequency of the shooting affrays that their methods of obtaining these supplies are not, in our ideas, legitimate. Knowing, too, the difficulty that we have in buying provisions for one hundred men only on the British side, and having seen the trade goods taken out by the Belgians, I am sure that "commandeering" is largely resorted to. Anyhow it is significant that all the natives on the Congo Free State side are retiring further and further inland, while the natives on the British side are rapidly resettling on the river-bank, from which they were driven by the Dervishes. Owing to the difficulty that the Belgians find in obtaining supplies, the ration per man is one small cup of millet a day; out of this he has probably to feed a slave boy, one or two wives, and Heaven knows how many children. Yet they all look sleek and fat. How do they manage it? The conclusion is obvious. When I was hunting with Captain Dugmore, the local natives on our side dare not go alone into the bush, as they said that they would be caught and eaten. Another great source of weakness is the Belgian method of treating their natives. They are too familiar with them, and then, when, as the inevitable result, the natives become impertinent, brutally severe. In treating natives it is indispensable to emphasize the distinction between black and white, yet at the same time to let the native see that you respect him in his own line, but take your own absolute superiority for granted. Hair-splitting justice is a *sine qua non*; and, I believe, herein lies our success with inferior peoples; it is the one thing that they can understand, and which inspires more respect than anything else.

On the third day we met the first Dinkas, miserable, amphibious objects, eking out a precarious existence on a semi-submerged island; here we camped, in a visible—nay, tangible—atmosphere of rotting fish, mud-caked niggers, marabouts, and kites; and at sunset, with a long-drawn expectant howl the mosquitoes arrived: little ones, big ones, black ones, mottled ones, a whirling, wailing fog of miniature vampires, that kept up the mournful dirge till the cold hour before sunrise, when with a sigh of relief we pushed off in our boat, and after five hours' paddling reached Bohr, which lies on the right bank at a sudden bend of the river. The original zaribas of the Dervishes and the more substantial earthworks thrown up when they heard of the occupation of Kero are already falling to pieces, and the elephant now takes his midday siesta midst the grinning skulls and calcined bones that are scattered about, all equally regardless of the wanton brutality of the near past. The past fades fast in Africa; yet another year, and the cotton-bush will have hid the mouldering relics of the earthworks, and the white ant will have seen the last grin of those gruesome jaws.

The fort of the Dervishes was of very considerable extent; about five hundred yards by six hundred yards, the long side lying on the river. There are still signs of a primitive effort at drainage, and the enormous quantity of cotton shrubs are a proof of the suitability of the soil to this product could it be brought within touch of a market. There are also unlimited numbers of gum-trees and tamarinds.

We had a few dynamite cartridges with us, and we obtained a good supply of fish by a couple of explosions. Amongst the numerous kinds that floated up to the surface was a curious fish similar to the species that I have mentioned as having been brought to me from the Ruo river near Chiromo. It was a long, eel-like fish, with the eyes covered by skin, the dorsal fin running down to and joining the diminutive tail. The snout was long and tubular, and the flesh lay in long, thin, delicate flakes like the flesh of the skate. Another species had the head and fore-part of the body encased in an adamantine shield armed with dangerous spikes on the back and by the pectoral fins. Its tail was shaped like the tail of a shark, which it resembles in general form, although the mouth was not underneath as with the shark's. A third species, very common all over this section of the Nile, much prized, and justly so, for the richness of its flesh, is covered with disproportionately enormous scales of circular form; its general form approximates to that of a red mullet. The commonest kind was the gorgeous tiger-fish, which is one of the most beautiful fish that swim.

There are large numbers of natives in the vicinity, and when we had at length convinced them of our pacific intentions, they brought milk and quantities of fish and fowls. It appears that such was the anxiety of the Dervishes in departing that the Dinkas succeeded in relieving them of their cattle. As a protection against mosquitoes the natives smother themselves in wood-ash, and the long lines of tall, gaunt, grey spectres slowly threading their way into the bush, each with a bright, broad-bladed spear, and a small gourd of milk or a decaying fish, present a very curious spectacle. Having stopped for a day to buy supplies, amongst which was a goat, rather less meaty than my hand, whose two hind legs combined would have had no chance against an English mutton-chop, we once more launched forth into the weary waste. We camped successively on a mud-bank tenanted by a few forlorn natives, from whom we obtained a small supply of grain at an exorbitant rate, and on a network of sun-dried hippo-holes whose authors resented our intrusion all night, expressing their disapproval by that strange variety of coughs, bellows, grunts, squeals, and roars peculiar to that misshapen pachyderm. Here we fired the 20 ft. reeds to modify the mosquito plague. They were very dry except at the base, and the terrific sheet of flame, capped by a vast cloud of smoke catching the red lights from the fire, afforded a picture of indescribable grandeur. It thundered away like a mighty sea of molten iron, licking up the country as it sped eastward; and we "smiled loud out" to think of the billions of mosquitoes that were perishing in its line; and the funny old hippo roared in astonishment, blinking their pink eyes at the alarming spectacle.

On the third day, having seen throughout the whole voyage from Bohr one tree at a distance of several miles, we were startled during lunch by the cry of "Steamer!" and rounding a bend in the river we saw the British steam-tub labouring up-stream with a bunch of ribbons that had once been a Jack flying at her stern. She was soon alongside, and we found on board Mr. Mulders, a naturalized American Dutchman, who built the Belgian steamer, in command, and two Belgians, one of whom was confined to his bed by a severe attack of sciatica which necessitated his return to Kero. In answer to our eager inquiries we learnt that they had spent the three months in the sudd, making prodigious efforts to cut a channel, and that eventually, after living waist-deep in water, sleeping on water, eating strange birds and being eaten by mosquitoes, steaming for miles in search of a stick or grain, they had abandoned their steamer, leaving her in charge of a few Askaris, and the whole party, including the French officer from Shambeh, who daringly followed them in a flotilla of native canoes, had started in the boats with the idea of dragging them by main force over the vegetation. The British boat was sent back with the sick men for supplies and mails, and with orders to return and patrol the vicinity of the obstructions at intervals of a week, blowing her whistle and endeavouring to find out whether the party would return, and, if no news had been obtained by the middle of March, to return with the Belgian steamer to Kero.

I consider this successful attempt of Capt. Gage of the 7th Dragoon Guards, and Dr. Milne, as one of the most daring feats ever accomplished in the history of African travel. They suffered indescribable hardships for nearly four months, during all which time they hardly slept one night on land; but were compelled to see the long hours of darkness through, night after night, cramped up in a small boat or lying on the vegetation, tormented by myriads of mosquitoes, and with very little more substantial than native porridge to keep their spirits up. Day after day, nothing but that vast expanse of weed of a hopelessness beyond civilized conception; day after day dragging their boats through and over stinking bogs and spongy masses of weed tenanted by a thousand crocodiles—not knowing where they were, nor, in characteristic British fashion, caring, yet ever keeping their face forward, strong in the knowledge that perseverance must succeed. Their food ran short, and to return was impossible. Had they not come unexpectedly upon Major Peake's steamers they would probably all have perished. Very few people can ever have any conception of the magnitude and apparent hopelessness of their task. The terror of those stupendous wastes! They have eaten like rust into my very heart, as they must do with all those who launch forth into their seemingly unending desolation.

From information I found it was impossible to land anywhere north of Bohr on the right bank, so decided that the only course open to me was to return to that salubrious resort. Commandant Renier kindly offered to take me on if I thought it worth while to make the attempt; however, it was obviously useless, and with a heavy heart I started back on my tracks. We steamed up-river until we came to the enormous Lake Powendael, which lies between the river and the left bank six hours north of Bohr, and there we anchored till morning, when we sent a boat ashore in search of wood. The lake is about twenty miles by ten, and very shallow, numerous banks covered with ducks, geese, pelicans, and other strange birds showing above the surface. The Dervishes were reported to have sunk their steamer here, but an exhaustive search by the small boat failed to find sufficient water to cover it; probably it was sunk in the channel near Abu-kuka or Shambeh, as these are almost the only spots where it is possible to reach the left bank. The following day we reached Bohr, and as one of my Wa Ruanda who had been sick was finished off by mosquitoes, and my Dinka had bolted with what he could lay his hands on, my numbers were reduced to my four Watonga, two small boys, one Ruanda, the criminal lunatic, and the youth from Kero. With these it was obviously impossible to start, and Commandant Renier kindly offered me some Askaris. Five boys from Sierra Leone turned up in answer to a call for volunteers, and with my numbers swelled to the vast total of fourteen, I made a start on December 30th.

CHAPTER XX.

IN DINKA-LAND.

The native information as to my route was decidedly discouraging, but knowing by now the value of native information, it was with reasonable hopes of success that I disposed of my bed and other luxuries, and put the first of three hundred miles behind me. As I started late, I camped at the first large village that I met, a distance of six miles from Bohr. Here there was an enormous population living round the extensive lagoons that stretched in all directions, and after the first few minutes of suspense, a brisk trade started in fish and grain, and eventually in milk. On the following day we succeeded in dodging several lagoons, but had to wade up to our necks and cross another nearly a mile wide on a very treacherous layer of vegetation. Skirting the edge of the water, we came on a herd of twenty elephant, and I dropped a good bull with a couple of .303's in the head. The quantities of goats and sheep possessed by the natives were extraordinary, enormous herds grazing in every direction in the rich vegetation growing in the swamps. After cutting off meat from the elephant, I followed one of the numerous paths which led inland, and meeting hundreds of natives on the way, arrived at a large, scattered village, where we camped.

The main population, which is very dense, lives in the bush at a distance of sometimes several miles from the river, and water is one of the most expensive supplies, though, except in seasons of severe drought, such as when I passed through, there are evidently numerous pools scattered all over the bush. Owing to the drought there was no grain obtainable, and the natives were eating the seeds of a water-plant resembling a crown-artichoke (the nenuphar) and the kernels of the before-mentioned plums. A very affable and intelligent gentleman, who had accompanied me for some miles, offered his services as guide, which I gladly accepted, and after marching for an hour I arrived at another extensive village. Here, as elsewhere, all the huts were isolated and surrounded by a fence of thorns to ward off the lions, which were very numerous. On the path we met hundreds and hundreds of natives, many of enormous stature, 6 ft. 4 to 6 ft. 6, who were going to cut up the elephant, and they were all very friendly. At the village I waited for my boys to close up, but after some time one was still missing, and as boys whom I sent back told me that they could not find him, I packed my people and belongings into one of the thorn-fences, and went back with one soldier and some Dinkas whom I persuaded to accompany me.

About a mile away I met my headman and my guide of the morning returning with the delinquent, who was none other than the criminal lunatic. It appears that he had decided to return home, and, as a preliminary, had distributed my blankets, mosquito-curtain, and clothes amongst the natives. By an extraordinary stroke of luck I recovered them intact, with the trivial exception of one of my two shirts; it was due to my guide, and he and the two men who brought them in were handsomely rewarded; so was the runaway. The flies by day, the mosquitoes by night, rendered life well-nigh impossible, and with visions of impassable swamps, waterless deserts, and famine in front, I heartily wished myself quit of Africa and all its abominations, as I have so often done before, and shall no doubt so often do again. In the afternoon, at the urgent request of many hungry Dinkas, I sallied forth and slew a good bull elephant. I had chased him for several miles, pouring in lead whenever I could see him, till at last he stood. This gave me my chance, and he dropped to a shot in the head. But as I was going up to inspect him, he suddenly rose and sloped away. I fired four shots from the 10-bore at him as he passed. At the fourth he stopped, turned his head towards me, and quite deliberately began to advance, examining carefully with his trunk every palm-bush. There was no unseemly haste about his action. He meant investigating the matter. My position was most uncomfortable, as, if I fired, I should give him my whereabouts, and certainly could not drop him; while, if I moved from the cover of the diminutive palm-tree behind which I was standing, he would immediately see me, and the country was too open to escape. So, for lack of another alternative, I waited. On he came quite quietly, that snake-like trunk writhing round every corner, till there were but two more palm-trees between him and me: out went that trunk once more; he stopped, swayed slowly to and fro, and fell with a mighty crash—dead. His tusks must have weighed about 60 lbs. apiece. It was heart-breaking to leave them lying there, and to think that I had had to kill such a magnificent beast for the sake of his meat. The natives were very much delighted, and evidently thought me a great institution, and for several days afterwards I was pestered with requests to shoot elephant, till I began to wish I had never seen such a beast. They promised to take the tusks of those I had slain to Bohr, and to give them to the steamer when she returned, but I don't suppose I shall see them again.[18]

The river, which is here one vast sea of grass, the opposite bank being quite invisible even from an eminence of 20 ft., continually branches inland in the form of long, narrow, meandering lagoons, which, I suppose, are apologies for rivers in this part of the world. As some of them are several miles in length, progress is very difficult, and every moment I dreaded to see a new one. However, I successfully dodged most of them, but had some trouble with one a mile broad, which we eventually passed by wading, the water being in places up to my boys' necks. At one time my small boy, with my revolver, prismatic compass, and coat, disappeared completely, but was extricated by an obliging Dinka of about 6 ft. 7 in. The prevalence of crocodiles, and a slimy bottom pitted with elephant-holes, did not facilitate matters.

Enormous numbers of Dinkas came to see me beaten by this obstruction; and after two hours' exhausting conversation in signs, during which I displayed all my remaining trade goods, I had still failed to induce a guide to show me the way across. In native fashion they all wanted to see what I would do. At last, utterly disgusted, I

---

[18] They turned up seven years later, the natives having kept them for me till a Government station was established.

started to wade, intending to swim if we could not manage otherwise, as I dare not waste the two or three days that would be necessary to march round. When they saw that I was quite determined, several came with me and showed me the shallowest path across. They were hugely delighted when I presented them with a Jubilee medal and some beads, but said that they dare not go any further, as the next village was not their village, signifying that if they went they would be speared. A short march soon brought us to the village in question. The natives were rather nervous at first, but soon brought us plenty of rotten fish and a little milk. Here my surviving Ruanda man succumbed to the attacks of the mosquitoes, which defied description; he had been ailing for some time, and being too desperate to keep them off, he was literally sucked dry. It was absolutely necessary to turn in half an hour before sunset and to make all the preparations possible for the night. I piled all my belongings round the edge of my net, and kept a green wood fire burning at each end: then I lay inside, smoked native tobacco (of remarkable pungency), and prayed for morning. As soon as the sun went down they started operations. It was like having a tame whirlwind in one's tent. They could not possibly have been worse: had there been thousands more it would not have mattered, as not a single one more could have found room on any exposed part of one's anatomy. Every night two or three hundred contrived to enter my net; I have no idea how. The most pernicious and poisonous kind was a very small black mosquito, that might possibly have penetrated the mesh. I used to turn out in the morning feeling perfectly dazed from the amount of poison that had been injected during the night. The natives of the country obviate the nuisance by lining their huts with a deep layer of burnt cow-dung, in which they lie. They also smear a paste made of this ash and cow's urine all over their bodies. The women carefully collect all the dung and spread it out to dry. In the evening, when the cattle are brought in to be milked, they burn it. The smoke serves to keep the flies from the beasts during the milking. Then all the ash is collected and placed in the huts.

Following the river, we made good progress till a halt was called by the presence of a stupendous old bull elephant with magnificent tusks, who was dozing on the path. We shouted to him to get out of the way, and he slowly turned round, stalked towards us, and when within fifty yards curled up his trunk, spread his ears, rumbled and came. Crash went every load, and I found myself in a medley of tent and boxes, pots and pans, with a double .303 loaded with soft-nosed bullets, looking at him in amazement; but the shot fortunately turned him, and away he went, screaming and trumpeting, giving my blankets a parting kick as he swung round. This is the only time I have seen one aggressive without due cause. Owing to the absence of water and the quantity of plum-trees, of which they are very fond, there were enormous numbers of elephant along the river-bank, and except where they were on the path we scarcely noticed them, every day passing several herds. I was wild when I thought of the prodigious but futile efforts that Sharp and I made round the volcanoes to find them, when we had porters galore, while now, having no porters, I looked upon them as a nuisance, owing to the delay they caused. Here, and for some days afterwards, close to the line of bush, there was a well-defined river with a stream of one and a half to two miles an hour, which would be navigable for flat-bottomed punts. The numbers of hippo were incredible, literally thousands and thousands. At every two hundred yards there was a great purple bank of twenty, fifty, or a hundred lying with their bodies half exposed, while others were wandering about in every direction on the vegetation, islands, and mud-banks. They practically ignored our presence, though we often passed within ten yards of them. Other game was scarce; I only saw a few waterbuck, bushbuck, and once the track of a giraffe, though plenty of guinea-fowl, and a few ducks and geese; but these were of little use, as, on opening my last box of shot-cartridges, they fell to pieces, being eaten through and through with rust. At one village a native produced a recent number of *Black and White*, carefully wrapped up in a piece of goatskin, and pointed out with great glee a picture of Dreyfus; as I had no interpreter, and the natives no longer understood my ten words of pigeon Arabic, I have not the remotest conception how it came into this outlandish spot. It was very difficult to obtain supplies, owing to the general famine, so I shot another elephant, which came down to water near camp, and made my boys smoke a three-days' supply of meat. The following day we saw two large herds of elephant, one mainly composed of good bulls. Some, showing splendid ivories, refused for a long time to leave the path. We were compelled to stone them. Then, making good progress, we camped opposite a ferry, which led to an island where I could see some natives. They quickly collected, and in a few minutes there was a crowd of several hundred, with a solid hedge of spears glinting in the sun. At first they were very doubtful; then, suddenly realizing that it was all right, they swarmed across, yelling and whooping, and in one minute my diminutive camp was one howling black mass. At first things looked rather anxious, but some slaps on the back and a long-winded repetition of arâm, which appears to be the local form of salaam, quickly spread a broad grin over the mass; they brought me a present of about thirty large fish, and there was soon a brisk trade in milk, of which they had an unlimited supply, so that all my men had a good wholesome feed. They proved very friendly, and I much regret that our conversation was strictly limited to arâm, which, however, appears to have considerable significance, being invariably responded to by much grunting and a peculiar clucking noise like the soliloquy of an old hen. Every one in Dinka-land carries a long-bladed spear, a pointed fish-spear, and a club made of a heavy purple wood, while the important gentlemen wear enormous ivory bracelets round their upper arm; strict nudity is the fashion, and a marabout feather in the hair is the essence of *chic*. They are all beautifully built, having broad shoulders, small waist, good hips, and well-shaped legs. The stature of some is colossal. It was most curious to see how these Dinkas, living as they do in the marshes, approximate to the type of the water-bird. They have much the same walk as a heron, picking their feet up very high, and thrusting them well forward. Their feet are enormous. Their colossal height is, of course, a great advantage in the reed-grown country in which they live. They are the complete antithesis of the pigmy, as the country in which they live is the complete antithesis of the dense forest that is the home of the dwarfs. Many of these strange African peoples form most interesting reading to a student of evolution. The adaptability of a race to its surroundings is wonderful. The favourite pose of a Dinka is in reality the favourite pose of a water-bird. It is most interesting to note that surroundings should produce a similar type in families as remote from one another as birds and men.

My headman woke me in the morning with the pleasing information that my home-sick criminal had disappeared in the night, so the body of my tent had to go by the board, a severe loss, as afterwards transpired. During this day's march and a part of the next, the population changed entirely, the well-bred Dinkas giving place to a miserable fishing-folk, who are presumably the Woatsch spoken of, as reported to live here, by Sir S. Baker. They are an extraordinary people, of a very low stage of civilization, and showed abject terror at the sight of beads and cloth. I imagine they took me for a god, as each village, man, woman, and child, persisted in escorting me for a mile or so, doing the honours with a deafening chant, and continually pointing to the sun; this, though very flattering, hardly acted as a sedative on my fever, and I was heartily thankful to leave them behind; at one spot there must have been fully five hundred men who formed a solid phalanx round me, and sang at the top of their voices for a distance of two miles. They appeared not to have the remotest conception of barter, and hid their faces when I produced any of my trade goods, so that it was impossible to buy any food. Even during the night small bands approached to a respectful distance and chanted, and at one watering-place about a hundred loathsome hags danced a wild fandango around me, uttering the shrillest cries conceivable, and accompanying them with a measured flap-flap of their long pendant dugs; then, as a grand finale, all threw themselves on their faces at my feet, and with one ear-piercing shriek dispersed into the bush, leaving me under the impression that I was in the Drury Lane pantomime, outside two bottles of champagne. Never in all Africa had I met such embarrassing and impossible people. In the intervals of these trying performances I noticed that the country was slightly more elevated, and that there was a profusion of large trees. This would be the best position for a Government station. But it soon settled down again into the dismal flat of sun-baked clay, thorn, and palm-scrub, which in places recedes, leaving large plains that are flooded in ordinary seasons; here there were numbers of small buck, and I saw a beautiful male *Cobus maria*. It was a most handsome little beast, and was running with a large herd of other waterbuck, and had the same action as the Uganda kob. I was much disappointed, from lack of porterage, to lose the opportunity of procuring such a rare specimen. The variety of aquatic birds was enormous; amongst others, a beautiful black-and-white ibis; but I looked in vain for *Balæniceps rex*. The kites, marabouts, and vultures were a great nuisance. On several occasions a kite actually took my dinner out of the frying-pan on the fire while the cook's back was turned.

After the singing gentry, it was with no little relief that I met some respectable Dinkas again with large herds of cattle; they, too, appeared to be ignorant of the elements of barter, and it was only after an hour's dumb-crambo business that they brought an antediluvian fish as a feeler; this I immediately bought at great price, and then they realized that there was something in the idea, and brought a good supply. They have absolutely none of the fear of, and respect for, the white man that one finds all over Africa except in the regions of Exeter Hall legislation, but merely regard one as a great joke, and, on the whole, not such a bad sort of fool. They are all the most inveterate, pertinacious, and annoying beggars, and evince the greatest astonishment when one refuses to distribute one's belongings gratis amongst them. One in particular amused me, a 6 ft. 4 giant, who took a fancy to my last pair of trousers, and when, pleading modesty, I refused his request, he stamped and howled like a spoilt child. He then proceeded to make himself very objectionable, and forced his way into my tent, refused to quit, and brandished his club. This was too much, so I suddenly took him by the scruff of the neck and the seat of where he wished my trousers to be, and, trusting in the superiority of a beef and beer diet over one of fish and thin milk, to his intense amazement, ran him out of camp, and imparted a final impetus with a double-barrelled drop-kick, backed by a pair of iron-shod ammunition boots. I was surprised to find how weak he was, despite his colossal stature. The others took it as a huge joke, and an hour afterwards he returned and behaved himself very well, on the morrow guiding me for some miles.

From here the country changes completely, opening out into a limitless plain, dotted here and there with clumps of borassus palm, growing on small, flat-topped eminences which are the only possible camping-grounds. The channel (which I christened the Gertrude Nile, and which had never hitherto been more than half a mile from the bush) bends away to the west and spreads out into large marshes, though its course is still obvious, and the plain, which is a mass of matted, half-burnt reed, hippo and elephant holes, is scored with numerous channels of water and mud, and towards the bush, which is soon at least fifteen miles from the river, is covered with small ant-hills. There is an enormous population on these plains, with huge herds of cattle and goats, though it is impossible to say where they live, and they are wonderfully clever at hiding their cattle, and light smoke fires to prevent them from making a noise. I marched for hours without seeing a native, but when pitching camp I could see hundreds and hundreds advancing in Indian file from all directions, or if I took a line that led far from water, a group would appear like magic to put me right. There was something uncanny about knowing that one was watched by hundreds without ever seeing more than an occasional individual perched on one leg, the other foot resting on his knee, on the top of a far ant-hill, and looking like a long black stork. The first day that I camped in the plain I was visited by at least a thousand natives.

With the exception of one or two slight fracas with my boys, they were well-behaved, and I bought a large supply of fish; but the second day about fifteen hundred turned up, and having nothing to sell, became very obstreperous. They tried to steal, so I ordered the vicinity of my tent to be cleared, and hustled several fairly roughly. One turned on me, and I knocked him down, cutting my hand badly on his teeth. They took my rough handling very well, but immediately resented any movement of my boys, and one silly young blood danced a dangerous war-dance, brandishing his spear round one of my Askaris, till I broke it for him, and gave him two or three reminders with a heavy hippo-whip. They then became very much excited, and I spent the rest of the afternoon with my hand on my revolver, momentarily expecting a general *émeute*, when, no doubt, we should have fared badly. Fortunately, there were two respectable old gentlemen who did their best to keep the younger blades quiet. One man bolted with a bit of cloth; a miss-fire from my .303 saved his life, and one of the old gentlemen, not knowing that I had pulled the trigger, signed to me to hold, and had the cloth fetched back; he then succeeded in clearing the camp of about half the turbulent rabble, for which I was very thankful. They then began to slowly file off, but about a hundred, including some of the most noisy ruffians, remained; these I quickly cleared with a heavy whip in one hand and my revolver in the other. They did not like the whip and smiled at the revolver, evidently thinking it a sort of club, till I shot a confiding marabout which was watching the proceedings, when there was a race for first place to less dangerous quarters.

On the march we came upon a belated hippo out on the plain, and there was a great hunt, about two hundred natives chasing him and plunging their spears into his body, till at last, covered with blood, he turned to bay, when I finished him off with a shot in the head.

A few miles further on I shot a Senegal hartebeeste, which gave us a supply of meat. On the third day we succeeded in shaking off our too attentive friends, and although we marched for six hours only made seven miles, owing to the necessity of feeling one's way round the swamps and the difficult nature of the ground. In many places the burnt vegetation was of the consistency of coke, and severely cut my boys' feet. The plain still widened, and the Gertrude Nile tended more decidedly towards the west. The bush was no longer visible, but to the west of the swamps there appeared to be a slight ridge with a dense covering of borassus.

We camped near a cattle village, and the people seemed friendly, though, as usual, somewhat turbulent. Two came into the camp after dark, evidently to see if we were on the alert, and were summarily ejected. In the morning about a hundred came and gave considerable trouble, and persisted in following us on the march. I noticed that two or three were closing round each of my boys, while at the same time about twenty were packing behind me. I turned round to drive them off, when my fools of Watonga were suddenly seized with a panic, and, throwing their loads down, ran towards me, shouting, "We are all lost!" Of course that started the game, and my best Congo soldier fell, stabbed to the heart, and two more went down with cracked skulls. I took the chief and his right-hand man with a double barrel, then turning round, found my boy had bolted with my revolver. At the same moment a Dinka hurled his spear at me; I dodged it, but he rushed in and dealt me a swinging blow with his club, which I fortunately warded with my arm, receiving no more damage than a wholesome bruise. I poked my empty gun at his stomach, and he turned, receiving a second afterwards a Dum-dum in the small of his back. Then they broke and ran, my army with eight guns having succeeded in firing two shots. I climbed up a high ant-hill that was close, and could see them watching at about three hundred yards for our next move, which was an unexpected one, for I planted a Dum-dum apparently in the stomach of one of the most obtrusive ruffians, whom I recognized by his great height. They then hurried off and bunched at about seven hundred yards, and another shot, whether effectual or not I could not see, sent them off in all directions, and the battle was finished. It was all over in a shorter time than it takes to tell the tale, but while it lasted it was fairly warm. I never expected to see my happy home again, nor did I feel much happier when I had time to look round. I was alone; at my feet lay my Congo Askari, in the last spasmodic shudder of death; a few yards away lay three more of my men, streams of blood slowly trickling from gaping wounds in their heads. The distorted figures of the three Dinkas, shot at close quarters, were the only other breaks in the dismal monotony of the marsh. I shouted, and slowly—one by one—my miserable curs emerged from patches of reed and bog-holes. Then the three wounded came-to from their swoon; one was very slightly hurt, but the other two were quite mad for days after. It was necessary, therefore, to throw away still more of our belongings. There was only one thing that could go, and that was Sharp's 60g. Holland and Holland paradox, half of which is peacefully reposing under some scrub, while the other half is at the bottom of a mud-hole. After dressing the heads of the two soldiers, who, with the trifling exception of insanity, did not seem much the worse, one for a gash 2 in. long and down to the bone on his temple, and the other for two gaping holes on the top of his skull, we hurried on, fearing the Dinkas might return *en masse*. But they contented themselves with watching us, and when I dropped the topmost man of a bunch of five on an ant-hill at six hundred yards, they only made further observations at a distance of a mile.

The news spread like wildfire, for, several miles further on, when passing within half a mile of a village, a band of ten old men came towards me, waving their arms in the air to show that they were unarmed. I went to meet them, and when quite close they started the old singing business, so I hurried off, after treating them to several arâms with an attempted pacific intonation. They then sent milk after me, but I waved them off, thinking it advisable to try by forced marches to break the line of communication.

Shortly afterwards, crossing a swamp on a dangerous bridge of weed burnt to the water level, I saw a specimen of *Balæniceps rex* standing quite close to me. I was on the point of firing, when a hippo put his head through the bridge at about ten yards, and regretfully I had to shoot him instead for his beef. Half a dozen Dinkas appeared, and, after making a great pacific demonstration, approached and helped to finish him off. He took several shots, and each time I fired they ran to a distance of at least two hundred yards, so they had evidently heard of the morning's proceedings. After cutting off some meat we continued our march, and it was not till 4 p.m. that I found another place where it was possible to camp, having buried most of my beads on the road to further lighten the loads. For the same purpose, in the evening I made a distribution of cloth and burnt a quantity, together with all my boys' rags.

The night passed peacefully, though I thought it advisable to put on a double sentry, and on the morrow, weary of swamps, I struck east towards the great burnt plain, and then marched due north, trusting to luck for water. I found numerous holes where the water had not quite dried up, and met many isolated groups of desponding natives spearing a loathsome four-legged reptile or fish, some of which, for lack of more delicate fare, I had to eat; and after marching for about fifteen miles, I again came on extensive swamps which stretched far to the east, and seemed likely to give me much trouble, if not to effectually prevent me going further. Being totally ignorant of the country, and without means of asking the simplest question of the natives, I had been fearing all along that I should arrive at some impassable obstacle. I was very anxious on this point, as it would have been impossible to return. Arriving unexpectedly on the edge of the first pool, I found it one mass of small duck, with a spur-winged goose standing up in the middle. I fired at him with my .303, and he dropped, the bullet striking him with most unusual noise. My boy, wading in, returned not only with the goose, but also two duck. The bullet had struck the goose's back, removing his intestines and half his breast, then cut off the head and broken the wing of No. 1 duck, and neatly cleaned No. 2. It was a Dum-dum, and must have exploded like a shell. I have often noticed that the bullets with the most penetration, such as the solid, nickel-coated, and the Dum-dum, shatter small animals and birds more effectually than the more expansive bullets, such as the Jeffrey and the lead-nose. This stroke of luck provided a very welcome change to my mournful diet of doubtful fish, occasional milk flavoured with cow's urine, which is used for washing the dairy utensils, and a strange cheese of my own manufacture.

We camped on the top of a layer of burnt vegetation overlying a morass, and my tent nearly disappeared in the night, while I was seized with furious bouts of vomiting, caused by the quantity of salt in the water. To make matters more cheerful, I discovered that my last two tins of tobacco were mouldy, and I only wished that I could enjoy it as much as the mosquitoes appeared to do, who settled in clouds on the rim of my pipe waiting their turn for a space on my epidermis. Several either climbed inside or bit me through a pair of ammunition boots. I had a severe cold and a stiff arm; my cook boy had dysentery; one of the Congo soldiers had a dreadful foot, which rendered walking a terrible torture; and the two gentlemen with cracked skulls were semi-delirious, so that, on the whole, we were a jovial party, our joviality being materially increased by the impossibility of making a fire, owing to lack of fuel.

In the morning we repeated the same tactics, and after finding plenty of water early in the march, only reached a camping-place at sunset. The country became slightly more cheerful, several trees about the dimensions of a healthy cabbage appearing on the horizon, and I saw the spoor of several giraffe, though where the giraffe themselves contrived to hide was more than I could guess. Our camp was near a large village where there were at least one thousand five hundred head of cattle, besides sheep and goats, and the chief brought me a fine fat bull-calf, which settled the nervous question of food for two days. These people, too, had evidently heard of the fracas, and only approached my camp in small bands, for which I was very grateful.

There were numbers of Dinkas fishing here. Their method is as follows: About a dozen men, each taking a large basket open at the bottom and with a hole at the top, advance in line through the shallow portions of the lagoon. Grasping the basket by the hole at the top, they dash it down on to the mud in front of them. I suppose if they catch a fish inside they pull it out of the hole at the top. I never saw them catch one, although they appeared to be quite hopeful.

The styles of coiffure affected by the Southern Dinkas had now changed, the prevailing fashion being to wear the hair long and frizzed out like a mop, while some of the young exquisites caked it with a white clay brought out to a peak behind. The rambling village, with its groups of figures and long lines of home-coming cattle dimly seen in the smoke of a hundred fires as I approached at sunset, was very picturesque.

CHAPTER XXI.

IN NUERLAND.

The following two days I still kept to the plain, on the first day finding plenty of water, and camping near a mud-trough where the water was flowing west; but on the second day we wandered into a waterless wilderness, and taking a north-west course marched for hours before we reached a stream. Our sufferings were intolerable, increased as they were by the salt nature of the water which we had been drinking for days. Half the boys fell by the road, and lay helpless till relieved by the water I sent back. I was beginning to despair of saving them, when from the only ant-hill for miles I saw a flight of birds, and after an hour's sharp burst I arrived at a large vlei, where to my joy I found that the water was flowing north, and was less salt. At an early stage of that day's march I had to leave yet another load. Soon after starting I saw a herd of at least four hundred hartebeeste, and on the vlei, where we camped, the numbers of ducks, geese, and pelicans were extraordinary. At my first shot I killed two large spurwings, and a few more rounds provided geese for all the camp, while I revelled in the luxury of *pâté de foie maigre*; but the little plump teal, knowing that I had no shot-gun, kept flighting backwards and forwards in thousands. Two guns might have had an evening's sport that they would have remembered for a lifetime. A few miles from camp I met some Nuer who had come to meet me. The chief, who was very sociable, though, like all, an incorrigible beggar, had been to Fashoda in the old times, and again my classic Arabic came into play. He asked after Emin, and seemed surprised to hear of his death, and also after Wadelai and Lado, and was particularly anxious to know if there was still a zariba at Bohr. He laid great stress on this point, asking me over and over again, so I imagined he wished to verify reports he had received of the flight of the Dervishes.

The following day I marched to the junction of the Kohr with the Bahr-el-Zaraf. In Justus Perthe's old map it is suggested that this Kohr is the outlet of the streams crossed by Lupton Bey in the hills east of Gondokoro. This cannot be so, as the natives at Bohr assured me that there was no water many days east; and if these streams are the feeders of this Kohr, they must, by the contour of the country, pass close to Bohr. Nor could the channel be dry, as the Kohr held plenty of water. Hence I am inclined to think that Lupton's streams either flow into the Nile south of Bohr, or pass down the other side of the watershed into the Pibro, the largest tributary of the Sobat. As Lupton went overland from Gondokoro to Bohr, and does not mark any significant feeder of the Nile, it is probable that the latter hypothesis is correct. That is, that they flow into the vast marsh recently located as the headwaters of the Pibro. If this is correct, the Kohr must also drain out of the Pibro marsh, in which case the country between the Sobat and the Bahr-el-Zaraf is an island.

The whole length of the bank was cut up with giraffe and elephant spoor, and as I could see for miles and miles in every direction and never saw one, I suppose they come great distances for water. The Kohr, though evidently from the exposed mud-flats of considerable width in the rains, was here not more than twenty yards wide and four feet deep; and the numbers of hippo and clouds of pelicans and cranes made sleep almost impossible.

The surrounding country assumed a little more character, long lines of palm-trees enlivening the awful monotony of that heart-breaking plain. The Nuer, though well-set-up, appear not to have the same unusual stature as the Dinkas; they wear circlets of cowries round their hair, which they grow long like a mop; the woolly buttons of the negroid, though visible from time to time up till now, have quite disappeared. Nothing impressed me so much as the vast flocks of birds. With five shots from a rifle I killed three geese, eight duck, and two pelicans, and that from camp: had I fired at some of the flocks I saw on the march I might have doubled the result.

Following the river, which has a very devious course, I saw large numbers of natives, and they were all very friendly, insisting on indulging in the trying practice of spitting in one's hand or on one's chest, which signifies intense respect; the Dinkas have the same objectionable custom.

For two days I saw numbers of natives with large herds of cattle and plenty of small palm-tree canoes, but a very limited supply of grain, and on the third day I came to a small Kohr with about a dozen large villages. Hundreds of natives came out to meet me, and I had some difficulty in driving them off, as, confident in their numbers, they were inclined to be boisterous.

A few miles further on, one of my Congolese soldiers, who, against all orders, lagged behind a few minutes, mysteriously disappeared, and an exhaustive search failed to find any trace either of him or of natives. The country was very open, and he was carrying a rifle, so they must have spirited him away very cleverly. From here to the mouth of the Zaraf there is only one village, so that for food I was entirely dependent on my rifle. At first there was no difficulty, as the river swarmed with hippo, and there were numbers of hartebeeste, Mrs. Gray's waterbuck, leucotis, reedbuck, waterbuck, and roan. A magnificent bull of the latter species I at first took to be a sable, owing to the extraordinary length of his horns, and with the cussedness of his kind he stood and watched us all pass at a distance of thirty yards. But for several days afterwards I had the greatest difficulty in obtaining meat, subsisting entirely on pelicans, one day being even reduced to marabout soup, and it was not till within thirty miles of the mouth that I again came into a game country, where the bush comes down to the river. Here I saw numerous giraffe, and one day marched for hours through small herds of cow elephant. It was curious that I saw nothing but bulls on the Nile swamps, while on the Zaraf there were huge numbers of breeding cows, and I only saw the spoor of a very few bulls, and those were mostly small. For days the muddy tide rolls slowly on between banks of sun-baked mud, unrelieved by swamps or vegetation. The flocks of birds no more break the depressing monotony, naught but great, loathly crocodiles, that slip without a sound into the turgid flow, bald-pated marabouts, and screaming kites. No sign of hope; a vast reserve for God's foulest creatures, and a fitting one. Ye gods, what a land! The old boyhood's desire to shriek and break something that invariably recurred on Sunday morning broke out afresh, and I felt that I was near that indefinable boundary beyond which is madness.

About thirty miles south of the Abiad an extensive Kohr, which was dry when I passed, flows into the Zaraf. Close by there is a small ridge a few feet above the level of the surrounding country; here I camped and saw a great variety of game. Four giraffe came and peered over a bush at me while I was having my bath, and thoroughly enjoyed the novel spectacle. They showed no inclination to move away, and I had a splendid chance of having a good look at them. The situation was quaint. It struck me as an admirable study for René Bull or Mr. Shepherd.

Soon after sunset two grand old lions commenced calling to one another, and I could hear them gradually approaching across the plain. They met about a mile from my camp, and after a round of hearty greetings, settled down into silence. As the wind was in their direction, I ordered all my boys up close to my tent and made two large fires. They still remained silent, so I knew that they were near; but after waiting some time I concluded that they did not mean business, and turned in. I had only just crept inside my mosquito-curtain when the sentry called out to me that they were in camp. I scrambled out, but was just too late! They had calmly strolled past in the full light of the fire, and I saw a tail disappear round the corner of a bush. Snatching up a blazing log, we dashed out, but, of course, never saw them, as there was too much bush; however, they were not in a hurry, and an occasional sniff showed that they were still inspecting, but they would not show in the firelight again, and, whenever I went out, sneaked off, till, getting tired of the game, they strolled away grumbling across the plain, and treated me to a farewell roar that will long linger in my ears as Savage Africa's farewell!

For on the morrow my troubles ended. We were plodding wearily along, wondering how to tide over the next four days, which I had estimated as the time necessary to reach the Sobat, when I saw in the far distance a curved pole swaying in the wind. For a long time it puzzled me; then I realized that it must be the mast of a boat, but dared not believe it, though certain that no palm-stem could swing to that angle. Presently I saw figures moving to and fro, and then one in white cloth, and soon we had evidently been noticed. A short council of war took place, and then an unmistakable Soudanese soldier came out to meet me, carefully inserting a cartridge in his rifle as he approached. Throwing my rifle on to my left shoulder, with a conciliatory and pacific smile I advanced with outstretched hand, and evidently convinced him that I was at least harmless, for with a 3 ft. 6 grin he drew his cartridge and shook the proffered hand with vigour. I learned that Captain Dunn, R.A.M.C., was up the Zaraf for a few days' shooting, and that he was expected back in camp in a few minutes.

I could scarcely believe that it was all over, that my troubles were ended! Those four days, that I imagined still remained, had been a nightmare to me. All my men were sick; the majority of them had to be pushed along at the point of the spear, to prevent them from lying down and giving up the struggle. There were no more hippo and very little game: all our grain had long been exhausted, and but two pipefuls of sour tobacco remained. And then, at a sudden bend of the river, all this nightmare was dispelled! It was over! From being so long without vegetables, my hands had begun to turn black, and the continual anxiety of the last month, day and night, had told its tale on my nerves. With what unspeakable content I sat down and waited for Dunn's arrival it would be impossible to describe. I had not to wait long, for a few minutes later Captain Dunn emerged from the bush. The following conversation ensued:—

Captain Dunn: "How do you do?"

I: "Oh, very fit, thanks; how are you? Had any sport?"

Dunn: "Oh, pretty fair, but there is nothing much here. Have a drink? You must be hungry; I'll hurry on lunch. Had any shooting? See any elephant?"

Then we washed, lunched, discussed the war, and eventually Dunn asked where the devil I had come from, saying that at first he had taken me for another confounded Frenchman, and was trying to hunt up some French. All this six hundred odd miles from anywhere in the uttermost end of the earth—the Nile swamps. Verily we are a strange people. How De Tonquedec, the Frenchman, laughed at the tale!

Then we dropped slowly down-stream in the boat, and in the light of the myriad stars discussed the strange world into which the Father Nile was slowly carrying me. A whirl of thoughts made sleep impossible, and as I pondered over many things I thought long on the Fashoda incident. In the course of a chequered career I have seen many unwholesome spots; but for a God-forsaken, dry-sucked, fly-blown wilderness, commend me to the Upper Nile; a desolation of desolations, an infernal region, a howling waste of weed, mosquitoes, flies, and fever, backed by a groaning waste of thorn and stones—waterless and waterlogged. I have passed through it, and have now no fear for the hereafter. And for this choice spot thousands of homes might have been wrecked, and the whole of civilization rushed into a cockpit of mutual slaughter. Let me recommend France to send the minister responsible for the Marchand expedition for a short sojourn in the land: no fitter punishment could be found. What a sensible idea it would be if ministers of rival nations, foreseeing a dispute, were to buy in a large store of choice wines and cigars, leave them at home, and decide to spend the time, till the dispute should be amicably settled, in the bone of contention.

CHAPTER XXII.

THE SOBAT TO CAIRO.

I awoke in the morning to find the gyassa[19] moored off the base camp of Major Peake's sudd-cutting expedition. Close by lay a trim, smart-looking gun-boat. AH was bustle and stir on board, and it was obvious that they were getting up steam. I drank in the sight, momentarily expecting to see it fade before my eyes, and to find myself once more wearily plodding through those maddening swamps. The transition from ceaseless anxiety and hungry misery to full-bellied content and tobacco-soothed repose had been so sudden; I was as a man who, after long time staggering in the dark, is suddenly thrust into the full glare of sunlight, and could hardly grasp that it was at last all over. Nothing to do but sit and be carried along towards clean shirts, collars, glasses, friends—all that makes life a thing of joy. How many people realize what all these things mean? How many people have ever caught the exquisite flavour of bread-and-butter? the restful luxury of clean linen? the hiss of Schweppe's? One must munch hippo-meat alone, save one's sole shirt from contact with water as from a pestilence lest it fall to pieces, and drink brackish mud for days, to realize all this. Sensations are but contrasts, and in the strong picture contrasts must be strong. We all have our allotted portions of black and white paint; how we lay it on is a question of temperament. One mixes the pigments carefully and paints his life an even grey. Another dashes in the light and shade with a palette-knife. Such an one is the wanderer in strange climes.

Captain Hayes-Sadler, the Governor of Fashoda, was in command of the gunboat, and kindly offered to take me down to Khartoum. They told me that Captain Gage, Dr. Milne, Commandant Henri, Lieut. Bertrand, and Lieut. de Tonquedec had all passed about four days before. De Tonquedec, a most delightful and entertaining man, was the last Frenchman to evacuate the Nile. He had been sent up to supplement the occupation begun by Marchand, and had done by far the finest work of all. No undertaking has ever been more absurdly overrated than Marchand's expedition to Fashoda. It was seized upon by the military party, and boomed to the echo as a set-off to the Dreyfusards. As a matter of fact, he never touched an inch of new country, but merely carried out successfully a very able bit of transport organization with everything in his favour—sound lieutenants, unlimited funds, and one of the best-equipped expeditions that ever set foot in Africa, supported by excellent native troops in his Senegalese. All the labour of the country was retained for him, and compulsion used where there was any difficulty in obtaining carriers. Hundreds of miles of navigable water took his goods almost to the Congo-Nile divide, and thence it was simply a question of moving from post to post till the watershed was crossed, and he

[19] Nile sailing-boat.

could place his boats on the navigable waters of the Nile. The only real difficulty, that of reoccupying the Bahr-el-Ghazal posts, had been already accomplished by the Belgians, whom the French kicked out. Once on the navigable Nile, they had but to go with the current till they reached Fashoda; the waters of the Bahr-el-Ghazal and Lake No happening to be comparatively free from sudd obstructions. They were strong enough to defy resistance at the hands of the Shilluks, who have nothing but ambatch canoes, and once entrenched at Fashoda they would have been poor creatures if they could not have beaten off a handful of Dervishes. As an able example of African transport it stands in the van of similar undertakings, but as a daring or dangerous feat it does not stand in the same class as Gage and Milne's descent of the Nile, or De Tonquedec's performance. His duty was a most hazardous one, as, with nothing but a handful of Senegalese and a sous-officier, he penetrated overland through the terrible Dinkas to the Upper Nile, and occupied Gaba Shambeh. Marchand is a world-word. When I arrived at Marseilles and inquired after De Tonquedec, nobody had ever heard of him.

Fortune favoured me when I started on the descent of the Nile. I knew that Khartoum had fallen, but nothing more. I had imagined that the Redjaf Dervishes were still occupying Bohr and the Upper Nile, and that the Khalifa was still at large on the Fashoda district of the Nile. But shortly after I started the Dervishes fled from Bohr before the advance of the Belgians, and while I was wearily plodding along, Sir Francis Wingate killed the Khalifa, and annihilated the Dervish army at Om Debrikat. The Abyssinians had finally retired from the Sobat, and by this happy combination of luck I had a clear route, though I did not know it, and my anxiety lest I should unexpectedly stroll into a Dervish or Abyssinian camp was considerable. Captain C. G. Steward, R.A., D.S.O., was in command of the base camp, and was sadly fretting at having had his orders to proceed to South Africa cancelled.

There were several gunboats employed on the sudd-cutting operations. Many of the Dervish prisoners had been sent south for the work, and were looking uncommonly well, which speaks volumes for the efficient transport system. The method of procedure was as follows:—The sudd, which at times is 30 ft. thick and sufficiently solid for the elephant to pass over, was cut into large blocks. A wire hawser was then attached, and the mass was pulled away by two steamers. When it floated clear it was cut up, and allowed to drift away with the stream. Many of these floating masses had accumulated opposite the base camp, and bade fair to form another sudd obstruction. In places where a portion was cut out, the water from the pressure caused by the pent-up river surged forth like a wave, bringing up water-logged canoes, bloated crocodiles, and various other unexpected apparitions. The fish rose in incredible swarms to these breathing-places. At one place the men took off their loose trousers, tied the ends, and baled out over four hundred large fish in less than an hour. The work was so hard that no one had time to get fever, and the health of the expedition had been excellent. After several months of desperate toil, the undertaking is now happily completed, and there is a clear riverway from Khartoum to Redjaf; and Fort Berkeley, the outpost of the Uganda Protectorate, instead of being nearly four months from Mombasa, is now within one month of Cairo. A weekly service of steamers should effectually prevent the sudd from re-forming. By judicious treatment, possibly on the lines that I have suggested in a subsequent chapter, the waterway might be made permanent, and its navigable facilities greatly improved. There is, undoubtedly, as pointed out by Gordon, the great difficulty of fuel, but probably in the near future oil will obviate this.

A few hours' steaming took us past the Sobat junction, where there is now but a small post of Soudanese under a native officer, and to the world-famed Fashoda. Here I handed over the first trans-continental post-bag, which I had brought through with me, to Captain Hayes-Sadler, who stamped the post-cards with the gorgeous red seal of Fashoda. Here, too, I received the first letter that had reached me for eighteen months, in which I learned that my oldest friend had fallen at Glencoe, at the very beginning of the war—to wit, Lieut. John Taylor, of the King's Royal Rifles. Curiously enough, the last letter that I had received on leaving civilization had been from him. Verily Africa is an accursed land. Many of the good friends whom I had met during our journey have already gone, and again and again I hear of fresh gaps in the chain.

I went and looked at the little French fort built of bricks that were taken from the ruined buildings of Fashoda. It is a very insignificant structure, and I should have been very sorry to be inside with a seven-pounder playing on the fort. There are still a few pawpaw trees planted by Marchand, the shrivelled fruit of which we took on board, and utilized as vegetable marrows. The Rek or King of the Shilluks lives near Fashoda; he is the descendant of a hundred kings, or something of that kind. I am not sure that his pedigree does not go back to the time of the Pharaohs. I had the pleasure of seeing his mop-headed Majesty ride past, attended by numerous courtiers. The Shilluk villages are about a mile away from the channel of the Nile, to avoid being flooded during the rains. The Dervishes kidnapped many thousands of the flower of their youth for military service. The Rek is a delightful old gentleman, and presented Captain Hayes-Sadler with an order not unconnected with crocodiles. The Shilluks are a most moral people, and live contentedly under an ample code of laws admirably suited to their social condition and mode of life. Any attempt to interfere with the belief and customs of such a people seems unwise. In view of the appalling misery and want at home, it is difficult to justify the large sums of money spent in upsetting the, in many cases, admirable existing state of society in Africa. Centuries have evolved a state of society most suitable to the surroundings and conditions of life. Why try to upset it? On the voyage down to Fashoda I saw many Shilluk fishermen wading in the shallow water, and endeavouring to spear fish. The spear used is of great length, and the pointed end is tied back to form a bow, by which means the point is induced to run along the top of, instead of sticking into, the mud. It seemed an unprofitable business, but, like most natives, they appear quite hopeful. They train their hair into gigantic mops, and dye it red with cow-dung. Many of the men have splendid features, and are extremely handsome. They hunt the hippo with great daring, pursuing the beasts in tiny ambatch canoes, which are often broken up by the infuriated bulls. They plunge a barbed spearhead into the skin, and then paddle ashore with the end of the attached rope; every one lends a hand, and the struggling brute is eventually hauled ashore and despatched.

North of Fashoda we saw many herds of waterbuck, hartebeeste (*Senegalensis?*), and roan grazing on the flats which lie between the marshy banks and the bush. One evening I was standing on deck, and noticed ahead of the steamer an animal sitting on the top of the bank watching us. As we passed alongside, it moved, and we saw that it was a splendid leopard. It strolled away quite unconcernedly, watching us round its shoulder, and slowly swishing its long tail to and fro; then it went and sat under a tree, whence it lazily regarded us till we were out of sight. At Djebel Ain we had to leave the gunboat, as the extraordinarily low Nile prevented steamers from crossing the ford, and we were forced to proceed to the next navigable stretch in a large gyassa or native boat. Djebel Ain is the end of the northern telegraph line, and I could at last wire and relieve the anxiety of my friends and relations. It was just fourteen months since I had left the end of the southern, or Mr. Rhodes's, section. Hayes-Sadler's Soudanese orderly, who looked after me, was a most delightful old gentleman. He could not quite understand me, and was continually demanding explanations of me: "Whence comes he, this man?" "Is he a soldier?" Hayes-Sadler explained that I was not, but was travelling for the pleasure of seeing the country. "Ah! you are a strange people, you English Effendis: how comes it that he wears not the moustache even as the other Effendis?" He was informed that I was of a slightly different ginss (tribe) to the others, and was quite satisfied at the explanation. After that he referred to me as "the Great White Effendi from the South." "He is a strange man, and verily comes from afar; yet I like that man—I look upon him as the apple of my eye," he informed his master. He was a splendid fellow, and I much enjoyed his polite and gentlemanly attentions after the dirty creatures with whom I had so long been in contact.

At the northern end of the ford we found the steamer waiting for us, and I first met Captain Gage and Dr. Milne, of whom I had heard so much. We were a numerous and jolly party on board, and with the exception of a morning's sand-grouse shooting, in the course of which eight guns bagged something over one hundred and fifty brace in a couple of hours, we arrived without further incident at Omdurman. Here we were bewildered with true Egyptian Army hospitality, and our time was spent in wildly flying from mess to mess.

The Sirdar gave a great dinner, at which he invited all the British and Egyptian commanding officers to meet the "tourists" from the south. Our simultaneous arrival was an extraordinary coincidence: Milne and Gage from the east, De Tonquedec, Bertrand, and Henri from the west, I from the south, and Hayes-Sadler from the north, and that in what was almost the uttermost end of the earth. After the dinner there was a great Soudanese dance; all the battalions broke up into their tribes and danced their tribal dances by torchlight: the spectacle was most weird. Sir Francis Wingate kindly asked me to stay with him at the Palace, which is already nearly completed.

The Soudan railway soon carried us down to Wady Halfa, thence a steamer to Assuan, and again the railway, and we once more stood in the roar of multitudes at the station in Cairo. And now it is all over. A few dangers avoided, a few difficulties overcome, many disappointments, many discomforts, and those glorious days of my life are already dim in the haze of the past. Here I stand, in the prosaic land of certainty and respectability! But far, far away, on those Urema flats, where the night-wind sighs to the grazing herds, my thoughts soar to the plaintive wail of the fish-eagle, and my heart throbs in unison with the vast sob-sob of the grandest of all created beasts, that mighty sound that is the very spirit of the veld, the great untrammelled field of Nature, far from all carking cares, pettiness, hypocrisy, and cant: where men may stretch themselves in generous emulation, find their apportioned level, and humbly worship at the great shrine of creation.

CHAPTER XXIII.

THE TRANS-CONTINENTAL RAILWAY.

Of the railway as far as Tanganyika I will say little, as I did not follow the route that has been selected. Its main scheme is already laid down.

But the route to be followed beyond the south end of Tanganyika is another matter, and one that will need much discussion.

Mr. Rhodes told me that he intended to take it across from Ujiji to the south end of the Victoria Nyanza, where presumably it would connect with Uganda and the railhead of the Mombasa railway at Ugowe Bay by steamers. Thence it would pass through the Lake Rudolph district and along the western base of the Abyssinian highlands to the Blue Nile. The arguments for this route are wood-supply, the supposed wealth and the supposed comparative salubrity of the countries traversed. Before offering my suggestion it win be advisable to inquire into the aims and objects of the Cape to Cairo railway. As far as I have seen, no individual of those who furiously denounce or optimistically uphold the project has ever grasped the real essential of such a connection; they have either sneered at it as a wild dream, or concluded that it is intended to run as an opposition means of transport to the ocean liners. This, of course, it will never do, nor yet is it a wild dream. The railway and the telegraph are to be the vertebra and spinal cord which will direct, consolidate, and give life to the numerous systems that will eventually connect the vast central highroad with the seas.

Building railways is a speculation, but one that up to date has proved very satisfactory in Africa. There is a saying that "trade follows the flag," but I think it would be more correct to say that "the flag reluctantly follows trade," and I know that "trade hurries along in front of the railway." The amount of small industries and unexpected traffic that crop up on the advent of the railway is wonderful; I suppose because there is no trade in virgin Africa strictly speaking, and the line wakes it to life by opening up new possibilities and ideas to the native.

Until the railway comes no one can judge of the capabilities of the country; it lies dormant. The appalling transport question, the inaccessibility, and the high cost of living weigh too heavily upon the land. The magic talisman, gold, alone will lead men far from touch with civilization.

But apart from all commercial considerations, on moral grounds alone the railway or a through connection is an immediate necessity—in fine, a duty inseparable from the responsibilities that we have assumed. Lord Salisbury, in speaking of the Uganda railway, recognizes this when he says: "That" (*i.e.* the completion of the railway) "means the subjugation, and therefore the civilization, of the country. Nothing but that railway could give us a grip of the country which would enable us to take the responsibility of such a vast extent of territory."

No other system than the through connection would have the same wide-reaching influence for the same expenditure; and the start that its completion will give to radiating enterprise is incredible. It is but the vertebral principle in Nature, and applies as surely to a continent as to a worm.

The moral obligation, I repeat, is immediate and inseparable from our bounden duty to develop the country, to "subjugate" and thereby "civilize" the natives, and thus justify our assumption of rights in Africa.

But I also feel convinced that commercially the enterprise is sound. It is, of course, well-nigh impossible to form estimates of returns in a country that is absolutely stagnant, reposing in abysmal depths of barbarism; but the soil is there, the climate is there, the wild luxuriance of Nature is there, the labour is there, and it needs but the magic touch of the railway to weld them all into one producing whole. It is experimental, I allow, but all enterprise is based on experiment. We are too apt to take things as they are, and not to inquire into what things were before, and by analogy what things similarly placed are likely to become. We reason—"Africa is a waste; India is a garden; and India will remain a garden, and Africa will remain a waste." The day is not far distant when Africa will pour out her wealth of cattle, grain, minerals, rubber, cotton, sugar, copra, spices, and a thousand other products to a grateful world. And over and above this, will give a home of comfort to millions of Europeans now suffocated by lack of breathing-space, and afford a field of investment for the pent-up millions of capital that are crowding returns down to an impossible minimum. What better advertisement to draw these millions into circulation than a railway opening up the unknown!

The extension of the railway northwards from Buluwayo through the Mafungabusi, Sengwe, and Sangati coal-fields and the Bembesi, Lower Sebakwe, and Lower Umfuli gold-finds is, of course, a commercial certainty; and the second section through the notoriously wealthy Lo Maghonda gold-field is equally assured. But beyond that, after it crosses the Zambesi at the Victoria Falls, all estimates must be mainly hypothetical. The Katanga copper-fields, the enormous quantities of rubber, which are now giving such magnificent returns to the few traders in the country, and the recently-reported gold-finds by Mr. George Grey augur well for the future; but I cannot agree with Mr. Rhodes in some of his contentions urged on an unresponsive Government as arguments for their support of the northern extension.

He urges the native labour question, hoping to bring large supplies of natives south to work in the mines. This wholesale exportation and importation of labour, I am sure, is most pernicious to the general welfare of the country. It raises the cost of labour throughout the districts affected, and, as I have attempted to show elsewhere, is bound eventually to bring all labour up to the highest rate that has been obtained.

Say, for the sake of argument, that there are ten thousand natives in Buluwayo working for £4 a month, and ten thousand natives are induced to come south from

Tanganyika, having contracted to work for so many months at 10s. a month. The Tanganyika natives will discover the current rates at Buluwayo, and will think that they have been swindled; if they do not break out into open revolt, they will return to their homes and spread the news, thereby prevent others from coming south at the 10s. figure, and raise the price of labour in their country far above its original level of 3s. a month. More may be induced to go at, say 30s. a month, and thus by degrees the price of labour throughout Africa south of Tanganyika will rise to £4. The original Buluwayo native will never work for less than the £4, and if crowded out by the imported natives, will form a most turbulent element in the country, and still the rate will go on rising. Exactly this process is going on now, but gradually, owing to the number of natives who come south being insignificant compared to what it would be with the facilities offered by a railway.

If the natives can be induced to settle, well and good. But it is not right that other districts should be made to pay for the administrative follies of districts which have not tackled the native question in the beginning. But more than this, the natives whom Mr. Rhodes wishes to bring to the mines do not exist; the country between the Zambesi and, Tanganyika is not densely populated as a whole, and even now the labour supply is not adequate to the demand on the Tanganyika plateau.

Again, he urges that the line will benefit the British Central Africa Protectorate by affording a means of transport of greater regularity and efficiency than the present system of river transport. This will never be. With organization and concentration the river route to Nyassaland will have no equal in South Africa for cheapness. From Chickwawa to Chinde at the mouth of the Zambesi there is an uninterrupted waterway of two hundred and fifty miles. It is obvious that a railway, two thousand miles long, with considerable haulage to the railway, can never compete with a waterway of two hundred and fifty miles. But he touches the right note again when he points out the necessity for providing against a repetition of the horrors of the Matabele rebellion with the turbulent tribes north of the Zambesi. The Angoni may yet, and the Awemba certainly will, prove a most turbulent element in society in Northern Rhodesia.

Such are roughly the pros and cons of the question of the advisability of a through connection.

From Cape Town to Buluwayo, a distance of one thousand three hundred and sixty miles, the railway is completed, and already giving handsome returns for the capital invested. From Buluwayo there will be a line passing through Gwelo to Salisbury to connect the Beira line, which, owing to its comparatively short mileage, will tap much of the commerce of Rhodesia.

The main line will branch north-west from Buluwayo, pass through the district of the Guay river, and cross the Zambesi at the Victoria Falls, where the curious formation will offer but slight difficulty to the construction of a bridge. Thence it will pass north to a point near Sitanda on the Upper Kafukwe, and east along the Congo-Zambesi watershed to a point near the Loangwa river, then again north along the watershed till it crosses the Chambesi, and from there to Kituta at the south end of Lake Tanganyika.

Thus far is a practical certainty of the next few years, the distance yet to be spanned amounting to eight hundred and sixty miles.

Beyond Kituta there is room for discussion. A splendid waterway of four hundred miles leads to the mouth of the Rusisi river, which might be navigated for thirty miles. This, however, might be rendered inadmissible by the existence of a bar which I consider probable, in which case the lake steamer could not navigate the river, as flat-bottomed boats cannot weather the seas on these lakes. Usambora would be the most suitable port at the north end, and from here a light railway could be laid for sixty miles along the flat bottom of the Rusisi valley with no more difficulty than the Soudan railway was laid.

From this point to Lake Kivu, which would be best touched at the loch immediately to the west of Ishangi, the distance is thirty miles, and a rise in level of 2,000 ft. has to be negotiated. But the configuration of the eastern valley, which I have mentioned as the probable old course of the Rusisi, would to a certain extent facilitate the sudden rise.

From this point to the bay at the north-eastern corner of the lake there is an excellent waterway of sixty miles. From this bay a light railway would pass through the neck between Mounts Götzen and Eyres, having to rise a further 2,000 ft. to the highest point that the line would attain to throughout its entire length. Thence by easy gradients it would drop to the Albert Edward Plains, which lie 3,000 ft. below the crest of the pass. Although this drop takes place in a distance of twenty miles, the contours of the country offer every facility. The line would then pass along under the eastern wall of the trough up the eastern side of the Albert Edward, across the narrow neck of Lake Ruisamba, and thence to Fort Gerry, or probably round the west of Ruwenzori and down the Semliki valley to the Albert Lake. It will be seen that I ignore the waterway afforded by the Albert Edward, although seventy-five miles long. I will explain my reasons subsequently. The objection to utilizing the Semliki valley is that, owing to the supineness of the British Government, it is in the Congo territory. Why we should have deviated from our policy of insisting on our rights in the Nile valley at this point I never could imagine, unless the ministers or delegates responsible were ignorant of the fact that the Semliki is as much a portion of the Nile as is the Bahr-el-Djebel. It is the obvious route for the railway, being the course of the huge rift valley that contains all these lakes, and although there is a drop of 1,500 ft. before the level of the Albert Lake is reached, it has immense advantages over the Fort Gerry route. Passing by Fort Gerry, the line would have to climb 2,000 ft. and then descend 3,000 ft. down the precipitous face that hems in the Semliki valley north-east of Ruwenzori proper. Another most important point in favour of the Semliki valley is that it is densely wooded, while to the east there is very little wood.

From the south end of Lake Albert to Dufilé at the head of the rapids there is a waterway of two hundred miles. From Dufilé to Redjaf the river is broken and rendered unnavigable by about one hundred miles of shallows and rapids. This stretch would have to be spanned by another light railway which would branch and tap the Shuli country to the east. Finally from Redjaf there is an uninterrupted waterway of one thousand miles to Khartoum, whence there is rail and steamer communication with Cairo. As an alternative to this, the Dufilé-Redjaf line could be continued at very trifling cost across country to the Sobat Junction, which would perhaps be necessary to avoid the navigation and fuel difficulties of the Bahr-el-Djebel waterway. The line could be carried slightly to the east of my route through the swamps, and the hard, flat, well-wooded bush country presents no difficulties to railway construction. I was debarred from passing that way by the dearth of water consequent on the extraordinary drought. Such is the route that appears to me to have undoubted advantages. When once Kituta is reached, now merely a matter of a few years, a further construction of four hundred and ten miles of railway will render steam communication between the Cape and Cairo an accomplished fact. The scarcity of fuel on this route has been suggested as a difficulty. I will now return once more to Kituta, and point out the fuel centres on the line I have suggested.

There are ample forests on both shores of Tanganyika, which will afford an inexhaustible supply of fuel for ages. By utilizing the waterway both shores are tapped, and the well-nigh insurmountable obstacles to railway construction offered by the precipitous mountains that hem in the lake are turned.

From Tanganyika to Kivu there are no difficulties, with the exception of the rise that I have mentioned just south of the Kivu Lake. Again, by utilizing the Kivu Lake enormous difficulties are avoided in the impossible country that surrounds the lake. The hills are very high, very steep, very numerous, very erratic, and often disconnected by ridges or any gradients that would assist construction. Immediately north of the lake the country again becomes easy, and another inexhaustible supply of fuel is found on the volcanoes, while the country is extremely rich, and wonderfully healthy, and carries the densest population that I have seen in Africa.

The Rutchuru valley offers no difficulties, and another fuel country is found at the south-eastern corner of the Albert Edward Lake, while the country along the eastern side to Katwe is so easy and flat that it would probably be worth while to ignore the waterway as I have already indicated.

Of the Semliki valley I can only speak from observation of the northern half, which is as flat as a billiard-table; but as the drop is not very considerable, the southern half should present no serious obstacle, while it offers a magnificent fuel supply. The Semliki is a well-defined river, and could be easily bridged. Thus the whole course is free of natural obstacles, sufficiently provided with fuel, supplies, and labour, and, over and above, being direct, taps all these lakes, which in themselves are the foci of the trade of large districts. By adopting this course, in an incredibly short space of time, and at a figure many millions short of the estimated cost of a through line, the first and most important objects of the connection will be attained: namely, the consolidation of our influence—the strengthening of the Administration, and thus the lessening of the numbers of soldiers necessary to ensure order—immense cheapening of communication and of the cost of telegraph up-keep. Even were the through railway cheaper, this combination of rail and steamboat will be sufficient to feel the pulse of the country, and if the results justify the further expenditure, the line can easily be completed, while its main objects have been attained years earlier than would otherwise be possible. As all porterage has to be done by natives in Central Africa, a railway is even more necessary than where wagon transport is available. Owing to the impossibility of bringing anything heavy into the country, many industries are debarred even from being experimented upon. There is still a considerable amount of ivory in native hands throughout the lake region, and the amount of rubber is stupendous; both these products will bear heavy transport charges, and are in themselves sufficient to make a beginning until a brisk trade has been stimulated in other products.[20]

These lakes, and the vast rift valley that contains them, are the natural highway which is fed by both sides of the continent. It must be remembered that Africa differs from other continents in the paucity of its outlets and means of outlet; no continent is so poorly endowed with harbours and navigable rivers for its size, excepting, perhaps, Australia, which is the antithesis of Africa in that its wealth lies along the coasts, while the centre is the pearl of Africa. Hence any route which offers natural advantages is of supreme importance.

The chief argument against this combination of rail and boat is the amount of handling that it will entail. I believe this is of no significance:—

First, because, as I have pointed out, there will be no through traffic. All the traffic will be local, in that it will be destined to feed the nearest radius that leads to the coast, or for the interchange of local produce.

Secondly, because of the immense difference in the capital to be sunk, and the cheapness of water transport compared to rail transport.

Thirdly, because of the large area tapped. Much of the freight would have to be brought in either case by water to the railway, and might as well be brought to one point as to another.

Fourthly, because labour is so plentiful, and as yet so ridiculously cheap that the cost would be very trifling.

Trade is allowedly conservative, but once it has been directed into a certain channel it needs a huge effort to divert it. Let us, then, establish a route as speedily as possible.

Finally, I wish I could induce some of the numerous philanthropists at home to see that by aiding enterprise of this description they strike at the very root of the slave trade, Belgian atrocities, cannibal raids, and the numerous other African diversions; and that in a few years they will assist to educate, elevate, civilize, and perhaps

---

[20] *E.g.* the Congo railway.

eventually to Christianize, the African natives more effectually than would be done in centuries by spasmodic mission work.

CHAPTER XXIV.

NATIVE QUESTIONS.

The enormous extent of Africa, and the consequent infinity of tribes widely divergent in origin, character, and habits, make it almost impossible to generalize on this most abstruse subject.

Still some principles may be laid down for the great negroid population of Africa which, as far as my experience goes, apply in most instances. I will ignore platitudes as to the equality of men irrespective of colour and progress, and take as an hypothesis what is patent to all who have observed the African native, that he is fundamentally inferior in mental development and ethical possibilities (call it soul if you will) to the white man.

He approaches everything from an entirely different standpoint to us. What that standpoint is, what his point of view is, by what mental refraction things are distorted to his receptive faculty, I cannot pretend to explain. I have failed to find any one who could. But the fact remains, that if a native is told to do anything, and it is within the bounds of diabolical ingenuity to do it wrong, he will do it wrong; and if he cannot do it wrong, he will not do it right. I can but suggest as an explanation that he is left-minded as he is generally left-handed. The following anecdotes will illustrate my meaning. They all came under my personal observation, and tend to show the impossibility of following a native's reasoning, if he does reason.

When I engaged the Watonga on Lake Nyassa, I informed them of all the salient features that they would see on the road, such as lakes, mountains that spat fire, mountains so high that the water became as stones, etc. As we passed each of these features I reminded them of what I had said, showing them that I had not lied, as they had imagined before starting. When the journey was nearly finished, I pointed out that everything had appeared as I had said, and asked them what they thought of it. Then spake the headman: "Lord, you are a wonderful lord. You told us of the four lakes, and how many days' journey it would take to pass them; you told us of the smoking mountains and the great mountains of the white water; of the elephants and the meat with necks like trees (giraffe); yet you have not been there before, as we well know. And as you would not have us, your servants, think you a liar, *you put them there.*"

Again, I had told them of the size of the white man's houses; and when we arrived at Khartoum I showed them the palace as an example. They smiled and said: "Yes, it is very wonderful; but that is no house, *it has been dug out of a hill.*"

When travelling up the Zambesi, I gave Sharp's Somali boy a Van Houten's cocoa-tin to open, telling him to make cocoa. He disappeared for a time, and returned with a tin-opener with which he proceeded to tear off the bottom of the tin. Having successfully accomplished this, he thrust a spoon in and pushed the lid off, with the result that all the cocoa fell out on to the ground. Then he looked at me with an expression of supreme contempt, as though to say: "I always thought the white men fools, but not quite such fools as to make a thing like that." He must have opened hundreds of tins before, both hermetically sealed ones and ordinary ones. Yet to this day he thinks me an idiot.

The small boy who was responsible for arranging my tent had been carefully instructed always to place my belongings in a certain order. Occasionally, through his having put my bed on an uneven piece of ground, I would tell him to change it to the other side, which meant reversing my boxes and table to bring them into the correct relative position. In doing this he was never satisfied till he had also reversed the square mat, and when I laughed at him for doing so he left the mat and put the boxes wrong, nor could he put them right till he had reversed the mat. This was most curious, and I could never grasp to my satisfaction what his train of reasoning was.

One day, when hauling a canoe up a very shallow tributary of the Nile, one of my boys, finding that he could not pull to advantage from the bed of the river, climbed inside and made superhuman efforts to drag it along. He quite failed to see the cause of my laughter, sulked, and refused to pull any more.

The answers of some natives who had been taken to England after a trip across Africa were instructive as showing the trend of a negro's mind. Questioned as to what appeared most wonderful to them, one replied: "The white man, when he wants anything, goes to the wall; then he obtains what he requires, light, drink, servants—in fact, everything." Another replied: "The selling-houses with rows and rows of meat, countless sheep and lumps of meat." And the third replied: "The little houses that run about the roads with horses." Of all the marvellous sights of civilization, three impressions stuck—bells, butchers' shops, and omnibuses. These few instances are sufficient to indicate in what unexpected channels the native's thoughts flow. His character is made up of contending elements, and is best explained by saying that he has no character at all. It is a blend of the child and the beast of the field. He is swayed by every wind that blows, yet may seize upon an idea and stick to it with remarkable tenacity, in spite of the most cogent arguments to and obvious advantages involved in the contrary.

He is as imitative as a monkey, and consequently is very apt at picking up crafts, gestures, and styles that are new to him, but is so bound down by tradition and custom that he never applies the improved methods of the white man to anything that he is accustomed to do in his own way.

His mind is so inactive and blank that he can carry for miles loads that he cannot pick up from the ground, by merely sinking his entity. He becomes mentally torpid, with the result that the effort is solely physical. A white man, though physically stronger, would fret himself into a state of utter fatigue in a quarter of the time.

In trifles he is impatient, yet will argue a question for a week till it is threshed out to the bitter end, and will accomplish with unceasing thoroughness a piece of carving or basket-work that takes months to perfect.

In debate he is extremely subtle, and in politics differs materially from the white man in that he can hold his tongue. On principle he never tells the truth, and consequently never expects to hear it. He is extremely suspicious, and his maxim is, "Mistrust every one." Yet a judicious laugh will inspire him with complete confidence. "When in doubt laugh," I have found a safe maxim in dealing with natives, and a well-timed laugh saved many ugly situations during our sojourn in the land.

He hates to be hurried; with him there is no idea of time. "Do not the days succeed one another?—then why hurry?" is his idea. He cannot understand at all the hurrying man.

His stage of evolution, which is but slightly superior to the lower animals, is the explanation of many of the seemingly inexplicable traits in his character, traits which are conspicuous in the bees and ants, and in varying degrees remarkable in other animals that have attained to some more or less complete communism. For instance, a native will share as a matter of course the last bite with any one of the same clan (a relationship that is expressed by the word "ndugu"), yet he will watch starve with the most perfect equanimity another native who, even though of the same tribe, does not come within that mystic denomination. Should, however, even his "ndugu" become very sick or otherwise incapable of taking his part in the battle of life, he is left to take care of himself as best he can, and everything is devoted to the sustenance of those who are still capable. In this respect the native is inferior to the elephant, who will at considerable risk to themselves endeavour to assist a wounded comrade from the field of battle. The fundamental basis of native society is local communism and disregard for all outside that commune; though at times the various communes that constitute a tribe will combine for some object of equal benefit to all. The rarity, however, of this combination for a purpose is what constitutes the essential weakness of all African peoples. The old Zulu *régime*, and the till recently remarkable cohesion of the Ruanda people, are the conspicuous exceptions, and are proof of what possibilities lie to the hand of dusky Napoleons in Africa. The Arabs fully realized and availed themselves of this inherent lack of combination amongst the tribes. The success of their policy of disintegration should serve as a useful example for our African statesmen. Many of our failures are to be attributed to our not having grasped the dominant fact that every chief who is left in possession of his power is a source of strength to ourselves, to be used as a counterpoise to every other chief similarly placed. It stands to reason that several definite units—to wit, clans consolidated under the ægis of responsible men— can be more easily brought to focus than a heterogeneous mass, incomplete in itself, and which will be bound to gravitate to any adventurer who may acquire a temporary hearing. The great mass, strangled as it is by innate superstition, hidebound by tradition, and so situated as to be incapable of enlightenment other than the most microscopically gradual, can never be brought thoroughly under white rule. It must be ruled by its constituted and therefore accepted chiefs, who alone can be made responsible to the Administration. How to bring these chiefs under our influence without lessening their local prestige, and how to infuse the necessary element of competition *inter se*, are the problems the solution of which will materially facilitate the thorny path of African administration. A curious quality, and one in some degree referable to this low stage of evolution, is their inability to grasp the idea of a natural death. If a man's head is smashed, they can associate the obvious cause and effect, but any death less easily explained is attributed to some such factor as the "evil eye." This is invariable with the Soudanese tribes, and is a source of unending trouble to the officers in command of Soudanese troops. Again, the utter disregard for the future would argue a social stage inferior to the bees. No native can be induced to look to the morrow. Over and over again we served out rations to our men, for, say, a week, and informed them that by no possible means could they obtain food during that week; yet on every occasion they ate it all the first day or threw away what they could not eat, trusting, in their characteristic optimism, that something would turn up. Nor do they ever learn from experience. Every year that the rains fail or their crops are for some reason deficient, they are caught and philosophically starve, yet two days more of work would place them beyond all possibility of famine.

Another very essential factor has to be taken into consideration in an endeavour to grasp the native character. That is the lack of the two sentiments, gratitude and pity, which enter so largely into the workings of the European mind. As far as I am aware, in all the Bantu dialects there is no word that remotely suggested either of these virtues. In the Swahili tongue the word asanti (thank you) has been borrowed from another language for the benefit of the mixed Hindu-Persian and Arab elements who constitute Swahili society. A few anecdotes will exemplify this lack.

I was paddling across the Shiré river to Chiromo, when a native asked me to give him a lift across. I did so, and no sooner had he landed, than he asked me for a present for having done so.

Another boy, who had been bitten by a deadly snake, came to me for treatment. With considerable difficulty, and the expenditure of my last bottle of whisky, I saved his life. Having completely recovered, he helped himself to such of my movables as he could conveniently annex, and absconded.

Their lack of the sense of pity is shown in their brutal treatment of animals, of the sick, and of those who are too old to work. Even the Portuguese or Spanish treatment of animals is Christian compared to a native's method. They are impervious to the sufferings of others, and rather regard them as a joke. On one occasion several boys were standing under a tree, when a snake dropped from a branch, and bit one of the boys on the cheek, causing the most intense pain which ended only in death. The other boys thought it great fun, and were distorted with laughter at the agonized convulsions of the unfortunate.

A further proof of the lack of these senses is their utter inability to understand them in others.

An amusing case that came to my notice is a proof in point. An official had engaged a cook at 10s. a month, who for three months gave complete satisfaction. At the end of that time he called the native before him, and explained that as he had done his work so well, his wages would be raised to 15s. a month. The cook appeared to be rather puzzled, and went away. The following morning he returned and demanded 15s., arguing that he was the same now as he had been before and that therefore he ought to have 5s. more for each of the three months which he had spent in his service. From that day he became useless, and eventually left, firm in the conviction that he had been swindled out of 15s.

Another man of my acquaintance saved a small child from a crocodile. The child's hand was badly torn, but after careful tending, with the help of a doctor brought at considerable expense from the nearest station, he was sent home completely cured. Thereupon the child's father and mother arrived on the scene, and demanded a large present because the child had been kept so long.

Gratitude or pity in others they attribute to fear, or the desire to get the better of them. They look upon kindness as a thing suspicious, a move to cloak some ulterior design. Nor can they understand leniency, but consider it weakness. They themselves are either abject grovellers or blustering bullies. The Arab understands this, and rules with a rod of iron; the natural result of which is that natives prefer Arab service to British, the philanthropy of which they do not understand, and either mistrust or despise. Strict justice they do understand; but it must be based on the "eye for an eye, tooth for a tooth" school. The unreasoning philanthropy which is the latest phase of our "unctuous rectitude" is as pearls before swine, and, as with other nations, so with natives, merely renders us objects of pity.

I trust that these few points are sufficient to indicate the difficulties that lie before the student of native character. Yet in spite of this, there exists a certain section of the community at home who presume to dictate the methods to be adopted in dealing with natives. Strong in their magnificent ignorance of the local requirements, racial characteristics, and the factors that make society, men are found who will condemn such acts as the desecration of the Mahdi's tomb. These individuals, unless specialists, would never dream of discoursing on the treatment of horses, spectral analysis, or any other subject requiring special study, yet, with a confidence sublime in its assurance, they will launch forth into the still more abstruse subject of native administration. Nothing is more to be deprecated than this meddling on the part of the stay-at-homes, in the methods adopted by the men specially selected to undertake the difficult task of ruling these peoples. We select the men whom we think most capable of promoting the prosperity of the countries in question, and instead of allowing them to find out by experience the methods most productive of good, we cramp their efforts by well-intentioned but fatal limitations on points of which we are necessarily profoundly ignorant. If, as a section of the press would lead us to believe, we are compelled to assume that every man who leaves this country *ipso facto* becomes an abandoned ruffian, the sooner we shut up our branch shops, and retain our servants under the watchful eye of the man in blue, the better for all concerned. But if, on the other hand, we are confident that we are promoting the welfare of the community at large by assuming these responsibilities, and believe that we can find reliable men to carry on the work, the least that we can do is to allow those men to profit by and regulate their methods on the experience that they must necessarily acquire, and which is necessarily denied to us. The fact that the method most productive of good in Africa is not the same as the method most productive of good at home is no evidence of the inadvisability of its adoption. A thousand and one factors known only to the man on the spot must be assumed. In the halcyon days that are no doubt coming, no one will be allowed to hold an important position in the Government who has not gone through the mill of travel. "What do they know of England who only England know?" What indeed! In an empire like ours, of which the British isles are already but the viscera, it is inconceivable that men who are largely responsible for the administration of that empire should display the gaping ignorance of the elements of which it is composed, which daily passes without comment. This external interference is of paramount importance. It is crushing all our African ventures, and with the rapidly-increasing facility of communication attendant on telegraphic construction, its effect is becoming daily more conspicuous. In the old days men were bound to act on their own initiative; now the tendency is to shirk responsibility by appealing to headquarters. This paralyzes decisive action, which alone is effective in dealing with natives. A general outline of policy should be adopted on the recommendation of the best available experts, but every possible detail should be left to the discretion of the local official. Many of the ridiculous restrictions that are made are nothing short of insults to the men affected by them. Imagine placing one man in charge of a district such as Toro—Toro is larger than Ireland, and consequently the position is one of enormous responsibility—and telling that man that he must not give more than twenty-five lashes to a native. It is grotesque. Twenty-five lashes would kill an average Toro native, but a hundred lashes barely make the dust fly off a Manyema porter. Surely details of this description should be left to the judgment of the man who can weigh the facts of the case.

But few people at home realize what an alarming and ever-growing difficulty has to be faced in the African native problem. It is a difficulty that is unique in the progress of the world. In Australia, Tasmania, New Zealand (in a minor degree), and America the aborigine has faded out of existence before the irresistible and to him insufferable advance of the white man. But not so the African, who in this sense differs entirely from other savages. Under the beneficent rule of the white man he thrives like weeds in a hot-house. Originally, the two great checks on population were smallpox and internecine strife. These have been minimized by the advent of white rule, and the resulting rate of increase is one to stagger the statistician. The stately Maori, the wild Australian, the chivalrous Tasmanian, and the grim Redskin have given up the struggle, and are fast going the way of the mammoth and the dodo, but in white-teethed content the negro smiles and breeds apace, mildly contemptuous of the mad Englishman who does so much for him and expects so little in return. What is to be done with this ever-increasing mass of inertia? We have undertaken his education and advancement. When we undertake the education of a child or beast we make them work, realizing that work is the sole road to advancement. But when we undertake the education of a negro, who, as I have endeavoured to show, is a blend of the two, we say, "Dear coloured man, thou elect of Exeter Hall, chosen of the negrophil, darling of the unthinking philanthropist, wilt thou deign to put thy hand to the plough, or dost prefer to smoke and tipple in undisturbed content? We, the white men, whom thy conscience wrongly judges to be thy superiors, will arrange thy affairs of state. Sleep on, thou ebony idol of a jaded civilization, maybe anon thou wilt sing 'Onward, Christian Soldiers!'"

A good sound system of compulsory labour would do more to raise the native in five years than all the millions that have been sunk in missionary efforts for the last fifty; but at the very sound of "compulsory labour," the whole of stay-at-home England stops its ears, and yells, "Slavery!" and not knowing what "slavery" is, yells "Slavery!" again, nor ever looks at home nor realizes that we are all slaves. Have we not compulsory education, taxes, poor-rates, compulsory this and compulsory that, with "jail" as the alternative? Nor are we paid by the State for being educated. Then let the native be compelled to work so many months in the year at a fixed and reasonable rate, and call it compulsory education. Under such a title, surely the most delicate British conscience may be at rest. Thereby the native will be morally and physically improved; he will acquire tastes and wants which will increase the trade of the country; he will learn to know the white man and his ways, and will, by providing a plentiful supply of labour, counterbalance the physical disadvantages under which the greater part of Africa labours, and thus ensure the future prosperity of the land, whereby, with the attendant security of tenure and of the rights of the individual, he will have that chance of progressive evolution which centuries of strife and bloodshed have denied him. Inducements might be offered to chiefs to make plantations of wheat, rice, coffee, and other suitable products, by exempting a number of their men, proportionate to the area cultivated, from the annual educational course.

This perpetual wail of "slavery," which is always raised to combat legitimate and reasonable discussion, is due to ignorance, to the inability to discriminate between the status of slavery and slave-raiding. Slave-raiding was a curse beyond belief, and is now, happily, to all intents a nightmare of the past, but the status of slavery is still widespread, and with many peoples is necessary and beneficent. The line between slavery and freedom is a very nice distinction. We can all be called upon to fight or to give up our goods for the common weal, or, as we phrase it, for the cause of progress. Then why should not other peoples be called upon to work for the cause of progress? There is a sound maxim in the progress of the world: "What cannot be utilized must be eliminated." And drivel as we will for a while, the time will come when the negro must bow to this as to the inevitable. Why, because he is black and is supposed to possess a soul, we should consider him, on account of that combination, exempt, is difficult to understand, when a little firmness would transform him from a useless and dangerous brute into a source of benefit to the country and of satisfaction to himself.

I invariably had trouble with my natives when they were not occupied. The native has no means of amusing himself, nor idea of making occupation, and consequently, like women similarly situated, has recourse to chatter and the hatching of mischief. Work, I am convinced, is the keynote to the betterment of the African; and he will not work for the asking. No amount of example will assist him. What are the results of several hundred years' communication with the Portuguese? A few natives wear hats, and the women's morals have deteriorated. Africa labours under many disadvantages—remoteness from markets, inaccessibility, dearth of waterways, and in parts a pestilential climate; but it has one great advantage in an inexhaustible supply of potential labour, which, if properly handled, should place it on terms of equality with countries more favourably endowed by Nature.

The first essential in opening up new country in Africa is for the Administration to fix a rate of pay, and to make that rate a low one. If it is left to competition the rate is bound to be forced up by contending trading companies. The first profits from new country are usually large, and the difficulty of obtaining labour very great before the native has gained confidence. Hence the rate dependent on competition is a fictitious one, and cannot be sustained under the conditions that will prevail subsequent to the harvesting of the first-fruits of the land. But it will be well-nigh impossible ever to lower the rate to meet diminishing profits. At first sight this seems severe on the native, but in reality it is not so. As he is, he has every necessary of life, and everything that we give him is a luxury. The taste for pay is a cultivated taste, and three shillings really gives him as much satisfaction as three pounds. The native on the Tanganyika plateau works more cheerfully for his three shillings a month than the Rhodesian native does for his two pounds, and yet beads and cloth are much more costly on the plateau than in Rhodesia. There is a short-sighted inclination amongst British officials to give the native more than he requires or even asks for, presumably simply because he is a native.

At one station I required a certain amount of labour, and as there was no precedent to go upon, we called up some of the local natives, and asked them for what sum they would be willing to do the work in question. They mentioned a figure which they evidently considered preposterous, but which, as a matter of fact, was very small. The official thereupon told them that they would get more. This naturally aroused their suspicions, and some of those who had at first been willing failed to turn up. It must always be remembered that the untutored native will work as readily for three shillings as he will for three pounds; and if he does not want to work, he will not do so for thirty pounds. The actual rate of pay carries no weight with him. It is merely a matter of whether he is in the mood. But, of course, if he has once received a certain figure he will never work for less, even if he is in the mood to do so. Were he to do so he would imagine that he had been swindled.

The Portuguese, for the simple reason that they themselves practically never pay their natives at all, failed to grasp the necessity of controlling the labour market in the Beira district, with the result that the wages of an ordinary carrier or labourer are one pound a month, and of an untrained house-boy from two pounds to three pounds a month. These sums were gladly paid in the original days of boom and prosperity, but in these days of comparative gloom they are feeling the pinch. Large supplies of labour are brought down from the Zambesi to minimize the difficulty, but with the sole result that this fictitious rate is spread to the regions that are being tapped when the labourers return to their homes. By this means the evil is gradually working up the Shiré river to British Central Africa. Rhodesia has, to a considerable extent, blighted her prospects by not grappling with the subject, in spite of the hysteria of those whose knowledge of natives, their ways, and of the best methods of dealing with them appears to be derived from week-end studies of the becollared fraternity who affect Margate and Brighton sands.

The name of Englishman is held high throughout Africa, and the Union Jack is the surest passport in the land. Let this be the answer to those who casually assume that because a man goes to Africa he necessarily becomes a brute, no matter what his social status, education, or previous mental condition. It is obviously to the interest of men who live as an infinitesimal minority amongst hordes of savages, to find out what means are most conducive to the proper control of those hordes, and to inspire them with that respect and assurance of justice, without which they will be in continual revolt, as has been the case with the natives of the Upper Congo since the substitution of Belgian and polyglot officials for the original staff of British and Americans. However, the damage is done, and I think the proposed remedy of importing "the teeming millions" of Lake Tanganyika (who, by the way, do not exist) a false and dangerous one. The imported natives, finding that they obtain less pay than the natives of the country, although they have come far from their own homes, break out in discontent, and, maybe, open revolt (as did the Angoni police, recruited and sent to Salisbury by Major Harding, C.M.G.), and when they return home spread the feeling of dissatisfaction far and wide. The Yaos who were sent to Mauritius were even a greater failure, and cannot but have the most pernicious influence on their return. Uganda has been similarly doomed as an agricultural country by the chaotic incompetence that supervened after the Lugard *régime*. British Central Africa alone of the young African States has steered a straight course through the stormy seas of labour questions. But British Central Africa has profited by its hitherto comparative insignificance, and, under the able guidance of Sir Harry Johnston, has found the right channel unruffled by the whirlwinds of adverse criticism, which have played with such unceasing ferocity upon Rhodesia. It seems hardly reasonable that one district should be called upon to pay for the mistakes made in another.

The establishment of native locations on a large scale in the districts that require labour will tend to ameliorate the labour scarcity and maintain wages at a reasonable level. On farms and plantations there is comparatively little difficulty in obtaining labour. The native is useless without his women-folk, but is easily induced to settle down in any spot required, if allotted so much land and allowed to bring his family, while at the same time a fillip is given to production when he finds that his women can add to his income by cultivating the various requirements of the white man.

To summarize; the questions of paramount importance are:—

1. *To make the Administration the sole labour agents.*

By this means the supply of labour can be evenly distributed through the year, or according to the country's requirements. The rate of pay can be fixed and maintained at a rational level. Undesirable people can be prevented from obtaining labour, and thereby adversely influencing the native. The native is protected against the employer, and guaranteed proper treatment by knowing that he has a court of appeal where he can obtain information and air his grievances.

2. *To rule through the chiefs, and refrain from injuring their prestige.*

Centuries cannot give the white man the power over the individual native that the recognized chief holds without question. The substitution of one chief for another is of no use unless the original chief is killed and his rightful heir instated. These matters are religion with natives. "Once a chief always a chief, even when dead," is their belief. To get a grip on an important chief and yet leave him his power is a difficult matter; and as these preliminary questions will affect the whole future of the country, the first step in administration should be entrusted to really able men, and not, as is too often the case, to any trader, hunter, or out-of-a-job who happens to be in the neighbourhood and to know a little of the language. By leaving the chiefs their power, administration is greatly facilitated by the resulting concentration of responsibility. All the petty questions and difficulties (which are often such dangerous ground, until the local customs are fully understood) devolve on the chief, and if there is any serious trouble the responsibility can be instantly located.

The prestige of the chiefs should be maintained in every possible way, such as exempting them from the hut-tax, allowing them a small armed escort, etc.

I realized the immense importance of this ruling through the chiefs when in the Chambesi district of Northern Rhodesia. Two chiefs of considerable influence, namely, Makasa and Changala, really administer the country under the direction of the collector. A criminal was wanted, and Changala handed him over in thirty-six hours; had he not done so, all the police in the district might have hunted for a year without success.

3. *More attention must be paid to maintaining the prestige of the white man.*

This is of paramount importance. There is rather a tendency amongst the officials to lower the non-official in the eyes of the native. This is fatal. The prestige must be maintained at all costs, as it is the sole hold that we have over the native. The rabble that is inseparable from a mining community is a great difficulty. But still much harm is caused by the ignorance of the youthful officials who are in positions for which they are in no wise fitted.

4. *Officials should be forced to acquire a knowledge of the language.*

The Germans set us a good example in their East Coast Protectorate, where a man must go through a preliminary course at the coast before being admitted to any position in the interior. I have seen much harm done by the employment of interpreters, who are invariably bribed, and only say what they wish to be said. This destroys the confidence of the native. I have always remarked the eagerness with which the native appeals to the white man who can converse direct with him.

5. *The constant moving of officials from place to place should be avoided.*

The native requires a long time to learn to know a white man and to feel confidence in him. In many places a game of general post with the officials seems to be the chief occupation of the Administration.

6. *The official should be enabled and encouraged to travel round his district.*

This is the surest means of inspiring confidence. At present most of the officials whom I met were tied to their stations by such statesmanlike duties as weighing out beads, measuring cloth, and copying out orders; all of which might be cheaply and effectually done by an Indian clerk. Travelling round and learning the natives is usually severely repressed at headquarters.

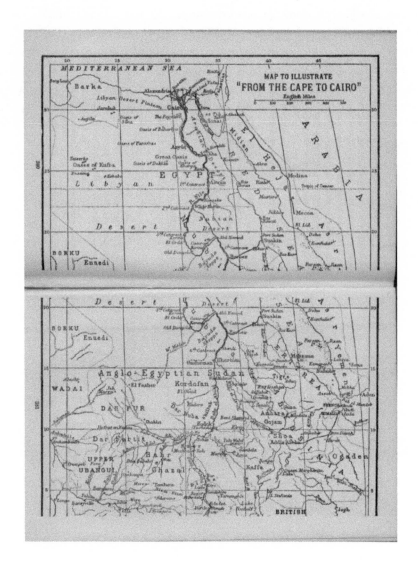

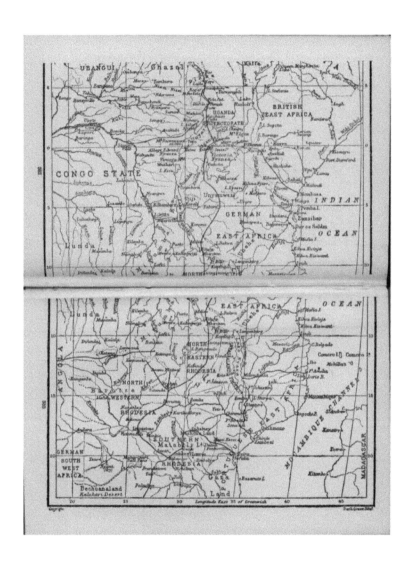